United States
Department of
Agriculture

Forest Service

Pacific Northwest
Research Station

General Technical
Report
PNW-GTR-828
October 2010

A Tale of Two Cedars: International Symposium on Western Redcedar and Yellow-Cedar

U.S. Department of Agriculture
Pacific Northwest Research Station
333 S.W. First Avenue
P.O. Box 3890
Portland, OR 97208-3890

Technical Coordinator

Constance A. Harrington, research forester, U.S. Department of Agriculture, Forest Service, Pacific Northwest Research Station, 3625 93rd Ave. SW, Olympia, WA 98512-9193

Credits

Cover photography by Constance A. Harrington and Joseph M. Kraft, U.S. Department of Agriculture, Forest Service, Pacific Northwest Research Station, 3625 93rd Ave. SW, Olympia, WA 98512-9193. Artwork on inside title page and section dividers by Jodie Krakowski, BC Ministry of Forests and Range, Research, Knowledge and Innovation Management Branch, Cowichan Lake Research Station, Box 225, Mesachie Lake, B.C. V0R 2N0

Pesticide Precautionary Statement

This publication reports on operations that may involve pesticides. It does not contain recommendations for their use, nor does it imply that the uses have been registered. All uses of pesticides must be registered by appropriate provincial, state or federal agencies, or both, before they can be recommended.

CAUTION: Pesticides can be injurious to humans, domestic animals, desirable plants, and fish or other wildlife – if they are not handled or applied properly. Use all pesticides selectively and carefully. Follow recommended practices for the disposal of surplus pesticides and pesticide containers.

A Tale of Two Cedars

International Symposium on
Western Redcedar and Yellow-cedar

U.S. Department of Agriculture
Forest Service
Pacific Northwest Research Station
Portland, Oregon
General Technical Report
PNW-GTR-828
October 2010

ABSTRACT

Harrington, Constance, A., tech. coord. 2010. A tale of two cedars – International symposium on western redcedar and yellow-cedar. Gen. Tech. Rep. PNW-GTR-828. Portland, OR: U.S. Department of Agriculture, Forest Service, Pacific Northwest Research Station. 177 p.

From May 24-28, 2010, an international symposium on western redcedar (*Thuja plicata*) and yellow-cedar (*Callitropsis nootkatensis* [syn. *Chamaecyparis nootkatensis*]) was held at the University of Victoria on Vancouver Island in British Columbia, Canada. The symposium was entitled "A Tale of Two Cedars" and brought together local, regional, national, and international experts to present cultural, biological, management and economic information on the two species. Although some papers or posters focused on just one of the cedars, many of the presenters covered both species and discussed the similarities and differences between them. This proceedings includes abstracts or short papers from all of the formal presentations or posters presented at the symposium.

KEYWORDS: Western redcedar, *Thuja plicata*, yellow-cedar, *Callitropsis nootkatensis*, *Chamaecyparis nootkatensis*, Alaska yellow-cedar, cultural use, ecology, soils, nutrient cycling, physiology, forest health, climate, genetics, wood properties, silviculture and forest management.

PREFACE

From May 24-28, 2010, an international symposium on western redcedar and yellow-cedar was held at the University of Victoria, on Vancouver Island, British Columbia, Canada. The symposium was sponsored by the Centre for Forest Biology, University of Victoria; British Columbia Ministry of Forests and Range; and U.S. Forest Service, Pacific Northwest Research Station. The Organizing Committee consisted of: Paul Hennon, U.S. Forest Service, Pacific Northwest Research Station, Juneau, AK; John Russell, British Columbia Ministry of Forests and Range, Research, Knowledge and Innovation Management Branch, Cowichan Lake Research Station, Mesachie Lake, BC; Constance Harrington, U.S. Forest Service, Pacific Northwest Research Station, Olympia, WA; Barbara Hawkins, Centre for Forest Biology, University of Victoria, Victoria, BC; Diane Douglas, British Columbia Ministry of Forests and Range, Tree Improvement Branch, Victoria, BC; and Jodie Krakowski, British Columbia Ministry of Forests and Range, Research, Knowledge and Innovation Management Branch, Cowichan Lake Research Station, Mesachie Lake, BC. We also acknowledge the support and helpful suggestions of Charles Peterson, U.S. Forest Service, Pacific Northwest Research Station, Portland, OR, in the initial planning stages for the meeting.

Canadian and U.S. scientists and managers have accumulated substantial knowledge and experience with western redcedar and yellow-cedar but there have been few opportunities to exchange this information. The primary goal of the meeting was to bring together experts in a broad range of fields to share information and experience and, where possible, to synthesize knowledge on these two species. Both of these cedars are culturally, economically, and biologically important, but they have been relatively poorly studied compared to other species of comparable importance. In addition, by addressing only two tree species, we hoped to delve deeply into various scientific disciplines—ethnobotany, ecology, soil science, physiology, entomology and pathology, climate, genetics, wood science, and silviculture. Many of the individual presentations in the sessions at the symposium addressed both cedar species and were multidisciplinary. We posed two related questions several times during the symposium: how are these two cedars similar, and how are they different?

The 4-day meeting began with 4 keynote speakers to set the stage for the rest of the meeting -- one each on cultural roles of the cedars, nomenclature and relatedness within the Cupressaceae, and two on wood properties and market opportunities. Dr. Nancy Turner shared her understanding of the traditional knowledge and use of cedars by First Nations people. Many First Nations peoples living in western North America have access to one or both of the cedars. They recognized that each cedar has unique properties for various cultural and daily necessities of life, and they used them accordingly. Dr. Damon Little covered the evolutionary history, taxonomy, and nomenclature of yellow-cedar and western redcedar and outlined key taxonomic changes in the Cupressaceae. The two cedars may look similar, but their descendants emerged from different branches of an ancient plant family long ago and are actually only very distantly related. The taxonomic classification of western redcedar is stable, but not so for yellow-cedar: it is in considerable flux. Drs. Chris Gaston and Ivan Eastin rounded out the keynote presentations by discussing the wood properties and commercial value of the two cedars and their different domestic and international markets. Both cedars are consistently the most commercially valued wood where they grow, but their woods have distinct properties, and very different North American and Asian market niches.

Our keynote speaker session was followed by others which were organized around several broad themes. The ecological sessions built a foundation of *where* on landscapes the two cedars could be conserved or actively managed. Information on habitat preferences, soils and nutrient cycling, physiology, forest health, genetics, and wood properties gave guidance on where cedars are best-adapted, both currently and in the future with a changing climate. This guidance came in the form of broad-scale patterns, such as physiological adaptation, climate envelopes, and the movement of populations to help ensure current and future adaptability. Speakers also addressed fine-scale features such as physiological plasticity in response to local climate, and ecological adaptation to wet soils through calcium and nitrogen uptake. Durable wood products from young-growth forests through silvicultural and genetic management are vital to the economic stability of our regions. Scientific information from related sessions outlined the progress that has been made to date as well as future research initiatives. These talks set the stage for the Friday management session which provided examples through field testing and operational experience of *how* cedars could be, and are being, managed with different silvicultural strategies and examined growth rates of these species with and without management. Our field trips reinforced many of the same themes. We experienced the beauty of old-growth forests and discussed the role of these cedars in forest management in areas within driving distance of Victoria. Population adaptation of the two cedars was witnessed first-hand, as were operational silvicultural successes and both ecologically rich and stressful environments. We thank: (1) Western Forest Products for providing staff to talk about their practices and for allowing access to multiple sites on a field trip where participants could view research installations, operational plantations, and natural stands of the species, and (2) Capital Regional District Watershed for allowing access to an exceptional old-growth stand.

The symposium included a poster session (abstracts or mini papers are included from that session in this proceedings) which covered a wide range of topics. A related workshop was held the following week to document the progress that has been made in tree improvement, through breeding, testing, and selection, to develop clones which are resistant to browsing by deer and elk and to discuss opportunities for broad-scale field testing. Information from that workshop is also included here.

As mentioned above, one of our keynote speakers, Damon Little, The New York Botanical Garden, covered the systematics of the Cupressaceae family. Based on recent information from molecular markers and knowledge of the taxonomic rules used in assigning scientific names, he suggested that we use *Callitropsis nootkatensis* for the species also referred to in the literature as *Xanthocyparis nootkatensis*, *Cupressus nootkatensis*, and *Chamaecyparis nootkatensis*. Most participants adopted that nomenclature for this proceedings. Dr. Little did not have an opinion on a standard common name but the majority of the meeting participants felt that yellow-cedar was the best common name as that name refers to the bright yellow color of the tree's heartwood and is widely used in British Columbia and Alaska where much of the range of the species exists. Other common names used include: Alaska yellow-cedar, Alaska cypress, Alaska cedar, Nootka false cypress, and yellow cypress.

Species from the Cupressaceae family are distinct from other conifers (i.e., in the Pinaceae) in many aspects that we addressed at the symposium. Our goal was to share information across topical and geographic barriers, and in this respect, the symposium was a resounding success. The symposium covered a wide range of topics and several participants expressed their enthusiasm at being exposed to subjects they might normally have thought little about. Discussion continued through the breaks, meals, and field trips and several attendees asked that a list of participants be included to facilitate future interaction (see the Table of Contents for this list). In addition, one of attendees, Bill Beese, wrote a song about the meeting and sang it, accompanying himself on the guitar, for the group (it was received with lots of laughter, clapping and cheers). He has graciously allowed us to print the lyrics from his song in the proceedings.

We thank Joseph Kraft for his assistance in preparing the proceedings. Although we asked the authors for their papers as "camera ready," we appreciate Joe's tweaking to get them to the desired final format.

Jodie Krakowski prepared the artwork (tree outlines, foliage and cones of western red cedar and yellow-cedar) used on the inside front cover and section dividers in this document; her artwork was also used on meeting handouts and printed on cups and wooden coasters given to speakers and meeting participants, respectively.

We hope that this printed proceedings will serve as a reminder of the topics covered for those who attended the meeting and as a synthesis of knowledge for these two important species. We closed A Tale of Two Cedars with the hope that a follow-on meeting will be held in 10 years to update our knowledge.

The Organizing Committee – A Tale of Two Cedars

2010 - A Tale of Two Cedars PNW-GTR-828

CONTENTS

SECTION A
KEYNOTE PRESENTATIONS

PALEOECOLOGY, ECOLOGY, AND HABITAT PREFERENCES

SOILS AND NUTRIENT CYCLING

PHYSIOLOGY

SECTION B
FOREST HEALTH

CLIMATE

GENETICS

SECTION C
WOOD

SILVICULTURE AND MANAGEMENT

SECTION D
ABSTRACTS AND PAPERS BASED ON POSTERS

WESTERN REDCEDAR DEER BROWSE RESISTANCE WORKSHOP

FIELD TOURS

SECTION A

KEYNOTE PRESENTATIONS

PALEOECOLOGY, ECOLOGY AND HABITAT PREFERENCES

SOILS AND NUTRIENT CYCLING

PHYSIOLOGY

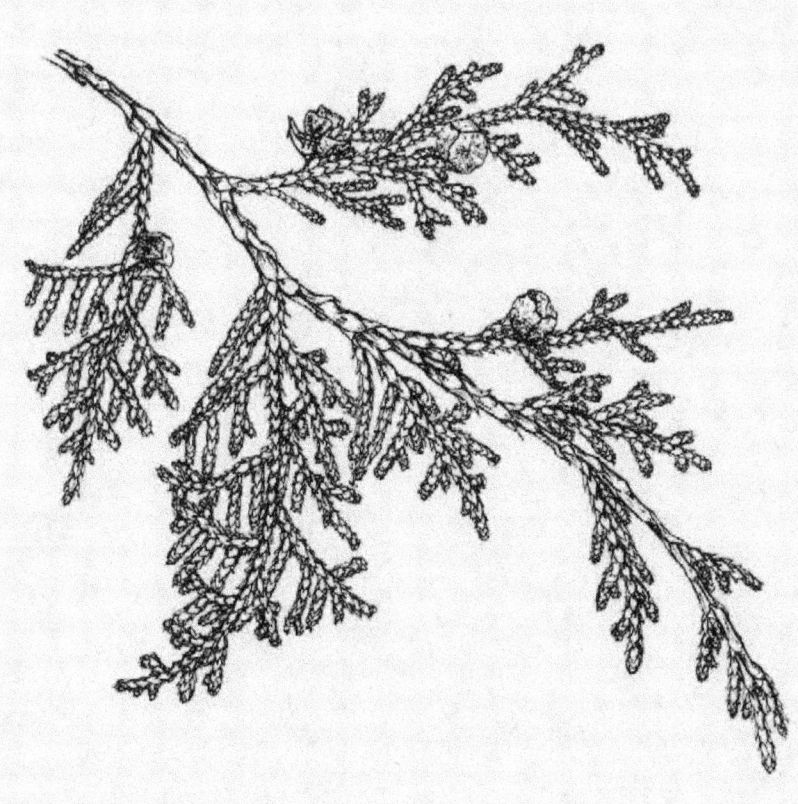

TREES FOR LIFE: THE CULTURAL ROLES OF WESTERN REDCEDAR AND YELLOW-CEDAR FOR FIRST PEOPLES OF NORTHWESTERN NORTH AMERICA

Nancy J. Turner[1]

ABSTRACT

Western redcedar (*Thuja plicata*) and yellow-cedar (*Chamaecyparis nootkatensis*) are both trees of immense cultural importance for First Peoples in northwestern North America. Western red-cedar is the main type of wood used for dugout canoes, as well as the posts and planks of Northwest Coast big houses and bentwood boxes, as well as being used for numerous smaller items, from fire tongs to fishing lures. Yellow-cedar is a preferred wood for canoe paddles, and is also used for carving masks, bows and other items. The fibrous inner bark of both species is woven into baskets, hats, mats, blankets and clothing. The tough, fibrous roots and branches of western redcedar are also used in basketry and for cordage. Both species are also used for a variety of medicinal purposes. The importance of these two species in material culture is mirrored in their roles in ancient narratives and in their spiritual values as reflected First Peoples' ceremonies and belief systems. First Nations have always used cedar trees with care and respect, often only partially harvesting cedar wood and bark to allow the trees to continue living – seen today in many places as culturally modified trees (CMTs). In many areas industrial logging has severely curtailed the availability of cedar for cultural purposes, but recent long-term management plans, and more widely adopted ethic of careful and caring use of these trees may help to alleviate this situation over time.

[1] School of Environmental Studies, University of Victoria, Victoria, B.C., Canada

WESTERN REDCEDAR (*THUJA PLICATA*) AND YELLOW-CEDAR (*CALLITROPSIS NOOTKATENSIS*): PHYLOGENY, NOMENCLATURE, AND ORGANISMAL CHARACTER EVOLUTION

Damon P. Little[1]

ABSTRACT

I aim to summarize our current knowledge of cedar evolution and the expression of that knowledge through botanical nomenclature. Red (*Thuja plicata*) and yellow cedar (*Callitropsis nootkatensis*) are members of the subfamily Cupressoideae—by far the largest and most diverse subfamily in Cupressaceae.

A number of organismal (anatomy, biochemistry, micromorphology, reproductive development, reproductive morphology, and vegetative morphology) and DNA sequence characters can be used to reconstruct the evolutionary (phylogenetic) history of Cupressoideae. Of particular interest are those characteristics that may be of adaptive significance. For example, wood secondary chemistry (the evolution of antimicrobial compounds), leaf architecture (the evolution of light tolerance), and transfusion tissue structure (the evolution of drought tolerance).

Phylogenetic reconstructions usually position the species of red cedar (*Thuja*) and asunaro (*Thujopsis dolabrata*) as the earliest branch within Cupressoideae. The nomenclature of red cedar is uncontroversial. Yellow cedar is reconstructed, remote from red cedar, in a more apical position along with the junipers (*Juniperus*), Old World cypresses (*Cupressus*), Vietnamese cypress (*Xanthocyparis vietnamensis*), and New World cypresses (*Callitropsis*). The arrangement of these groups varies somewhat depending on the source of data utilized, but yellow cedar is consistently resolved alongside of the Vietnamese and New World cypresses. This phylogenetic reconstruction had led to recent nomenclatural changes for New World cypresses (controversial in some quarters). In literature, yellow cedar is known variously as *Callitropsis nootkatensis*, *Xanthocyparis nootkatensis*, *Cupressus nootkatensis*, and *Chamaecyparis nootkatensis*. Until the relationship between yellow cedar, Vietnamese cypress, and the New World cypresses are satisfactorily resolved, the most conservative nomenclatural treatment is to recognize a single genus—*Callitropsis*—for all three.

---

[1] Cullman Program for Molecular Systematics, The New York Botanical Garden, Bronx, NY 10458-5126, dlittle@nybg.org.

A TALE OF TWO MARKETS: OPPORTUNITIES FOR WESTERN REDCEDAR AND YELLOW-CEDAR IN JAPAN AND THE U.S.

Chris Gaston[1] and Ivan Eastin[2]

ABSTRACT

This presentation will begin with an overview of the wood properties and markets for western redcedar and yellow-cedar. The specific attributes and properties of these two cedars will be covered from a supply, demand and competition perspective. Topics covered will include: BC/PNW production, shipments, international trade, end-uses, and market shares. This will provide a statistical overview of the opportunities for marketing these species. Our presentation will then focus in on two specific market opportunities.

Market Opportunities in Japan

There are a number of potential market opportunities for cedar lumber in Japan. These range from rough green lumber to planed and kiln-dried lumber to glue-laminated yellow-cedar sill plates (dodai). The most promising opportunities include yellow-cedar dodai for the post and beam market, 2x4 and 2x6 dimension yellow-cedar lumber for sill plates in the 2x4 market, yellow-cedar lamina for the glue-laminated beam industry, and rough, green or planed, kiln dried red or yellow cedar lumber for the shoji manufacturing industry. Strategic recommendations for selling cedar into Japan include: 1) develop comparative performance properties of species used for dodai, 2) develop a marketing campaign promoting the benefits of using yellow-cedar to homebuyers in Japan, 3) promote the idea of a yellow-cedar foundation system for houses, 4) sawmills should carefully analyze market segments to ensure a good match with their production capabilities, and 5) investigate opportunities for WRC and YC in products targeted to the R&R, DIY, and outdoor use markets in Japan.

Market Opportunities in Outdoor Decks in the US

The deck building industry is going through a period of rapid growth and dramatic change with respect to the types of materials available to build decks. To better understand material use and contractor preferences within the deck building industry, CINTRAFOR, with funding support from FPInnovations, recently completed a survey of deck builders and home builders across the US. The deck building industry is dominated by small to medium-sized firms. Just over 40% of deck builder projects were new (first time) decks built on existing homes while 25% were new decks built on new homes and almost a third were replacement decks built on existing homes. Material use in the substructure was dominated by treated lumber with a market share of over 90%. Material use in deck surface applications was dominated by wood-plastic composite products followed by treated lumber and western red cedar. Finally, approximately 30% of deck accessories were built using wood-plastic composites and treated lumber while an additional 18% were built from western red cedar. The results of the market research suggest that the target market for cedar should be deck builders located on the US west coast, comprised of California, Oregon and Washington. The survey results show that decks built in this market are larger, more expensive and more likely to use naturally durable woods.

This study also investigated the potential for Profile Decking, a new treated whitewood decking product that has grown out of research conducted at FPInnovations. This product, along with cedars, is targeting solid wood alternatives to plastic wood decking.

[1] FPInnovations, 2665 East Mall, Vancouver, BC, Canada V6T 1W5 chris.gaston@fpinnovations.ca
[2] Center for International Trade in Forest Products, University of Washington, Seattle, WA.

WESTERN REDCEDAR AND YELLOW-CEDAR DISTRIBUTIONS ALONG ELEVATION GRADIENTS IN SOUTHEAST ALASKA: IMPLICATIONS FOR CLIMATE CHANGE

John Caouette[1] and Paul Hennon[2]

ABSTRACT

The coast Alaska rainforest is a large relatively intact forest, largely managed by a single entity (the US Forest Service), relatively low in tree species diversity, and not vulnerable to fire. The combination of these characteristics makes coastal Alaska an ideal setting for studying relationships between tree species distributions and climate. We conduct analyses of red and yellow cedar tree species and their life stages across elevation gradients in southeast Alaska. We conduct our analysis in a meta-replicated manner, emphasizing repeatable outcomes across multiple forest inventory datasets. We keep our explanatory factors simple (i.e., elevation classes), so as to better illustrate and measure complex relationships amongst tree species and within species attributes (e.g., dead, live and regeneration). Elevation is used as the primary explanatory factor because of its strong correlation with climate. Thus elevation becomes a pseudo-climatic gradient from which we can observe species niche differentiation and migration. This type of analysis not only provides an additional perspective on forest-climate relationships, but also provides measurable indicators for tree species vulnerability assessments and monitoring programs related to climate change. Results show patterns of climatic niche differentiation for both red and yellow-cedar trees. Results also show climatic differentiation amongst dead, live, and regenerating for the yellow-cedar trees, but not for the redcedars.

[1] The Nature Conservancy, Juneau, Alaska

[2] US Forest Service, Pacific Northwest Research, Juneau, Alaska

DECLINE IN WESTERN REDCEDAR 1000 YEARS AGO AT SGANG GWAAY UNESCO WORLD HERITAGE SITE ON SOUTHERN HAIDA GWAII: SELECTIVE RESOURCE REMOVAL BY HAIDA PEOPLES

Terri Lacourse[1]

ABSTRACT

SGang Gwaay village at the southern tip of the Haida Gwaii archipelago (Queen Charlotte Islands, British Columbia), with its many standing monumental poles and the remains of cedar-plank houses, is recognized as the greatest *in situ* example of Northwest Coast architecture and monumental art. The late Holocene vegetation history of Anthony Island and the potential ecological impact of Haida villagers were investigated by conducting pollen and plant macrofossil analyses on sediments from a small pond near the village. Fossil pollen and plant macrofossil assemblages reveal 1800 years of relatively stable temperate rainforest vegetation. However, Cupressaceae (cedar) pollen percentages and accumulation rates decline about 1000 years BP, coincident with radiocarbon-dated occupation of the island by Haida peoples, who use *Thuja plicata* Donn ex D. Don (western redcedar) almost exclusively for house construction, dugout canoes, monumental poles, and many other items. Selective resource removal by Haida peoples offers the most likely explanation for this local decline in western redcedar. Given the long lifespan of cedar and since many standing western redcedar remain on Anthony Island, it appears that harvesting was conducted at a sustainable rate. This research provides independent paleoecological evidence for local changes in forest composition attributable to Indigenous peoples on the Pacific coast of Canada.

KEYWORDS: pollen analysis, plant macrofossils, *Thuja plicata*, human impact, selective harvesting

INTRODUCTION

The village of SGang Gwaay, on the eastern shore of Anthony Island on the Pacific coast of Canada, was designated a UNESCO World Heritage Site in 1981. The remains of a large Haida village with collapsed cedar-plank houses and standing monumental poles make SGang Gwaay one of the best examples of prehistoric Northwest Coast architecture and art. Acheson (1998) determined that SGang Gwaay was settled by Kunghit Haida around 1590 ± 160 ^{14}C years before present (yr BP). Settlement occurred after late Holocene decreases in relative sea level of about 5 m exposed new land suitable for human habitation (Hebda and Mathewes 1986, Lacourse et al. 2010).

This paper summarizes paleoecological evidence of prehistoric forest modification by Haida peoples on Anthony Island (Lacourse et al. 2007). Unlike archaeological and ethnobotanical remains, which are the direct products of human activities, paleoecological records offer independent data on the ecological impact of Indigenous peoples. Pollen and plant macrofossil analyses of a lake sediment core collected from SGang Gwaay Pond on Anthony Island are compared to the island's archaeological record, which spans the last 1600 years (Acheson 1998). We propose that localized selective harvesting of large *Thuja plicata* trees by Haida is reflected in the pollen record from this site.

[1] Dept. of Geography, University of Victoria, Victoria, BC V8W 3R4, tlacours@uvic.ca

ENVIRONMENTAL SETTING

Anthony Island (52°05.75'N, 131°13.25'W) is located at the southern tip of the Queen Charlotte Islands (Haida Gwaii), an archipelago of about 150 islands on the edge of the continental shelf on the North Pacific coast. Anthony Island is small (~1.5 km^2) and low in elevation (≤60 m a.s.l.). The island's hypermaritime climate is characterized by cool summers and wet, mild winters.

Anthony Island lies within the Coastal Western Hemlock biogeoclimatic zone, which occurs at low to middle elevations along the coast of British Columbia (Meidinger and Pojar 1991). Forests in this zone are dominated by *Tsuga heterophylla* (western hemlock) and *Thuja plicata* with varying amounts of *Picea sitchensis* (Sitka spruce), *Chamaecyparis nootkatensis* (yellow-cedar), and *Pinus contorta* ssp. *contorta* (shore pine).

SGang Gwaay Pond is located on the southeast side of Anthony Island (5.3 m a.s.l.), about 700 m south of the village. It is the only permanent body of water on the island and is very small (~0.3 ha), which suggests that most pollen deposited in the basin is of local origin. *Picea sitchensis*, *T. heterophylla*, and *P. contorta* ssp. *contorta* grow immediately around the pond. *Thuja plicata* trees, some of which are culturally modified, are scattered on the island.

METHODS

A 106 cm-long sediment core was retrieved with a Livingstone corer from SGang Gwaay Pond in 0.7 m of water (Hebda and Mathewes 1986). Two radiocarbon ages were obtained from the core: one on peat at 95 cm (1750 ± 120 ^{14}C yr BP, WAT 1197) and one on a *Picea* twig at 40 cm (1110 ± 40 ^{14}C yr BP, BETA 201518). These ^{14}C ages were calibrated to calendar ages (1665 and 1020 cal yr BP, respectively) using CALIB 5.0 (Stuiver and Reimer 1993). An age-depth model was then constructed using calibrated ^{14}C dates and a cubic spline curve. Sediment samples were prepared for pollen analysis following standard methodology (Fægri and Iversen 1989). A minimum sum of 500

terrestrial pollen grains was counted for each subsample. To calculate pollen concentrations, two tablets of *Eucalyptus* pollen (16,180 ± 1460 grains; Batch 903722) were added to each sample. Pollen accumulation rates were calculated using pollen concentrations and sedimentation rates and were used to evaluate trends in population size, since they avoid the statistical interdependence of percentage data.

RESULTS AND INTERPRETATION
Sediment and Chronology

The base of the sediment core consists of gravel and coarse sand with fragments of marine shells (Fig. 1). The age-depth model predicted an age of 1780 cal yr BP for the core bottom. Marine shells occur below 98 cm i.e., ca. 1675 cal yr BP, which represents the minimum age for marine regression. The area near present sea level would not have been available for human occupation prior to this time (Hebda and Mathewes 1986, Lacourse et al. 2010). Marine sediments are overlain by dark brown limnic detritus (Fig. 1).

Pollen Analysis

SGang Gwaay Pond pollen and spore percentages (Fig. 1) are dominated by *Picea sitchensis*, *Tsuga heterophylla* and *Alnus crispa* (Sitka alder). Cupressaceae (cedar), *Alnus rubra* (red alder), and total herb pollen each do not exceed 5% of the sum. Ericaceae (heather; e.g., *Gaultheria*) and Rosaceae (rose; e.g., *Rubus*) pollen are consistently present at low levels. Polypodiaceae fern spores including *Polypodium* account for about 20% of the sum on average. Uncommon pollen and spores not shown in Figure 1 include *Tsuga mertensiana* (mountain hemlock), *Taxus brevifolia* (Pacific yew), *Gentiana douglasiana* (swamp gentian), *Lycopodium* spp. (clubmoss), and *Selaginella wallacei*. Total pollen accumulation rates (PARs) are about 10,000 grains/cm^2/cal yr (Fig. 1), similar to PARs in temperate rainforest elsewhere along the coast (e.g., Lacourse 2005).

Cupressaceae pollen percentages and accumulation rates decline after 1000 cal yr BP

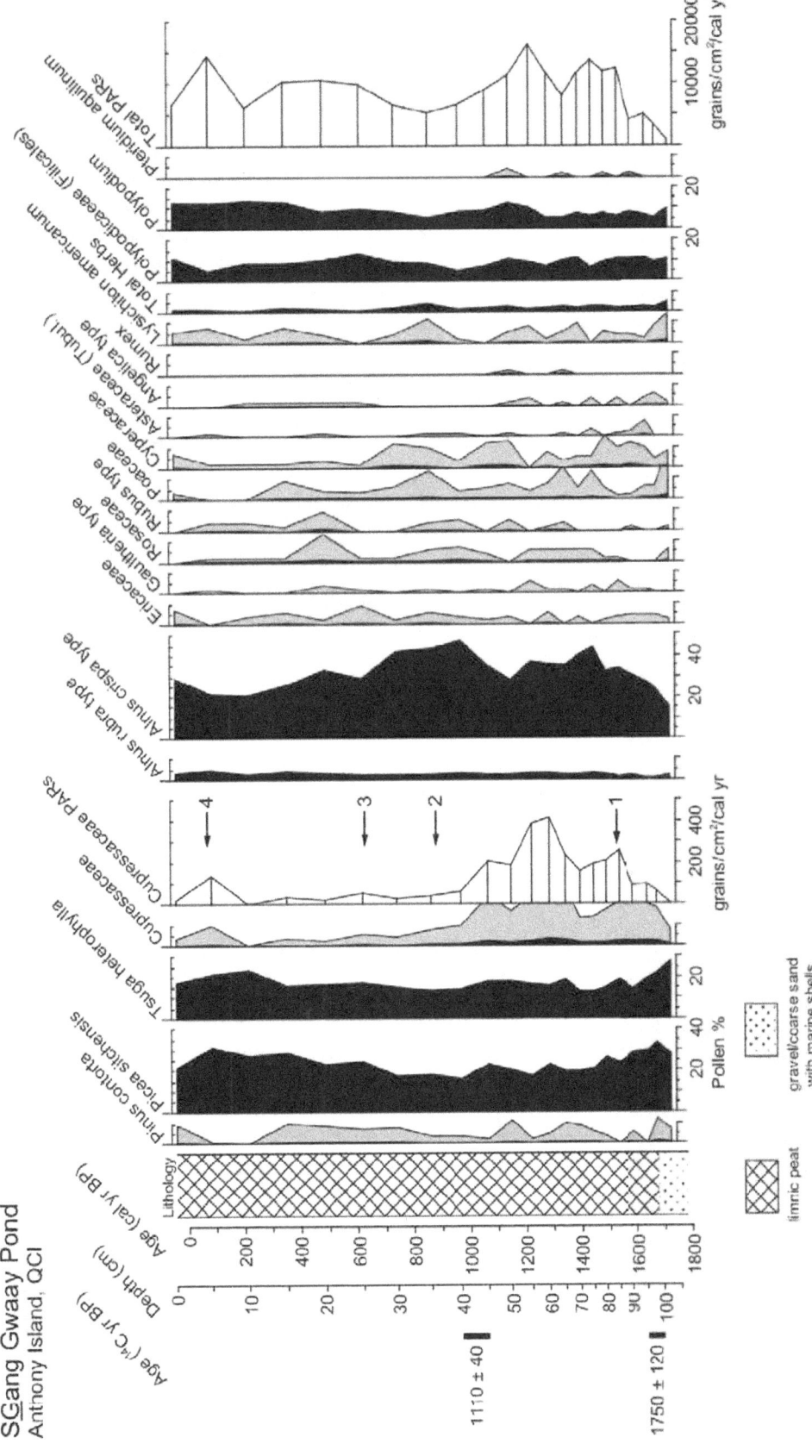

Figure 1 - Sediment stratigraphy and summary pollen and spore percentage diagram for SGang Gwaay Pond, Anthony Island including Cupressaceae and total pollen accumulations rates (PARs). Depth bars in Cupressaceae and Total PARs show the subsampling scheme. Grey curves represent 10x exaggeration. The archaeological record is summarized from Acheson (1998): 1 = establishment of SGang Gwaay village; 2 = establishment of Tc!u'uga ["to go for cedar"] village; 3 = expansion of SGang Gwaay village; and, 4 = abandonment of SGang Gwaay village.

9

(Fig. 1). *Thuja plicata* and *Chamaecyparis nootkatensis* have indistinguishable pollen morphologies, but *C. nootkatensis* does not grow on the island, so *T. plicata* is likely the only contributor of Cupressaceae pollen. Furthermore, an abundance of *T. plicata* branch fragments, seeds, and scale leaves in the sediment core confirms the local presence of *T. plicata* over the last 1800 years (Lacourse et al. 2007).

DISCUSSION

Our data from Anthony Island show few changes in forest composition over the last 1800 calendar years. The pollen record (Fig. 1) reflects closed rainforests dominated by *Picea sitchensis* and *Tsuga heterophylla* with abundant *Alnus crispa* shrubs and Polypodiaceae ferns. The one exception to this relative stability is the near disappearance of *Thuja plicata* after 1000 cal yr BP i.e., after about 500 years of occupation at SGang Gwaay. The most likely explanation is selective harvesting of *T. plicata* trees by Haida for construction of houses, dugout canoes, and other items. The proof of this harvesting lies only 700 m north of the pond in the cedar-plank homes and monumental poles of SGang Gwaay village. These structures were constructed from large *T. plicata* trees, suggesting that harvesting would likely have focussed on mature trees. The removal of such large trees would have influenced the local pollen rain most strongly. Tc!u'uga village, which means "to go for cedar", was established on the adjacent shore of Moresby Island around 980 ± 65 ^{14}C yr BP (~880 cal yr BP) (Acheson 1998) i.e., about 100 years after the decline in *T. plicata* pollen at SGang Gwaay Pond. The precontact Haida population size is unknown but intensification in settlement and cultural activity and increases in site size in the southern Queen Charlotte Islands after 800 ^{14}C yr BP (~715 cal yr BP) suggest increased population at that time (Acheson 1998).

Paleoecological records from coastal British Columbia demonstrate that low elevation forests have been more or less stable in composition during the late Holocene, dominated by *Tsuga*

heterophylla, *Thuja plicata*, and *Picea sitchensis* (e.g., Brown and Hebda 2002, Lacourse 2005). A number of other pollen records from coastal BC show a slight decline in *T. plicata* pollen percentages over the last two millennia (Hebda and Mathewes 1984, Brown and Hebda 2002, Lacourse 2005), although some records show stable values and/or slight increases in *T. plicata* (e.g., Brown and Hebda 2002). It is possible that a regional decline in *T. plicata* could be associated with climate variability. Temperatures inferred from varves in southern Alaska suggest relatively warm conditions during the Medieval Warm Period (AD 1000-1300) and cooler conditions during the Little Ice Age (AD 1500-1850) (Loso et al. 2006). Tree-ring records from southern Vancouver Island suggest that precipitation has been relatively stable over the last 2000 years, with short periods of drought as well as increased precipitation, particularly during the Little Ice Age (Zhang and Hebda 2005). Other paleoclimatic records from the region also document climate variability over the last 2000 years, but in general these changes would have been too low in amplitude to strongly influence the hypermaritime climate of Anthony Island. Climatic conditions remained within a range suitable for the growth of *T. plicata*. Also, the climatic preferences of *T. plicata* are more or less equivalent to other abundant species in the region such as *Tsuga heterophylla* (Thompson et al. 1999), which do not show a late Holocene decline in abundance. Climate variability may have facilitated a decline in *T. plicata* on Anthony Island, but the decline most likely reflects selective harvesting of *T. plicata* trees by Haida living on the island.

The Haida have relied almost exclusively on *T. plicata* for house posts and planks, dugout canoes, monumental poles, and smaller items such as storage boxes (Turner 1998). *Thuja plicata* bark was also used for clothing, mats, baskets, and cordage, and scars from bark-stripping are apparent on several living *T. plicata* trees on Anthony Island. Given the long life span typical of *T. plicata* i.e., >1000 years (Waring and Franklin 1979) and since many standing *T. plicata* remain on the island, it appears that harvesting of *T. plicata* trees was conducted at a sustainable rate. Indeed, sustainable practices were often used by Indigenous peoples (Deur and Turner 2005).

Pollen and plant macrofossil evidence indicated that *Thuja plicata* has been present in coastal British Columbia since about 9000 ^{14}C yr BP, although it was not abundant until after 6000 ^{14}C yr BP, when the climate became cooler and more humid. On the basis of paleoecological and archaeological evidence, Hebda and Mathewes (1984) argued that the development of macro-woodworking technology on the North Pacific coast was linked to the mid-Holocene expansion of *T. plicata* in coastal forests. Specialized woodworking tools and large wooden structures do not appear in the archaeological record until about 5000 and 3000 ^{14}C yr BP, respectively, i.e., only after *T. plicata* became abundant and large trees became available (Hebda and Mathewes 1984).

Our research highlights the contrast between prehistoric anthropogenic modification and disturbance of forests on the Pacific coast with the ecological impact of Indigenous peoples in parts of eastern North America, where large-scale clearing and burning of the land dramatically altered regional forest composition and structure (Delcourt and Delcourt 2004). On Anthony Island, forest modification was primarily through selective resource removal and limited clearing for village areas. In general, the impact of Haida and other Indigenous peoples on Pacific coast rainforests involved subtle changes and diffuse terrestrial resource use compared to other regions, which is sensible given the marine focus of Northwest Coast cultures. Our research also demonstrates the value of conducting paleoecological analyses on non-cultural deposits from locations close to archaeological sites for expanding our understanding of the ecological impact of Indigenous peoples over long time periods.

ACKNOWLEDGEMENTS
We thank the Haida Nation for permission to conduct this study in their territory and for support through the Kunghit Haida Cultural History Project. Financial support was also provided by NSERC of Canada through research grants to T.L. and R.W.M.

LITERATURE CITED
Acheson, S.R. 1998. In the wake of the ya'áats'xaatgáay ['Iron People']: A study of changing settlement strategies among the Kunghit Haida. British Archaeological Reports, International Series 711, Oxford.

Brown, K.J.; Hebda, R.J. 2002. Origin, development, and dynamics of coastal temperate conifer rainforests of southern Vancouver Island, Canada. Can. J. For. Res. 32: 353-372.

Delcourt, P.A.; Delcourt, H.R. 2004. Prehistoric Native Americans and Ecological Change. Cambridge: Cambridge Univ. Press.

Deur, D.; Turner, N.J. 2005. Keeping It Living: Traditions of Plant Use and Cultivation on the Northwest Coast of North America. Seattle, WA: Univ. Washington Press.

Fægri, K.; Iversen, J. 1989. Textbook of Pollen Analysis. 4th Ed. Toronto, ON: John Wiley & Sons.

Hebda, R.J.; Mathewes R.W. 1984. Holocene history of cedar and Native Indian cultures of the North American Pacific Coast. Science 225: 711-713.

Hebda, R.J.; Mathewes, R.W. 1986. Radiocarbon dates from Anthony Island, Queen Charlotte Islands, and their geological and archaeological significance. Can. J. Earth Sci. 23: 2071-2076.

Lacourse, T. 2005. Late Quaternary dynamics of forest vegetation on northern Vancouver Island, British Columbia, Canada. Quat. Sci. Rev. 24: 105-121.

Lacourse, T.; Mathewes, R.W.; Hebda, R.J. 2007. Paleoecological analyses of lake sediments reveal prehistoric human impact on forests at Anthony Island UNESCO World Heritage Site, Queen Charlotte Islands (Haida Gwaii), Canada. Quat. Res. 68: 177-183.

Lacourse, T.; Hebda, R.J.; Mathewes, R.W. 2010. Cultural and noncultural deposits reveal human impact on late Holocene forests on Anthony Island, Haida Gwaii. In: R.M. Dean (ed.), The Archaeology of Anthropogenic Environments. Center for Archaeological Investigations, Occasional Paper No. 37, Southern Illinois Univ., Carbondale, pp. 54-74.

Loso, M.G.; Anderson, R.S.; Anderson, S.P.; Reimer, P.J. 2006. A 1500-year record of temperature and glacial response inferred from varved Iceberg Lake, southcentral Alaska. Quat. Res. 66: 12-24.

Meidinger, D.; Pojar, J. 1991. Ecosystems of British Columbia. BC Ministry of Forests, Victoria, BC.

Stuiver, M.; Reimer, P.J. 1993. Extended ^{14}C data base and revised CALIB 3.0 ^{14}C age calibration program. Radiocarbon 35: 215-230.

Thompson, R.S.; Anderson, K.H.; Bartlein, P.J. 1999. Atlas of relations between climatic parameters and distributions of important trees and shrubs in North America. USGS Professional Paper 1650A. USGS, Denver, CO.

Turner, N.J. 1998. Plant Technology of First Peoples in British Columbia. Royal British Columbia Museum Handbook. Vancouver, BC: Univ. British Columbia Press.

Waring, R.H.; Franklin, J.F. 1979. Evergreen coniferous forests of the Pacific Northwest. Science 204: 1380-1386.

Zhang, Q.-B.; Hebda, R.J. 2005. Abrupt climate change and variability in the past four millennia of the southern Vancouver Island, Canada. Geophys. Res. Lett. 32, L16708, DOI:10.1029/2005GL02291.

ECOLOGY AND DISTRIBUTION OF WESTERN REDCEDAR AND ALASKA YELLOWCEDAR IN NORTHWESTERN WASHINGTON

Robin D. Lesher and Jan A. Henderson[1]

ABSTRACT

The ecology and distribution of western redcedar (*Thuja plicata*) and Alaska yellowcedar (*Callitropsis nootkatensis*, syn *Chamaecyparis nootkatensis*) were analyzed based on their occurrence and abundance on 5587 USFS ecology plots on National Forest lands in northwestern Washington. Western redcedar occurred on 40% of the plots, Alaska yellowcedar occurred on 10% of the plots. The ecology is described for these species relative to environmental gradients of elevation, temperature and moisture. Redcedar showed broad ecological amplitude, but was more frequent at lower elevations, warmer temperatures, and towards the drier end of the precipitation gradient, whereas yellowcedar was limited to cooler sites at mid to upper elevations and higher precipitation. The role of these cedars in forest succession and stand development is described based on their abundance and size-class distribution in different stand ages.

KEYWORDS: ecology, distribution, succession, stand development, northwest Washington

INTRODUCTION

This study provides baseline information on the current distribution and habitats of western redcedar and Alaska yellowcedar in northwestern Washington, their occurrence in different temperature and moisture regimes, and their abundance and size-class distribution during stages of stand development and succession. The Olympic and Mt. Baker-Snoqualmie National Forests (NF) comprise the 1 million ha study area. Beginning in 1979, a network of 5587 reconnaissance and permanent benchmark ecology plots were installed and re-measured to inventory and describe the vegetation on these two National Forests (Henderson et al. 1989, 1992). Data from ecology plots were used for results presented here; not all data were collected on every plot so sample size varies for the different analyses.

Western redcedar was well distributed across the study area, whereas yellowcedar was more limited in distribution (Fig. 1). Redcedar occurred on 2225 plots (40% of total) and

Alaska yellowcedar occurred on 538 plots (10% of total). Large diameter trees (>1m dbh) are infrequent (Fig.1): 14.2% of the plots with redcedar had trees in this size class compared to 8.7% for yellowcedar. Large diameter trees of both species tend to occur in moister sites and in older stand ages which is mostly related to the fire history of the area (Henderson et al. 1989).

Environmental Distribution

The distribution of the two cedar species was analyzed for the environmental gradients of elevation, precipitation and temperature (Henderson et al. in review). Redcedar had higher average cover than yellowcedar, and was most abundant at elevations below 1000 m (Fig. 2). Yellowcedar typically had low cover (averaging < 3%), with highest cover at middle elevations from 1200-1500 m.

Spatial analysis of the elevation gradient for the study area in the Cascades (Fig. 3) showed the land area between 1000-1400 m was most abundant. However, redcedar plots were more frequent at lower elevations (400-1000 m),

[1] Robin D. Lesher is a plant ecologist and Jan A. Henderson is area ecologist (retired) with Pacific Northwest Region, Mt. Baker-Snoqualmie National Forest, 2930 Wetmore Ave, Suite 3A, Everett WA 98201. rlesher@fs.fed.us

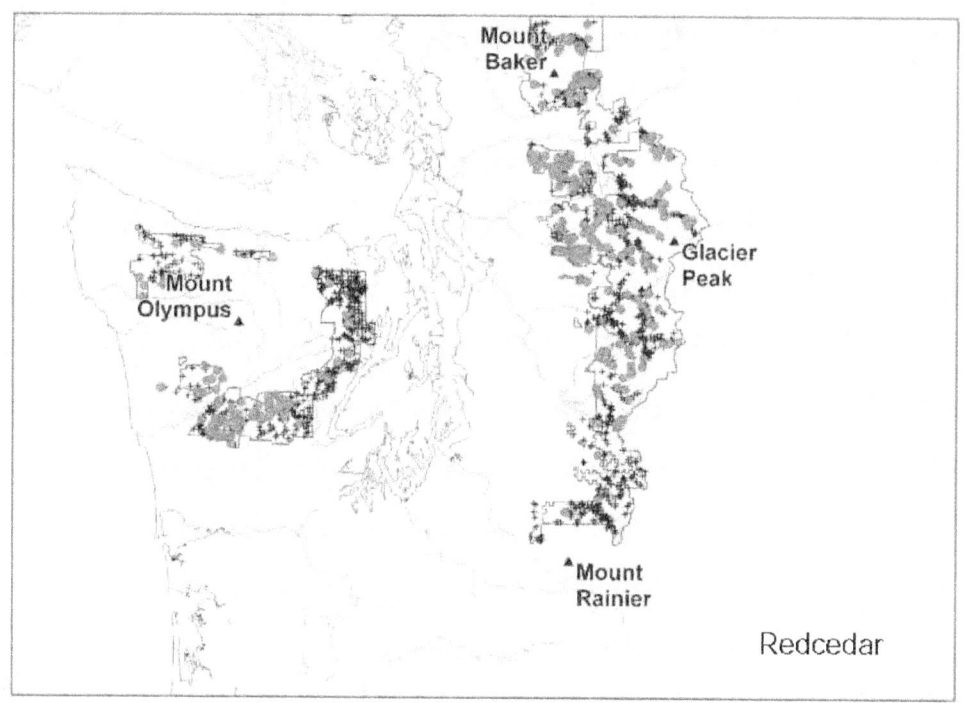

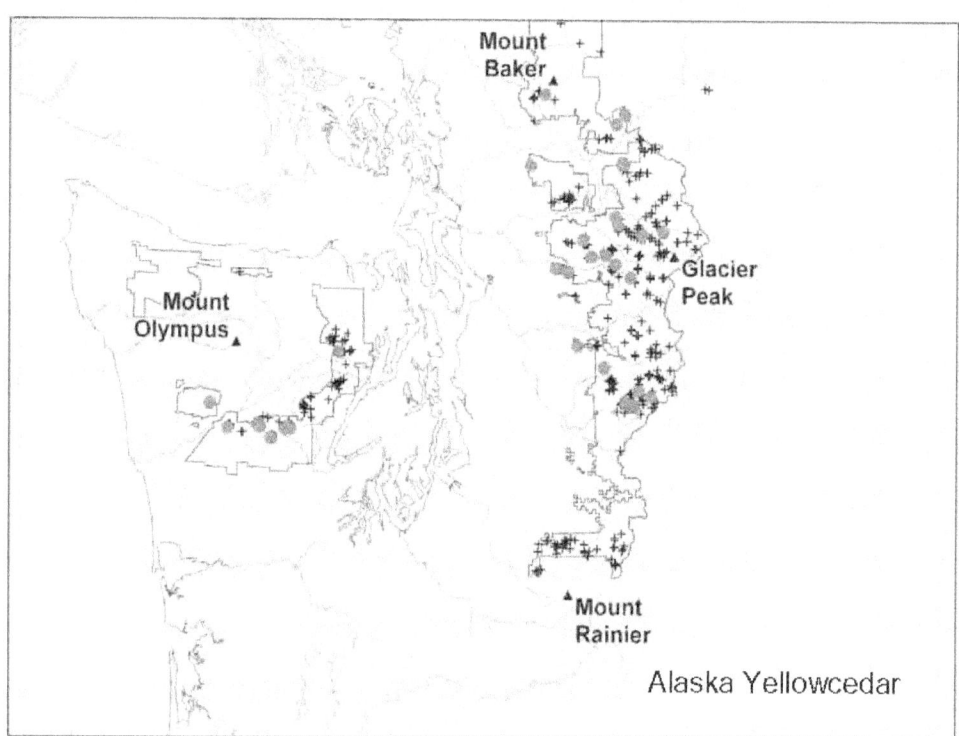

Figure 1 — Western redcedar distribution (upper map) on ecology plots (n=2225) on National Forest lands of northwestern Washington, circles indicate plots with trees >1m dbh (n=316). Yellowcedar distribution (lower map) on ecology plots (n=538) on National Forest lands of northwestern Washington, circles indicate plots with trees >1m dbh (n=47).

where yellowcedar plots were more frequent at mid elevations (800-1600 m).

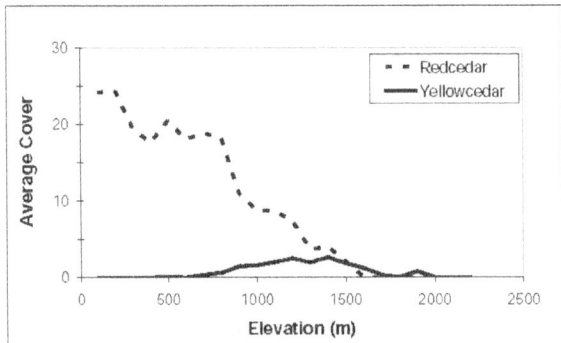

Figure 2 -- Mean cover of redcedar and yellowcedar by elevation for the western North Cascades.

The relationship of the frequency distribution for the species relative to the landscape displays ecological information on the importance of this complex variable (elevation) in the distribution of the species. If there was no relationship with elevation and redcedar, we would expect the distribution of redcedar to follow the distribution of the landscape (MBS NF) (Fig. 3). However, redcedar was more frequent at elevations below 1000 m (above the landscape (MBS NF) line), and less frequent above 1000 m (below the landscape (MBS NF) line).

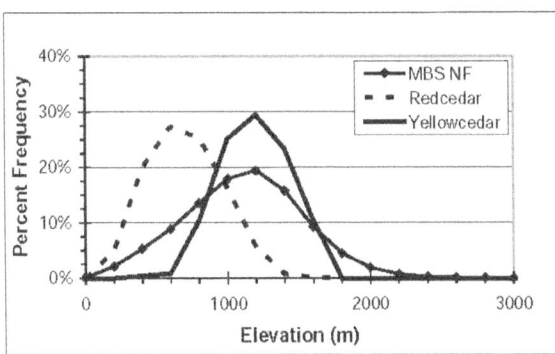

Figure 3 -- Frequency distributions by elevation class of redcedar plots (n=1099) and yellowcedar plots (n=231) compared to the frequency distribution of pixels (n=900,000) for Mt. Baker-Snoqualmie NF.

A similar analysis was done for the precipitation gradient, where the frequency distribution for the landscape was compared to the distribution of the two cedar species (Fig. 4). Redcedar had a similar distribution as the landscape for the precipitation gradient, but was more frequent at the drier end of the precipitation gradient. The frequency for yellowcedar was highest between 2000-4000 mm total annual precipitation. For the part of the gradient greater than 3200 mm precipitation, the frequency of yellowcedar was greater than the landscape frequency. This suggests that precipitation was an important predictor of the environment for yellowcedar for those areas on the landscape that receive more than 3200 mm of precipitation.

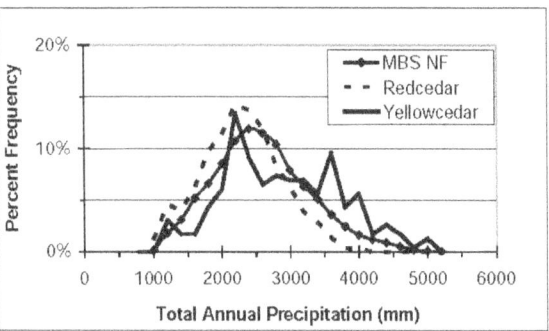

Figure 4 -- Frequency distributions by precipitation class of redcedar plots (n=1099) and yellowcedar plots (n=231) and the frequency distribution of pixels (n=900,000) for Mt. Baker-Snoqualmie NF.

The distribution of redcedar and yellowcedar for the gradient of mean annual temperature (MAT) were compared to the landscape (Fig. 5). The most common temperature classes for the western North Cascades were 4-5 deg C. The distribution of yellowcedar was centered on the MAT distribution for the landscape, and was most frequent from 3-6 deg C, where redcedar

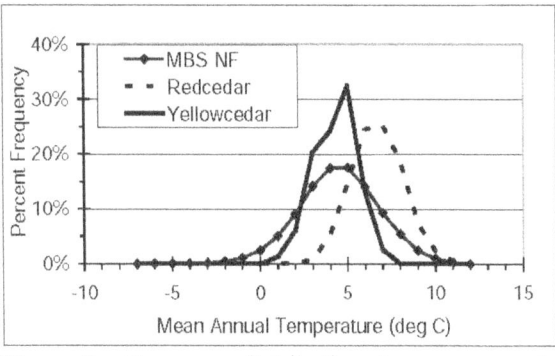

Figure 5 -- Frequency distributions by mean annual temperature class of redcedar plots (n=1099) and yellowcedar plots (n=231) compared to the frequency distribution (n=900,000 pixels) for Mt. Baker-Snoqualmie NF (western North Cascades).

was most frequent at warmer temperatures (6-8 deg C). The difference between the frequency curves for the landscape (MBS NF) and redcedar suggests that MAT was an important predictor of the environment for redcedar at temperatures above 5 deg C (Fig. 5).

The occurrence and abundance of redcedar were analyzed by potential vegetation types (plant association groups). Plant Association Groups (PAGs) are units of potential vegetation (broader than plant associations and narrower than vegetation zones or series) that represent a complex environmental gradient. Redcedar had high constancy and a fairly even distribution throughout the western hemlock zone PAGs, which indicates broad ecological amplitude for this species. However, redcedar was rarely abundant and averaged about 20% cover. In the middle elevation forests of the silver fir zone, redcedar had lower frequency and cover, but there was little difference in constancy and cover between dry and wet vegetation types.

Abundance of cedars and other tree species along age sequence
The cover of redcedar and yellowcedar for different age classes was compared to other tree species to understand the contribution of tree species composition and abundance to stand

development and succession in the western North Cascades. This analysis was done for the Western Hemlock/Swordfern-Mesic PAG (*Tsuga heterophylla/Polystichum munitum*) (Fig. 6). This PAG represents a relatively warm, mesic environment and is the most common PAG in the western hemlock zone in the study area. Cover of redcedar was fairly constant across the age classes and averaged about 20%. Most species showed a peak in cover between 50-120 years; Douglas-fir (*Pseudotsuga menziesii*) peaked early and declined in old stands; western hemlock increased over time and eventually dominated old-growth stands. Red alder (*Alnus rubra*) and bigleaf maple (*Acer macrophyllum*) had the lowest cover and occurred throughout the age sequence but at low abundance; however, these early seral species may also occur in old stands where they can be found in canopy gaps.

A similar analysis was done for the most common PAG in the middle elevation forests of the silver fir zone (Fig. 7). The Silver Fir/Alaska Huckleberry Moist PAG (*Abies amabilis/Vaccinium alaskaense*) occurs in cool moist environments with a persistent winter snow pack averaging 2-3 m. The cover of redcedar was fairly constant over time (Fig. 7), a

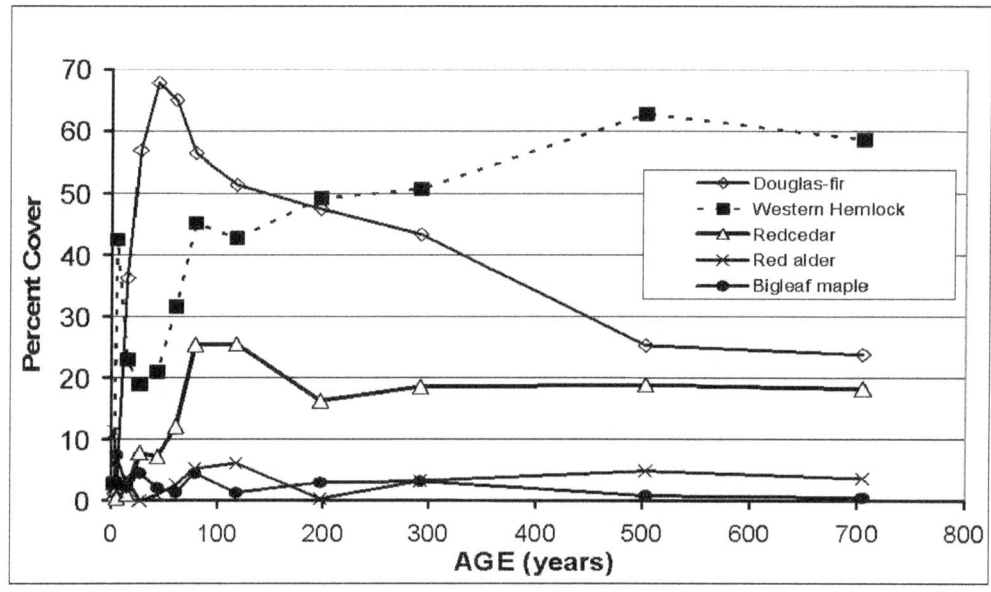

Figure 6 -- Averaged percent cover of major tree species by averaged stand age for the Western Hemlock/Swordfern-Mesic Plant Association Group, western North Cascades (n=403).

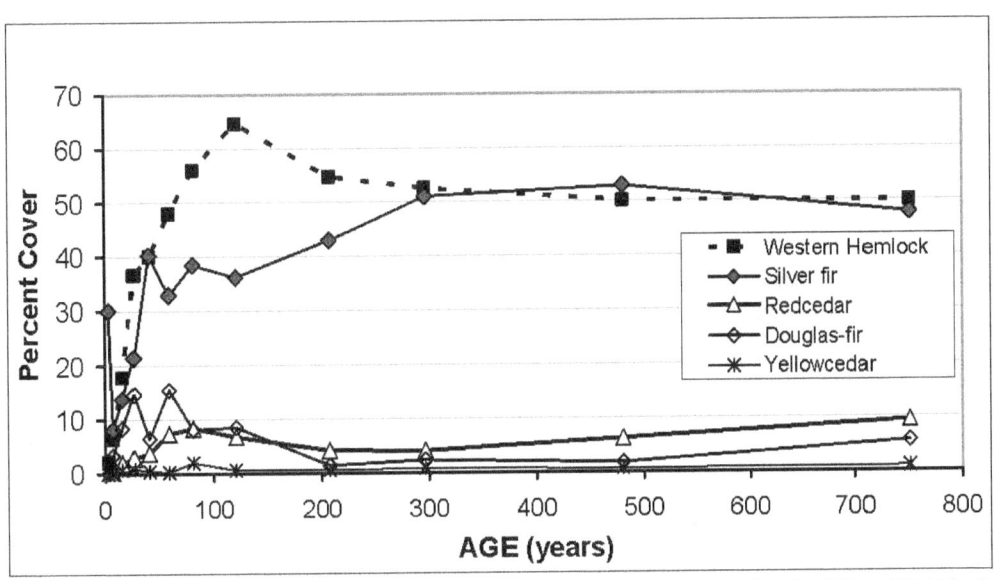

Figure 7 -- Averaged percent cover of major tree species by averaged stand age for the Silver Fir/Alaska Huckleberry-moist Plant Association Group, western North Cascades (n=813).

similar pattern to the western hemlock PAG (Fig. 6), but averaged about half the cover (10%) compared to the western hemlock zone PAG. Western hemlock and silver fir co-dominate in old forests, each averaged about 50% cover. Yellowcedar occurred in the silver fir zone PAG, but was typically a minor component. Douglas-fir was also a minor species in these environments, and the young age classes with Douglas-fir were mostly plantations.

Redcedar size class distribution by stand age
The abundance (cover) of redcedar by size class and stand age was calculated for the Western Hemlock/Swordfern-Mesic PAG (Fig. 8). Redcedar cover peaked in the 80 and120 year age classes, and then was fairly constant into the oldest age class. Beginning in mature stands (120 year age class), all size classes for redcedar were represented but the relative abundance changed across the age sequence. Pole size trees dominated until the 200 year age class, when the 3-10 dm dbh size class became more abundant. The cover of redcedar trees >1 m dbh was highest in the oldest stands.

A similar analysis was done for the distribution and abundance (cover) of redcedar by size class

and stand age for the Silver Fir/Alaska Huckleberry-Moist PAG (Fig. 9). In this cool moist environment, redcedar cover peaked in the 60 to 80 year age classes, and was fairly constant over time but at lower levels than warm mesic western hemlock PAG (Fig. 8). All size classes of redcedar were present in mature stands at about 80 years, but the relative abundance changed with age and larger diameter trees became more abundant over time.

The silver fir zone is a colder environment than the western hemlock zone. Redcedar trees achieved larger diameters in younger age classes in the silver fir zone PAG compared to the western hemlock zone PAG (figs. 8, 9). This pattern may relate to competition with associated species, where the dominant tree species in the silver fir zone PAG have similar shade tolerance. There is a bigger range in shade tolerance of tree species in the western hemlock zone PAG where Douglas-fir was a major component of most stands.

Alaska yellowcedar size class distribution by stand age
The abundance (cover) of yellowcedar by size class and stand age was calculated for the western North Cascades (Fig. 10). Most size classes of yellowcedar were represented in old-

growth stands beginning in the 300 year age class. Yellowcedar is a slow growing species, and the 3-10 dm dbh size class was not achieved until about 200 years. The oldest stands were dominated by yellowcedar in the 3-10 dm dbh and >1m dbh size classes, however the largest trees were uncommon until the oldest age class, which represented stands from 1000 to over 1500 years of age. If this oldest age class didn't exist on the landscape, there would probably be very few of these big old yellowcedar trees.

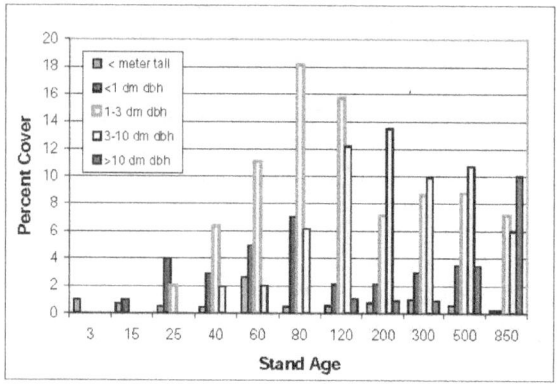

Figure 8 -- Cover of redcedar by size class and stand age (n=157) for the Western Hemlock/Swordfern-Mesic PAG in the western North Cascades. Age represents the midpoint of the class.

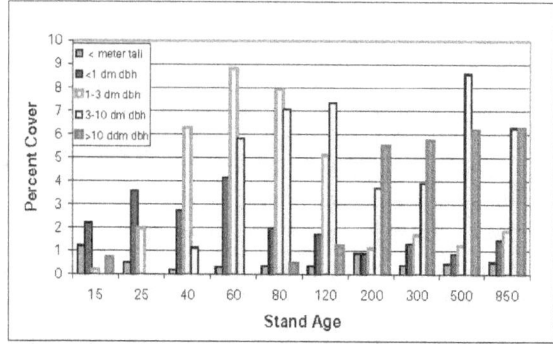

Figure 9 -- Cover of redcedar by size class and stand age (n=257) for the Silver Fir /Alaska Huckleberry-Moist PAG in the western North Cascades. Age represents the midpoint of the class.

Summary
Redcedar had broad ecological amplitude, tending somewhat to the dry end of the precipitation gradient. Redcedar was also more common at warmer temperatures and at lower elevations. The cover of redcedar was fairly constant over stand ages in both the western

hemlock and silver fir zone PAGs. Larger diameter redcedar trees became dominant at younger stand ages in the silver fir zone PAG compared to the western hemlock zone PAG.

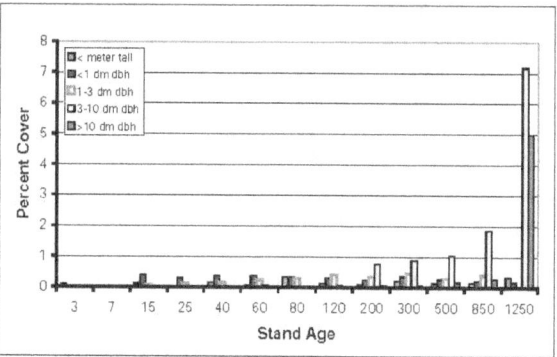

Figure 10 -- Cover of yellowcedar by size class and stand age for the western North Cascades (n=3837). Age represents the midpoint of the class.

Yellowcedar was less common on the landscape, and was limited to cooler sites at mid to upper elevations and with higher precipitation. The cover of yellowcedar was highest in the oldest stands. In the study area, the oldest trees were yellowcedar. It is a slow-growing species, and trees >1m dbh were uncommon in forests less than 500 years old.

LITERATURE CITED
Henderson, J.A.; Peter, D.H.; Lesher, R.D.; Shaw, D.C. 1989. Forested plant associations of the Olympic National Forest. Tech. Pap. R6-ECOL-001-88. Portland, OR: USDA Forest Service, Pacific Northwest Region. 502 p.

Henderson, J.A.; Lesher, R.D.; Peter, D.H.; Shaw, D.C. 1992. Field guide to the forested plant associations of the Mt. Baker-Snoqualmie National Forest. Tech. Pap. R6-ECOL-028-91. Portland, OR: USDA Forest Service, Pacific Northwest Region. 196 p.

Henderson, J.A.; Lesher, R.D.; Peter, D.H.; Ringo, C.D. A landscape model for predicting potential natural vegetation of the Olympic Peninsula USA using boundary equations and newly developed environmental variables. In review.

NITROGEN AVAILABILITY IN FOREST FLOORS OF WESTERN REDCEDAR: SURPRISES, CONUNDRUMS, SOLUTIONS

Cindy E. Prescott[1]

ABSTRACT

Western redcedar (*Thuja plicata* Donn ex D. Don) is thought to be an indicator of nutrient-rich sites, to preferentially take up nitrate and to create N-rich forest floors. Higher concentrations or proportion of nitrate (relative to ammonium) are also commonly reported in cedar forest floors. However, rates of net N mineralization in cedar forests floors are usually not greater than other species; nor are N concentrations higher, indicating that cedar does not create particularly N-rich forest floors. This is consistent with cedar foliar litter consistently having high C:N ratio, high recalcitrant content, and slow decay relative to other tree species. This conundrum may be related to the high concentrations of Ca and high pH of cedar forest floors relative to other species. Cedar forest floors also have been reported to have higher bacteria biomass (including ammonium-oxidizing bacteria) and lower fungal biomass, probably as a consequence of the higher pH and Ca. Therefore, the greater proportion of nitrate in cedar forest floors is probably more reflective of higher pH and associated changes in microbial populations, rather than an indication of high N availability. There is also little evidence that western redcedar preferentially takes up the nitrate form of nitrogen.

KEYWORDS: Nitrate, litter decomposition, calcium, pH, common-garden experiment.

INTRODUCTION

Although it has long been recognized that tree species influence the properties of the soils and forest floors that develop beneath them, it has proven surprisingly difficult to generalize about the nature of particular tree species' influences (Binkley 1995; Binkley and Giardina 1998). Western redcedar is no exception; in fact, recent evidence has called into question many of the ideas previously held about western redcedar and its influence on forest floor and soils. Cedar has traditionally been considered to be an indicator of nutrient-rich sites, and is thought to produce N-rich forest floors. These generalizations are based on cedar being generally associated with rich sites in ecosystem classification schemes (Klinka et al. 1989), evidence that cedar preferentially takes up nitrate (Krajina et al. 1973), and the observation that cedar has arbuscular mycorrhizae, which tend to be associated with nitrate uptake and nitrate environments (Read and Perez-Mereno 2003).

Cedar forest floors consistently have high concentrations of Ca and high pH relative to other species (Alban 1969; Turner and Franz 1985; Prescott and Preston 1994) and higher concentrations of nitrate or proportion of nitrate (relative to ammonium) (Turner and Franz 1985; Harmer and Alexander 1986). These observations understandably led to the assumption that western redcedar is a nitrophilous species.

Recent findings are not consistent with the conventional wisdom that western redcedar is an indicator of nutrient-rich sites, prefers nitrate and creates N-rich forest floors. On nutrient-poor cedar-salal sites on northern Vancouver Island, cedar grows better than other species, and responds less to fertilization with N and P (Bennett et al. 2003). There is also little evidence that cedar prefers nitrate – Bennett and Prescott (2004) found that cedar took up both nitrate and ammonium (Fig.1), and careful perusal of the early work of Krajina et al. (1973) does not

[1]Cindy Prescott is Professor and Associate Dean, Faculty of Forestry, University of British Columbia, 2005-2424 Main Mall, Vancouver, BC, Canada, V6T 1Z4 cindy.prescott@ubc.ca

support the conclusion that cedar prefers nitrate any more than does Douglas-fir (*Pseudotsuga menziesii* (Mirb.) Franco) or lodgepole pine (*Pinus contorta* Dougl. ex Laws. var. contorta). Foliar litter of western redcedar consistently has high C:N ratio, high "acid-unhydrolyzable residue" (AUR) content, and decays more slowly than foliar litter of other west-coast tree species (Harmon et al. 1990; Prescott and Preston 1994; Prescott et al. 2004). Rates of net N mineralization in cedar forests floors are usually not greater than other species (Prescott and Preston 1994; Prescott et al. 1995); nor are N concentrations higher (Ovington 1954; Alban 1969; Prescott and Preston 1994), indicating that cedar does not create particularly N-rich forest floors. In fact, at the Clonsast Bog trial in Ireland, cedar forest floors had the lowest rates of net N mineralization of 14 species, including *Calluna* (Prescott et al. 1995; Table 1).

THE CONUNDRUM

These observations lead to the question of how western redcedar can be associated with rich sites and nitrate, but also grow on N-poor sites, not respond to N addition, have recalcitrant litter and low-N forest floors, and not show a marked preference for nitrate.

A possible solution to this conundrum lies in the high calcium concentrations and pH that are a distinct characteristic of forest floors of western redcedar. Nitrifying organisms are known to be less active in acidic forest floors and soils, and so would be expected to be more active in cedar forest floors than other coniferous tree species. Cedar forest floors have been reported to have higher bacteria biomass (including ammonium-oxidizing bacteria) and lower fungal biomass (Turner and Franz 1985). The higher pH and Ca may also stimulate soil macrofauna, particularly earthworms. A positive association between Ca and pH in litter and forest floors, earthworm abundance and nitrate availability has been reported under certain broadleaf trees species (Reich et al. 2005; Hobbie et al. 2006; Laganiere et al. 2008).

This leads to the hypothesis that the high proportion of nitrate in cedar forest floors is a

Table 1 – Rates of net nitrogen mineralization and pH of forest floors under various species at the UBC Research Forest and Clonsast Bog (Ireland) field trials. Mineralization rates are based on 1-mo lab incubations. From Prescott et al. (1995).

Species	N Mineralization (μg N g^{-1} d^{-1})	pH
UBC Research Forest		
Douglas-fir	5.5	5.2
Western hemlock	3.2	4.2
Western redcedar	1.6	5.1
Clonsast Bog		
Sissile oak	22.6	4.7
Sitka spruce	15.1	4.8
Grand fir	15.1	5.0
Douglas-fir	13.9	4.4
Norway spruce	12.7	4.9
Western hemlock	8.9	3.9
Scots pine	7.4	4.7
Monterey pine	5.3	4.1
Calluna	4.1	4.6
Western redcedar	1.2	6.1

consequence of higher pH and associated changes in populations of soil fauna and microorganisms, rather than an indication of high N availability.

EP 571 SPECIES TRIAL

This hypothesis can be tested with data from the BC Ministry of Forests and Range Experimental Project (EP) 571 study sites on the west coast of Vancouver Island, British Columbia, Canada. Four installations were examined, each with two plots of each of four tree species: western redcedar, western hemlock (*Tsuga heterophylla* (Raf.) Sarg.), Douglas-fir and Sitka spruce (*Picea sitchensis* (Bong.)). The Upper Klanawa and Sarita Lake sites are near Franklin River; the San Juan and Fairy Lake sites are near Port Renfrew. The installations are in the Submontane Very Wet Maritime Coastal Western Hemlock (CWHvm1) variant on the windward side of the Vancouver Island Mountains (Meidinger and Pojar 1991). The soils are Ferro-Humic or Humo-Ferric Podzols but soil moisture and nutrient regimes vary among sites. Fairy Lake installation soils are in the drier, less nutrient-rich range, Sarita Lake is moderate, and Upper Klanawa and San Juan are moister and more nutrient rich. The study area initially supported old-growth stands of western hemlock, western redcedar, amabilis fir (*Abies amabilis* [Dougl.] Forbes), and occasional Douglas-fir and Sitka spruce, and was logged between 1958 and 1960, slash-burned in 1961 and planted in 1962. At each site, 81 seedlings were planted in each of two plots for each species at each of 2.7-m, 3.7-m, and 4.7-m spacing. In this study only the 2.7-m spacing plots were sampled, except at the Fairy Lake site, where one western hemlock plot failed so we sampled a 3.7-m spacing plot. Plots have been maintained since installation and volunteer conifers, (mostly western hemlock) have been periodically removed.

If the hypothesis is correct, then relative to the other tree species, cedar litter and forest floors will have higher pH and Ca, higher populations of bacteria, nitrifiers and soil macrofauna, and more available N in nitrate form, but will not have faster decay or greater N availability.

RESULTS

Consistent with our hypothesis, cedar litter at the EP 571 sites had lower N and higher Ca and AUR concentrations than the other litters (Table 2). Cedar foliar litter decayed more slowly than litter of western hemlock or Douglas-fir (Fig. 2).

Table 2 – Nutrient and carbon concentrations (mg g^{-1}) in foliar litter of western redcedar and other conifers at the EP 571 sites. AUR = acid-unhydrolyzable residue (recalcitrant material, %). Adapted from Prescott et al. (2000).

Species	N	C/N	P	K	Ca	Mg	AUR
cedar	5.46	102	0.48	0.6	16.7	0.8	48
	b		b	b	a	b	a
hemlock	5.26	109	0.43	0.6	8.2	1.2	37
	b		b	b	c	a	c
Douglas-fir	7.60	75	0.53	0.4	6.9	0.8	39
	a		b	b	c	b	bc
spruce	7.71	73	0.80	1.6	11.6	1.2	42
	a		a	a	b	a	b

Values are means with SE given in parentheses of four samples per species or site. For each parameter, means followed by different letters are significantly different (p < 0.05) based on Duncan's multiple range test.

Cedar forest floors also had higher pH, higher concentrations of Ca and Mg and lower N concentrations than the other species (Table 3).

Table 3 – Mass (Mg ha^{-1}), pH, and nutrient concentrations (mg g^{-1}) in forest floors of western redcedar and other conifers at the EP 571 sites. Adapted from Prescott et al. (2000).

Species	Mass	pH	N	P	K	Ca	Mg
cedar	59	4.8	8.6	0.93	0.83	9.7	2.4
	a	a	a	ab	c	a	a
hemlock	36	4.3	8.6	0.88	1.23	4.9	1.7
	ab	b	b	b	ab	b	a
Douglas-fir	32	4.5	9.0	0.87	1.04	6.0	2.0
	b	a	ab	b	bc	b	a
spruce	47	4.8	10.3	1.06	1.50	8.7	2.1
	ab	a	a	a	a	a	a

Values are means with SE given in parentheses of eight samples per species or site. For each parameter, means followed by different letters are significantly different (p < 0.05) based on Duncan's multiple range test.

Rates of net N mineralization and nitrification were highly variable within plots and differed greatly among sites, but average rates were slightly higher under cedar (Fig. 3). Lower fungal:bacterial ratios were found in cedar forest floors (Fig. 4). However, assessment of communities of soil invertebrates did not provide evidence for greater populations of earthworms, millipedes or enchytraeids in cedar forest floors (S. Berch, unpublished data).

CONCLUSIONS

In conclusion, the evidence to date is consistent with the suggestion that western redcedar produces recalcitrant, low-N litter which decomposes relatively slowly, but has high Ca concentrations which stimulate nitrification. This creates the unusual situation in which the forest floor is N-poor but dominated by nitrate. It follows that the presence of nitrate is not necessarily an indication of high N availability. There is also little evidence that western redcedar preferentially takes up the nitrate form of nitrogen.

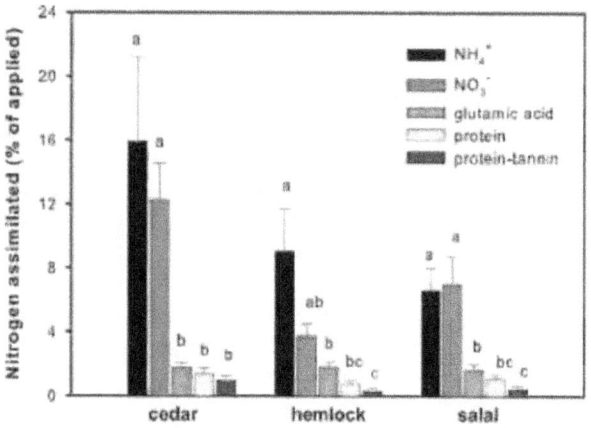

Figure 1–Uptake of ^{15}N-enriched solutions of $Ca(NO_3)_2$, $(NH_4)_2SO_4$, glutamic acid, plant protein, and plant protein-tannin complex by cedar, hemlock and salal seedlings following injection into the forest floor at the beginning of the 20-day greenhouse trial. Adapted from Bennett and Prescott (2004).

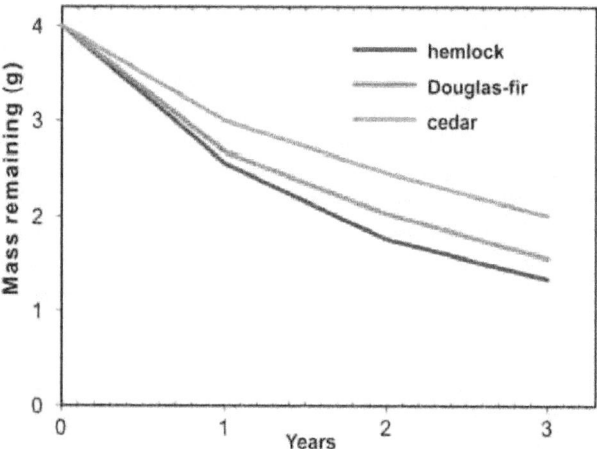

Figure 2–Mass loss of foliar litter of western redcedar and other conifers during 3 years at the EP 571 sites. Adapted from Prescott et al. (2000).

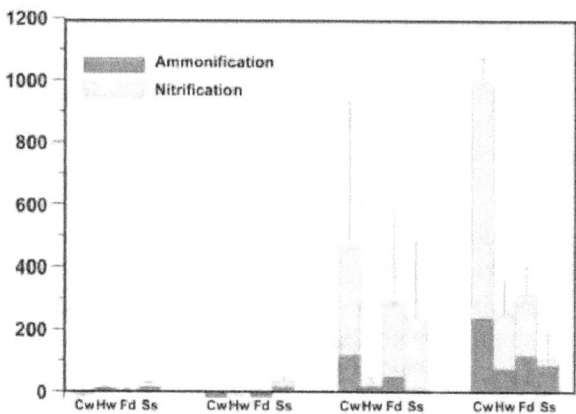

Figure 3–Rates of N mineralization and proportion of ammonium and nitrate (μg g^{-1} 25 d^{-1}) produced during a 25-day laboratory incubation of forest floors from four tree species at the four EP 571 sites. Error bars are standard errors (n = 2). Tree species abbreviations are as follows: Cw - western redcedar; Hw - western hemlock; Fd - Douglas-fir; Ss - Sitka spruce. Adapted from Prescott et al. (2000).

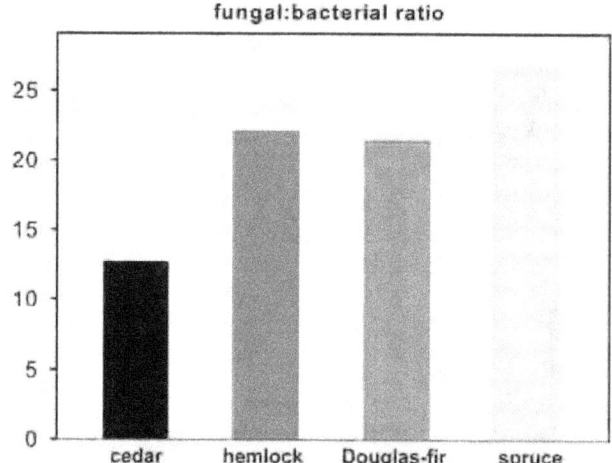

Figure 4–Fungal:bacterial ratios of forest floors from four tree species at the EP 571 sites. Adapted from Grayston and Prescott (2005)

LITERATURE CITED

Alban, D.H. 1969. The influence of western hemlock and western redcedar on soil properties. Soil Sci. Soc. Amer. Proc. 33: 453-457.

Bennett, J.N.; Prescott, C.E. 2004. Organic and inorganic nitrogen nutrition of western redcedar, western hemlock and salal in mineral N-limited cedar-hemlock forests. Oecologia 141: 468-476.

Bennett, J.N.; Prescott, C. E.; Barker, J.E.; Blevins, D.P.; Blevins, L.L. 2003. Long-term improvement in productivity and nutrient availability following fertilization and vegetation control on a cedar-hemlock cutover. Can. J. For. Res. 33: 1516-1524.

Binkley, D. 1995. The influence of tree species on forest soils: processes and patterns. Pp. 1-33 in: Proceedings of the Trees and Soil Workshop, Lincoln University. Edited by D.J. Mead and I.S. Cornforth. Agronomy Society of New Zealand Speical Publication # 10, Lincoln University Press, Canterbury, New Zealand. 122 p.

Binkley, D.; Giardina, C. 1998. Why do tree species affect soils? The warp and woof of tree-soil interactions. Biogeochemistry 42: 89-106.

Grayston, S.J.; Prescott, C.E. 2005. Microbial communities in forest floors under four tree species in coastal British Columbia. Soil Biol. Biochem. 37: 1157-1167.

Harmer R.; Alexander, I. 1986. The effect of starch amendment on nitrogen mineralisation from the forest floor beneath a range of conifers. Forestry 59: 39-46.

Harmon, M.E.; Baker, G.A.; Spycher, G.; Greene, S.E. 1990. Leaf-litter decomposition in the *Picea/Tsuga* forests of Olympic National Park, Washington, U.S.A. For. Ecol. Manage. 31: 55-66.

Hobbie, S.E.; Reich, P.B.; Oleksyn, J. 2006. Tree species effects on decomposition and forest floor dynamics in a common garden. Ecology 87: 2288-2297.

Klinka, K.; Krajina, V.J.; Ceska, A.; Scagel, A.M. 1989. Indicator plants of coastal British Columbia. University of British Columbia Press, Vancouver. 330 p.

Krajina, V.J.; Madoc-Jones, S.; Mellor, G. 1973. Ammonium and nitrate in the nitrogen economy of some conifers growing in Douglas-fir communities of the Pacific north-west of America. Soil Biol.Biochem.5: 143-147.

Lageniere, J.; Pare, D.; Bradley, R.L. 2008. Linking the abundance of aspen with soil faunal communities and rates of belowground processes within single stands of mixed aspen-black spruce. Appl. Soil Ecol. 41: 19-28.

Meidinger, D.V.; Pojar, J. 1991. Ecosystems of British Columbia. B.C. Ministry of Forests, Victoria, B.C. Spec. Rep. Ser. 6.

Ovington J.D. 1954. Studies of the development of woodland conditions under different trees. II. The forest floor. J. Ecol. 42: 71-80.

Prescott, C.E.; Preston, C.M. 1994. Nitrogen mineralization and decomposition in forest floors in adjacent plantations of western red cedar, western hemlock, and Douglas-fir. Can. J. For. Res. 24: 2424-2431.

Prescott, C.E.; Thomas, K.D.; Weetman, G.F. 1995. The influence of tree species on nitrogen mineralisation in the forest floor: Lessons from three retrospective studies. pp 59-68 in: Pp. 1-33 in: Proceedings of the Trees and Soil Workshop, Lincoln University. Edited by D.J. Mead and I.S. Cornforth. Agronomy Society of New Zealand Speical Publication # 10, Lincoln University Press, Canterbury, New Zealand. 122 p.

Prescott, C.E.; Vesterdal, L.; Preston, C.M.; Simard, S.W. 2004. Influence of initial chemistry on decomposition of foliar litter in contrasting forest types in British Columbia. Can. J. For. Res. 34: 1714-1729.

Prescott, C.E.; Vesterdal, L.; Pratt, J.; Venner, K.H.; de Montigny, L.M.; Trofymow, J.A. 2000. Nutrient concentrations and nitrogen mineralization in forest floors of single species conifer plantations in coastal British Columbia. Can. J. For. Res. 30: 1341-1352.

Read, D. J.; Perez-Moreno, J. 2003. Mycorrhizas and nutrient cycling in ecosystems – a journey towards relevance? New Phytol. 157: 475-492.

Reich, P.B.; Oleksyn, J.; Modrzynski, J.; Mrozinski, P.; Hobbie, S.E.; Eissenstat, D.M.; Chorover, J.; Chadwick, O.A.; Hale, C.M.; Tjoelker, M.G. 2005. Linking litter calcium, earthworms and soil properties: a common garden test with 14 tree species. Ecol. Lett. 8: 811-818.

Turner, D.P.; Franz, E.H. 1985. The influence of western hemlock and western redcedar on microbial numbers, nitrogen mineralization, and nitrification. Plant Soil 88: 259-267.

THE EFFECTS OF EXCESSIVE MOISTURE ON SOIL C AND N MINERALIZATION AND SITE PRODUCTIVITY IN COASTAL FORESTS OF BRITISH COLUMBIA

Toktam Sajedi[1] and Cindy E. Prescott

ABSTRACT

Conifers regenerating on cutovers of cedar-hemlock (CH) forests exhibit slow growth and nutrient deficiencies (N and P) which are not observed on adjacent cutovers of hemlock-amabilis fir (HA) forests. The underlying causes of the nutrient deficiencies are not understood. Our field investigations indicate that CH soils are wetter, oxygen-limited and potentially more anaerobic than HA sites. We hypothesize that these conditions will be associated with lower mineralization of C and N, changes in prevalent N forms and lower forest productivity. Forest floor and mineral soil from 5 CH and 5 HA sites were incubated for 4 weeks in the laboratory at four moisture levels (field moisture and three levels up to saturation), and total N and C, dissolved inorganic and organic N (DIN and DON), microbial biomass and CO_2 flux were measured.

Microbial biomass, C mineralization (CO_2 efflux) and the SIN:SON ratio all declined under water-saturated conditions. SON was the most responsive N form to the changes in soil moisture and redox. SON concentrations increased with increasing moisture and decreasing redox potential. Ammonium concentrations were most closely related to total N concentration, and nitrate concentrations were correlated with pH. Concentrations of SIN (especially ammonium) increased with increasing moisture in HA soils, suggesting that excessive moisture did not inhibit N mineralization in HA forests. In contrast, in CH humus and soil, the SIN pool was small and decreased with increasing moisture. Our results indicate that the low N availability on CH sites results from synergistic effects of higher phenolic contents of the organic matter and greater frequency of waterlogging of soils on CH sites.

Improving soil oxygen availability through the use of trenches can be an effective method to enhance timber growth by removing excess water from the rooting zone in wetland forests. The effects of drainage on site productivity and soil carbon stores was assessed by comparing tree growth, understory vegetation, soil C stores and C mineralization in drained and undrained areas in a cedar-swamp cutover that had been operationally drained 10 years earlier. Drainage improved tree growth and increased soil total C storage in the humus layer. However, laboratory incubation indicated that microbial biomass C and C mineralization (CO_2) efflux were not affected. Our results indicate that drainage could be a useful silvicultural practice for improving the productivity of cedar-swamp ecosystems in coastal B.C. and that it may be possible to improve tree growth without stimulating loss of soil C. This requires that drainage improve aeration in the rooting zone while maintaining redox levels of less than +300 mV in the bulk soil, a condition where oxygen level may be sufficient for plant growth but not for aerobic microbial decomposition.

[1] Faculty of Forestry, 2424 Main Mall, University of British Columbia, Vancouver, BC, V6Z 1L1, tsajedi@gmail.com

THE BIOGEOCHEMISTRY OF CEDAR FORESTS: THE CEDAR-NITRATE HYPOTHESIS

David V. D'Amore[1] and Paul E. Hennon

ABSTRACT

Yellow-cedar (*Chamaecyparis nootkatensis* (D. Don) Spach) and western redcedar (*Thuja plicata* Donn) are competitive in low productivity sites on wet, nearly saturated soils in forests of the Pacific Northwest, British Columbia and southeast Alaska. One means of surviving these marginal conditions is through exploiting a coupled calcium (Ca^{+2}) and nitrate (NO_3^-) nutrient cycle where trees assimilate N as NO_3^-, but must accumulate a counter-ion to NO_3^- such as Ca^{+2} to control their internal cell pH and provide electrochemical balance. This 'cedar-nitrate hypothesis' has been proposed as an explanation for the presence of yellow- and redcedar in ecotonal areas between open peatlands and well-drained soils. However, this process occurs preferentially near the soil surface where higher pH and aerobic soil promote nitrification leading to a potential susceptibility of the trees to freezing injury. Cedars must concentrate fine-root biomass near the soil surface to access Ca and NO_3^- and this physiological adaptation that makes these cedars more competitive on marginal sites also creates a vulnerability to periodic root freezing injury that is leading to the decline of at least one of them – yellow-cedar. The proliferation of shallow fine roots to facilitate this nutrient acquisition strategy is consistent with the findings that yellow-cedar has been subject to fine root freezing injury leading to widespread decline. Cedars influence the soils under their canopy by enriching the forest floor with calcium compounds leading to increases in pH. The availability of NO_3^- in cedar forests is favored by increased microbial activity and shifts in microbial community composition that is conducive to N mineralization and nitrification at higher pH. The cedar-nitrate process leads to fundamental shifts in the biogeochemistry of cedar forests. These biogeochemical changes have a potentially substantial cumulative impact on soil and streamwater that is incorporated into an entire watershed signal. We will provide evidence from a replicated yellow-cedar forest stand study to support the nutrient cycles associated with the cedar-nitrate hypothesis. We will also describe how the feedback mechanisms between the trees and soils of cedar forests impact watersheds. This information can be used to formulate management and adaptation strategies in the growing region of both yellow- and redcedar trees. We also explore the links to other cedars and the potential for the development of the cedar-nitrate acquisition strategy to guide the management and ecological understanding throughout the 'cedar' family.

---
[1] Forest Service, U.S. Department of Agriculture, Pacific Northwest Research Station, Juneau, AK 99801, U.S.A. ddamore@fs.fed.us (corresponding author), Tel: 907-586-7922, Fax: 907-586-7848; phennon@fs.fed.us

DECOMPOSITION AND NUTRIENT DYNAMICS IN WESTERN REDCEDAR/HEMLOCK AND DOUGLAS-FIR/HEMLOCK ECOSYSTEMS ON THE WESTERN OLYMPIC PENINSULA OF WASHINGTON

Emily E.Y. Moghaddas[1], John G. McColl[2], Robert L. Edmonds[3], and Barbara Cade-Menun[4]

ABSTRACT

Western redcedar and Douglas-fir are important tree species at lower elevations in the Pacific Northwest US and western Canada, but they differ ecologically. Despite these differences they grow together. Western hemlock is commonly associated with both species. This study was conducted to determine: (1) differences in soil between western redcedar/hemlock and Douglas-fir/hemlock stands on the western Olympic Peninsula of Washington, (2) differences in decomposition rates of a common woody substrate (birch sticks), (3) differences in nutrient immobilization and release, and (4) potential nutritional advantages for western redcedar and Douglas-fir to grow together. Stands ranged in age from about 75 years to old-growth. Birch sticks were placed in three western redcedar/hemlock sites near Kalaloch and three Douglas-fir/hemlock sites near Forks, Washington in May 1998 and retrieved after 6, 12 and 16 months. Sticks were analyzed for C, N, P, K, Ca, and Mg. Mass loss tended to be greater in sticks in Douglas-fir/hemlock than western redcedar/hemlock stands after 16 months (38% versus 34%), but not significantly ($p < 0.05$). Temperature and moisture conditions in the stands were similar. Nitrogen and P were immobilized in sticks in both stand types, but to a lesser extent in western redcedar/hemlock than Douglas-fir/hemlock. Calcium, K, Mg were initially lost from the sticks and then slightly immobilized in both stand types. Soil pH in the upper 10 cm of mineral soil was similar in western redcedar/hemlock and Douglas-fir/hemlock stands (3.9 versus 4.0). There were no significant differences in concentrations of C and N and C/N ratios in the A horizon soil in the Douglas-fir/hemlock and western redcedar/hemlock sites. However, concentrations of total P and Ca were significantly higher in the Douglas-fir/western redcedar sites than the western redcedar/hemlock sites. The A horizon depth was also significantly greater in the western redcedar/hemlock stands. Nutritionally western redcedar might benefit from the higher P levels provided by Douglas-fir and Douglas-fir might benefit from the deeper rooting western redcedar which would aid in nutrient retention.

KEYWORDS: Decomposition, nutrient cycling, western redcedar, Douglas-fir

INTRODUCTION

Western redcedar (*Thuja plicata*) and Douglas-fir (*Pseudotsuga menziesii*) are important tree species at lower elevations in the Pacific Northwest US and western Canada. However, they differ considerably ecologically. Western redcedar is tolerant of shade and high soil moisture, while Douglas-fir is intolerant of shade and high soil moisture. Douglas-fir is fire tolerant and western redcedar is fire intolerant. Western redcedars also tend to live longer than Douglas-firs. Furthermore, western redcedar is an arbuscular mycorrhizal species while Douglas-fir is an ectomycorrhizal species. They also differ nutritionally, with western redcedar thought to be a Ca accumulator. Western redcedar has a wider range tolerance of nutrient availability, and grows better on extremely N-

1 Pacific Southwest Research Station, USDA Forest Service, Taylorsville, CA 95983

2 Ecosystem Science Division, Department of Environmental Science, Policy and Management, University of California, Berkeley CA 94720

3 School of Forest Resources, University of Washington, Seattle, WA 98195

4 Agriculture and Agri-Food Canada, Swift Current, Saskatchewan, S9H 3X2, Canada

poor western redcedar-salal sites. Both species respond to N and P fertilization (Klinka and Brisco 2009).

Despite these differences they grow together. Western hemlock (*Tsuga heterophylla*) is a common associate of both and all three can occur together. Currently there is considerable interest in growing western redcedar with Douglas-fir in plantations instead of planting monocultures of Douglas-fir. However, western redcedar is heavily browsed by deer and is hard to establish.

Tree species can greatly influence litter substrate quality and have a large effect on the chemical and physical nature and decomposition of the forest floor (Prescott 1996, 2002; Prescott and Vesterdal 2005). Tree species also strongly influence the chemistry of throughfall and stemflow. Concentrations of PO_4, SO_4 tended to be higher in Douglas-fir throughfall and stemflow than western redcedar and hemlock in an old-growth rain forest on the Olympic Peninsula of Washington (Edmonds et al. 1991). Also stemflow had higher concentrations of Ca, K, Mg and Na in Douglas-fir. Ammonium concentrations tended to be higher in western redcedar throughfall and stemflow, but NO3 concentrations were similar.

Few studies contrasting decomposition and nutrient dynamics of western redcedar and Douglas-fir have been conducted. Our specific objectives were to determine (1) differences in soil between western redcedar/hemlock and Douglas-fir/hemlock stands on the western Olympic Peninsula of Washington, (2) differences in decomposition rates of a common woody substrate (birch sticks), (3) differences in nutrient immobilization and release, and (4) nutritional advantages for western redcedar and Douglas-fir to grow together. The data presented here are part of a larger study involving determination of decomposition rates and nutrient dynamics at the mineral soil/forest floor interface under Douglas-fir and incense cedar (*Calocedrus decurrens*) in the California Sierra Nevada and Douglas-fir and western

redcedar in the temperate rainforest of coastal Washington and the Mediterranean-type climate of California (Greinke 2000).

STUDY SITES

Study sites were located within or near the lower Soleduck and Hoh River valleys of the Olympic Peninsula, Washington. Three western redcedar/hemlock sites near Kalaloch and three Douglas-fir/hemlock sites near Forks were selected. There is little difference in climate among the sites. Total annual precipitation averages about 300 cm, mostly falling from October to May. Mean monthly air temperature ranges from 4° C in January to 16° C in August (National Climate Data Center, U.S. Dept. of Commerce). The relatively young soils are classified as Dystrustepts and Ustorthents, with solum depths ranging from 30 to 110 cm. Douglas-fir, western redcedar, western hemlock and Sitka spruce were overstory species on the Douglas-fir/hemlock sites while only western redcedar, western hemlock and Sitka spruce occurred on the western redcedar/hemlock sites. Oxalis oregana, Gaultheria shallon and Vaccinium parvifolium were the dominant understory species on Douglas-fir /hemlock sites and Blechnum spicant, Gaultheria shallon, Vaccinium ovatum and Vaccinium parvifolium dominated on western redcedar/hemlock sites.

MATERIALS AND METHODS
Soils
Forest floor depths and horizon depths were determined by digging soil pits at each site. Concentrations of C, total N, organic P, inorganic P, total P, available P, and Ca were determined in the A horizons. C/N ratios were calculated.

Decomposition
Highly uniform, untreated white birch (*Betula papyrifera*) craft sticks ($2 \times 18 \times 130$ mm) were obtained from Penley Corp, New Paris, ME. Sticks were linked together in sets of ten. In April, 1998, 15 sets of sticks were buried lying flat between the forest floor and mineral soil at each of the 6 study sites. Five sets were collected at each site in fall 1998, spring 1999,

and fall 1999, corresponding to 6, 12 and 16 months of decomposition, respectively.

Sample processing and nutrient analyses
Sample processing and nutrient analyses were conducted at the University of California at Berkeley, with the exception of C and N, which were conducted at the Division of Agriculture and Natural Resources Analytical Lab, University of California, Davis. Sticks were oven dried to constant weight at $65°$ C. Stick weights were corrected for ash content and mass loss was calculated. Sticks were ground in a Wiley mill (Thomas Scientific, Swedesboro, NJ) to pass a 40-mesh screen. Total ash content was determined by incinerating at $600°$ C for 16 h. A subsample was digested in nitric acid and analyzed for phosphorus (P), potassium (K), calcium (Ca), and magnesium (Mg) by ICP spectrometry. Carbon and total N were determined using a Nitrogen/Carbon Analyzer 112-200-11 (Carlo-Erba, Milan, Italy).

Statistical analysis
Student's t tests (Microsoft Office Excel 2007) were used to determine differences in variables between western redcedar/hemlock and Douglas-fir/hemlock sites. Statistical differences were determined at $p<0.05$.

RESULTS AND DISCUSSION
Soils
The O horizon depth was not significantly different between the Douglas-fir/hemlock (5.0+ 2.6 cm) and western redcedar/hemlock (7.0 + 2.0 cm) sites. However, the A horizon depth was significantly deeper in western redcedar/hemlock (24.0+ 4.4 cm) than in Douglas-fir/hemlock (7.5+ 6.1 cm).

There were no significant differences in concentrations of C and N and C/N ratios in the A horizon soil in the Douglas-fir/hemlock and western redcedar/hemlock sites (Table 1). Prescott and Vesterdal (2005) also found similar levels of total N in cedar forest floors relative to Douglas-fir and hemlock, but a higher proportion of nitrate relative to ammonium. They also found higher concentrations of Ca.

However, we found that concentrations of Ca in A horizon soils were significantly higher in the Douglas-fir/hemlock sites than the western redcedar/hemlock sites. Total P concentrations were also significantly higher in Douglas-fir/hemlock sites. Organic P, inorganic P, and available P concentrations also tended to be higher, but not significantly because of the high variation. Organic P tended to be the dominant form of P in the Douglas-fir hemlock sites, while inorganic P was the dominant form in the western redcedar/hemlock sites.

There were also no significant differences in the A horizon pH (Table 1). However, Prescott and Vesterdal (2005) found that western redcedar forest floors had higher pH (6.1) in comparison to Douglas-fir (4.4) and hemlock (3.9).

Table 1-Average ($\pm$ SD) A horizon soil nutrient characteristics and concentrations in Douglas-fir/hemlock and western redcedar/hemlock sites. P concentrations are in mg/kg while Ca is in cmol$_c$/kg. Averages with different letters are significantly different ($p \leq 0.05$).

	Douglas-fir/ hemlock	western redcedar/ hemlock
pH	4.0 ± 0.3a	3.9 ± 0.2a
C (%)	8.0 ± 2.0a	8.8 ± 1.7a
N (%)	0.4 ± 0.1a	0.4 ± 0.2a
C/N	21.7 ± 0.3a	24.8 ± 8.3a
Org P	1105 ± 798a	43 ± 20a
Inorg P	560 ± 180a	375 ± 220a
Total P	1665 ± 650a	418 ± 236b
Avail P	33.8 ± 30.2a	2.8 ± 2.0a
Ca	0.7 ± 0.2a	0.4 ± 0.1b

Decomposition of birch sticks
There were no significant differences in decomposition rate of the birch sticks in the western redcedar/hemlock and Douglas-

fir/hemlock sites after 6, 12 and 16 months (Fig. 1). However, decomposition tended to be faster at the Douglas-fir/hemlock sites after all time periods. Prescott and Vesterdal (2005) found that Douglas-fir and hemlock forest floors had faster decomposition than cedar forest floors. Also Graystone and Prescott (2005) found higher bacterial biomass and lower fungal biomass in cedar forest floors than Douglas-fir and hemlock forest floors.

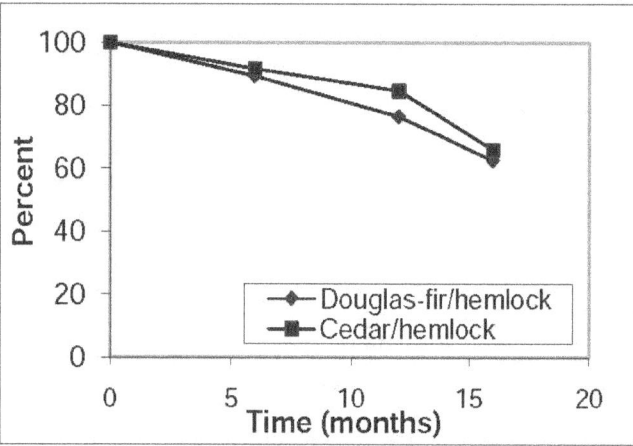

Figure 1 -- Percent mass remaining of birch sticks at the western redcedar/hemlock and Douglas-fir/hemlock sites after 6, 12 and 16 months.

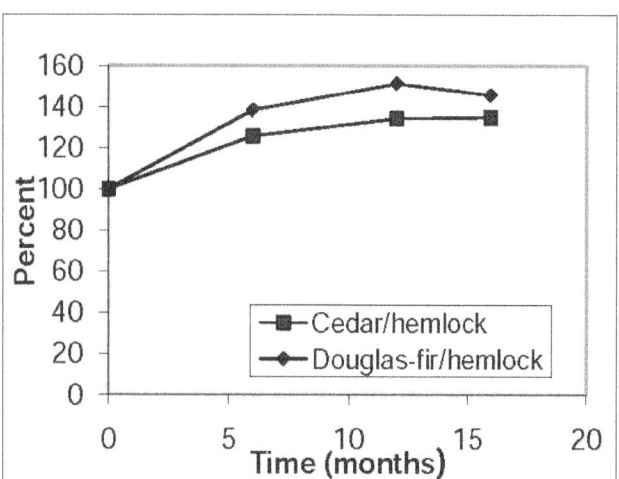

Figure 2 -- Changes in original percent N in birch sticks at the western redcedar/hemlock and Douglas-fir/hemlock sites after 6, 12 and 16 months.

Nutrient immobilization and release
Changes in percent original N mass in birch sticks with times are shown Figure 2. Nitrogen

was more rapidly immobilized in the Douglas-fir/hemlock sites than the western redcedar/hemlock sites. However, N began to be released after 12 months in the Douglas-fir/hemlock sites, but in the western redcedar/hemlock stand N continued to be immobilized for 16 months. The C/N ratio also decreased more rapidly with time in the Douglas-fir/hemlock sites than the western redcedar/hemlock stand. Like N, P was more rapidly immobilized in the Douglas-fir/hemlock sites than the western redcedar/hemlock sites (Fig. 3), and the·C/P ratio fell more rapidly in Douglas-fir/hemlock sites. In contrast to N and P, Ca, K, and Mg were initially released from the decomposing birch stakes, but then began to be immobilized at both Douglas-fir/hemlock and western redcedar/hemlock sites. However, even after 16 months the percent of original Ca, K, and Mg was less than 100%. The nutrient mobility series after 16 months was similar in both western redcedar/hemlock (K<Mg<Ca<N<P) and Douglas-fir/hemlock (K<Mg=Ca<N<P) with K being most mobile and P being least mobile.

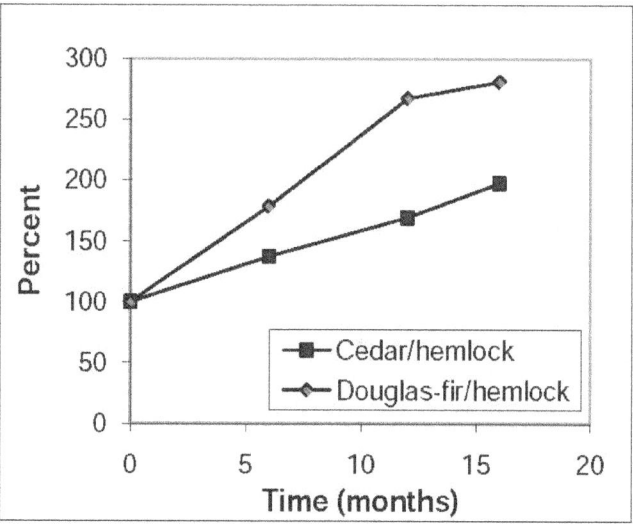

Figure 3 -- Percent P remaining in birch sticks at the western redcedar/hemlock and Douglas-fir/ hemlock sites after 6, 12 and 16 months.

Nutritional advantages for western redcedar and Douglas-fir to grow together
There may be a number of nutritional advantages for western redcedar and Douglas-fir

to grow together along with western hemlock. Western redcedar and Douglas-fir in particular have quite different throughfall and stemflow chemistry (Edmonds et al. 1991). Concentrations of PO_4, SO_4 tend to be higher in Douglas-fir throughfall and stemflow than western redcedar and hemlock. Also stemflow has higher concentrations of Ca, K, Mg and Na in Douglas-fir than western redcedar. Ammonium concentrations tended to be higher in western redcedar throughfall and stemflow, but NO_3 concentrations were similar.

We found that concentrations of P, particularly organic P, were much higher in the A horizon soil in Douglas-fir/hemlock sites than western redcedar/hemlock sites perhaps reflecting differences in throughfall and stemlow in western redcedar and Douglas-fir. The tendency for faster decomposition in the Douglas-fir/hemlock sites might also indicate that the presence of Douglas-fir could make N and P more available to western redcedar when they grow together. In addition, western redcedar growing with Douglas-fir could result in deeper A horizons since western redcedar tends to root deeper than Douglas-fir (Bennett et al. 2002), more C storage, less nutrient loss below the rooting zone, and greater site occupancy. Western redcedar will also increase soil biodiversity since it has arbuscular mycorrhizal fungi and Douglas-fir and hemlock have ectomycorrhizal fungi.

LITERATURE CITED

Bennett, J. N.; Andrew, B.; Prescott, C.E. 2002. Vertical fine root distributions of western redcedar, western hemlock, and salal in old-growth cedar-hemlock forests on northern Vancouver Island.

Edmonds, R.L.; Thomas, T.B.; Rhodes, J.J. 1991. Canopy and soil modification of precipitation chemistry in an old-growth temperate rainforest. Soil Sci. Soc. Am. J. 55: 1685-1693.

Graystone, S.J.; Prescott,C.E. 2005. Microbial communities in forest floors under four tree species in coastal British Columbia. Soil. Biol. Biochem. 37: 1157-1167.

Greinke, E.Y.K. 2000. Wood decomposition and nutrient dynamics in California and Washington forests. MS thesis, University of California (Berkeley), Berkeley, CA.

Klinka, K.; Brisco, D. 2009. Silvics and silviculture of coastal western redcedar: a literature survey. B.C Min. For. Range, For. Sci. Prog., Victoria, B.C. Spec. Rep. Ser. 11.

Prescott, C. E. 1996. Influence of forest floor type on rates of litter decomposition in microcosms. Soil Biol. Biochem. 28: 1319-1325.

Prescott, C.E. 2002. The influence of the forest canopy on nutrient cycling. Tree Physiol. 22: 1193-1200.

Prescott, C. E. 2005. Decomposition and mineralization of nutrients from litter and humus. In:. BassirRad, H. (ed). Nutrient Acquisition by Plants: An Ecological Perspective. Springer-Verlag, Berlin: 125-41.

Prescott, C. E.; Vesterdal. 2005. Effects of British Columbia tree species on forest floor chemistry. In: Binkley, D. ; Menyailo, O., eds. Tree species effects on soils: Implications for Global Change, Springer, Dordrecht, The Netherlands: 17-29.

ECOPHYSIOLOGICAL PROCESSES OF WESTERN REDCEDAR (*THUJA PLICATA*) AND YELLOW-CEDAR (*CALLITROPSIS NOOTKATENSIS*)

Steven C. Grossnickle[1] and John H. Russell[2]

ABSTRACT

Each tree species has its own unique pattern of physiological response to field site environmental conditions. This presentation reviews the physiological performance of western redcedar (*Thuja plicata* Donn) and yellow-cedar (*Callitropsis nootkatensis* (D. Don) Spach) in relation to environmental conditions. It must be recognized that environmental conditions change daily, seasonally and yearly. These two species show physiological responses to these changing environmental conditions. Their physiological performance in response to the environment ultimately determines these species subsequent performance in relation to field site conditions. This presentation is a synthesis of two decades of research by the authors and others. The first part of the presentation centers around the gas exchange processes of western redcedar and yellow-cedar in relation to atmospheric (i.e., light, humidity, temperature) and edaphic (i.e., soil temperature and water) conditions that occur in the field. Where available, information on these species growth is discussed in relation to these atmospheric and edaphic conditions. The second part of the presentation focuses on the seasonal patterns of freezing tolerance and drought tolerance of western redcedar and yellow-cedar. Where available, the talk will explore the dynamic nature of physiological responses and growth patterns that occurs for these species in a yearly cycle.

KEYWORDS: western redcedar, yellow-cedar, ecophysiology, gas exchange, freezing tolerance, drought tolerance.

INTRODUCTION

Each tree species has its own unique pattern of physiological response to field site environmental conditions. The physiological performance of western redcedar (*Thuja plicata* Donn) and yellow-cedar (*Callitropsis nootkatensis* (D. Don) Spach) is driven by their response to environmental conditions. It must be recognized that environmental conditions change daily, seasonally and yearly. These two species show physiological responses to these changing environmental conditions. Their physiological performance in response to the environment ultimately determines these species subsequent performance in relation to field site conditions. The following sections briefly describe the major ecophysiological response patterns of these two species. Detailed discussions of the ecophysiological processes of western redcedar and yellow-cedar can be found in the list of publications by the authors (see attached list).

Photosynthetic Patterns

Western redcedar and yellow-cedar have specific photosynthetic patterns in relation to atmospheric (i.e., light, humidity, temperature) and edaphic (i.e., soil temperature and water) conditions that occur in the field. Photosynthetic patterns of these species are only minimally affected by air temperatures >15 °C. Below 15 °C there is a decline in photosynthesis with decreasing air and soil temperature, with western redcedar more sensitive of the species.

- Western redcedar declines at a faster rate (i.e. 46% greater decrease per 1 °C) than yellow-cedar.
- Yellow-cedar has greater photosynthetic capability at below freezing

[1] CellFor Inc., #4 6772 Oldfield Rd., Saanichton, BC, Canada V8M 2A3. sgrossnickle@cellfor.com
[2] Cowichan Lake Research Station, BC Ministry of Forests and Range, Box 335, Mesachie Lake, BC, Canada V0R 2N0

temperatures (i.e. 68% higher @ -7.5 °C).

Like air temperature, these species are only minimally affected by soil temperatures >15 °C. Below 15 °C there is a decline in photosynthesis with decreasing soil temperature, with western redcedar more sensitive of the species.

- Western redcedar declines at a faster rate (i.e. 58% greater decrease per 1 °C) than yellow-cedar.
- Yellow-cedar has greater photosynthetic capability at near-freezing temperature (i.e. 33% higher @ 0 °C).

Photosynthesis is at a maximum when western redcedar and yellow-cedar are exposed to well-watered conditions (predawn water potential (ψ_{pd}) of -0.5 MPa). Photosynthetic capability declines with decreasing soil water availability with both species comparable in their response to drought.

- Western redcedar declines to 20% of maximum photosynthetic capability at a predawn water potential (ψ_{pd}) of -1.4 MPa (compared to photosynthesis @ a ψ_{pd} of -0.5 MPa) and 9% of maximum photosynthetic capability at a ψ_{pd} of -2.4 MPa.
- Yellow-cedar declines to 32% of maximum photosynthetic capability at a ψ_{pd} of -1.4 MPa and 3% of maximum photosynthetic capability at a ψ_{pd} of -2.4 MPa.

Photosynthesis is at a maximum when western redcedar and yellow-cedar are exposed to vapour pressure deficits (VPD) of <1.0 kPa. For both species their photosynthetic capability declines with increasing VPD.

- Yellow-cedar is more sensitive to drying air with their photosynthetic capability declining at 11% to 19% greater decrease per 1 kPa increase in VPD than western redcedar.

Both species show a rapid increase in their photosynthetic capability as sunlight increases to 25% of full sunlight; thereafter both species have a continued gradual increase in photosynthesis as light level increase to full sunlight. Both species have a comparable photosynthetic response to light. However, under normal field conditions as light levels increase, VPD typically increases, thereby tempering the benefits of high light levels on these species photosynthetic capabilities.

GROWTH RESPONSE

Western redcedar and yellow-cedar growth patterns are responsive to critical seasonal environmental conditions. Both of these species are found to have optimum root growth at soil temperatures of ~22 °C. Low soil temperatures in the spring can limit root growth.

- Western redcedar has an 8% decrease in root growth per 1 °C as soil temperature declines from 22 °C.
- Yellow-cedar has a 7% decrease in root growth per 1 °C as soil temperature declines from 22 °C.

During the spring, shoot flush for both western redcedar and yellow-cedar is initiated after they have received 700 thermal hours (hourly average >5 °C).

Shoot growth is at a maximum when western redcedar and yellow-cedar are exposed to well-watered conditions (ψ_{pd} of -0.5 MPa). Availability of water is a major factor limiting shoot growth in the summer.

- Western redcedar shoot growth decreases 4% per -0.1 MPa decline in ψ_{pd} (compared to growth @ a ψ_{pd} of -0.5 MPa).
- Yellow-cedar shoot growth decreases by 7% decrease per -0.1 MPa decline in ψ_{pd}.

Shoot growth patterns of these species are only minimally affected by air temperatures >15 °C. However, there is a decrease in shoot growth when air temperatures are <15 °C in the fall.

- Western redcedar shoot growth slows by a rate of 17% decrease per 1 °C during the fall.
- Yellow-cedar has a decrease of 13% in shoot growth per 1 °C in the fall.

For both species shoot growth and mitotic activity cease at 4 °C.

FREEZING TOLERANCE

Freezing tolerance of western redcedar and yellow-cedar has a seasonal shift; from a low level of freezing tolerance during the active summer-early fall growing season to maximum freezing tolerance in the middle of the winter. Freezing tolerance then declines from the mid winter maximum to a low level by early spring. The shift in freezing tolerance from these maximum and minimum levels is driven, in part, by how these species respond to seasonal temperature changes.

Freezing tolerance increases in the fall in response to decreasing air temperature.

- Western redcedar has a 1.4 °C increase in freezing tolerance per 1 °C decline in average fall air temperature from 15 to 5 °C. After shoot growth activity ceases freezing tolerance continues to increase by 2 °C per 1 °C decline in average air temperature from 5 to 0 °C.
- Yellow-cedar also has a 1.4 °C increase in freezing tolerance per 1 °C decline in average fall air temperature from 15 to 5 °C. However, after shoot growth activity ceases freezing tolerance increase by 5 °C per 1 °C decline in average air temperature from 5 to 0 °C, more than double the acclimation rate of western redcedar.

Freezing tolerance decreases in late winter and early spring in response to increasing air temperature.

- Western redcedar has a 1.9 °C decrease in freezing tolerance per 100 thermal hours (from 0 to 500 thermal hours). After shoot growth activity is initiated freezing tolerance continues to decrease by 4.0 °C per 100 thermal hours.
- Yellow-cedar has only a 0.7 °C decrease in freezing tolerance per 100 thermal hours (from 0 to 500 thermal hours). After shoot growth activity is initiated freezing tolerance continues to decrease by 3.1 °C per 100 thermal hours.

DROUGHT TOLERANCE

Drought tolerance of western redcedar and yellow-cedar also has a seasonal shift; from a low level of drought tolerance during the active growing season to maximum drought tolerance in the middle of the winter. This shift in drought tolerance from these minimum to maximum levels is driven, in part, by how these species respond to late summer drought conditions and fall seasonal temperature changes.

Drought tolerance is low when western redcedar and yellow-cedar are actively growing and exposed to well-watered conditions (ψ_{pd} of -0.5 MPa). Drought tolerance increases in response to summer drought conditions.

- Western redcedar osmotic potential at saturation (Ψ_{sat}) decreases by 1.7% and osmotic potential at turgor loss point (Ψ_{tlp}) decreases by 3.5% per -0.1 MPa decrease in ψ_{pd} (compared to well-watered seedlings growing with a ψ_{pd} of -0.5 MPa).
- Yellow-cedar Ψ_{sat} decreases 0.8% and Ψ_{tlp} decreases by 0.9% per -0.1 MPa decrease in ψ_{pd} (compared to well-watered seedlings growing with a ψ_{pd} of -0.5 MPa).

Drought tolerance is low when western redcedar and yellow-cedar are actively growing and exposed to air temperatures >15 °C. Drought tolerance increases with declining temperature.

- Western redcedar Ψ_{sat} decreases by 7% and decreases by 13% for Ψ_{tlp} per temperature change of 1 °C (compared to well-watered seedlings growing at 15 °C).
- Yellow-cedar Ψ_{sat} only decreases 1% and Ψ_{tlp} decreases by only 3% per temperature change of 1 °C (compared to well-watered seedlings growing at 22 °C).

Conclusion

This review briefly describes how the physiological performance of western redcedar and yellow-cedar are driven by their response to environmental conditions. Overall, western redcedar displays ecophysiological patterns that allow this species to respond to environmental conditions typically found in lower elevation forests that have potentially drier summer conditions and milder winter temperature conditions. Yellow-cedar generally shows ecophysiological patterns that allow this species to respond to environmental conditions typically found in high elevation forests that have potentially wetter summer conditions and colder winter temperature conditions.

LIST OF PUBLICATIONS

Arnott, J.T.; Grossnickle, S.C.; Puttonen, P.; Mitchell, A.K.; Folk, R.S. 1994. Influence of nursery culture on growth, cold hardiness and drought resistance of yellow cypress. Can. J. For. Res. 23:2537-2547.

Fan, S.; Grossnickle, S.C.; Russell, J.H. 2008. Morphological and physiological variation in western redcedar (*Thuja plicata* Donn. Ex D. Don) populations under contrasting soil water conditions. Trees, 22:671-683.

Folk, R.S.; Grossnickle, S.C.; Arnott, J.T.; Mitchell, A.K.; Puttonen, P. 1996. Water relations, gas exchange and morphological development of fall- and spring-planted yellow cypress stecklings. For. Ecol. Manage. 81:197-213.

Folk, R.S.; Grossnickle, S.C.; Major, J.E.; Arnott, J.T. 1994. Influence of nursery culture on western red cedar. II. Freezing tolerance of fall-planted seedlings and morphological development of fall- and spring-planted seedlings. New Forests, 8:231-247.

Folk, R.S.; Grossnickle, S.C.; Russell, J.H. 1995. Gas exchange, water relations and morphology of yellow-cedar seedlings and stecklings before planting and during field establishment. New Forests, 9:1-20.

Grossnickle, S.C. 1992. Relationship between freezing tolerance and shoot water relations of western red cedar. Tree Physiol. 11:229-240.

Grossnickle, S.C. 1993. Shoot water relations and gas exchange of western hemlock and western red cedar seedlings during establishment on a reforestation site. Trees, 7:148-155.

Grossnickle, S.C.; Fan, S.; Russell,J.H. 2005. Variation in gas exchange and water use efficiency patterns among populations of western redcedar. Trees, 19:32-42.

Grossnickle, S.C.; Russell, J.H. 1990. Water movement characterization of yellow-cedar (*Chamaecyparis nootkatensis* (D. Don) Spach) seedlings and rooted cuttings. Tree Physiol. 6:57-68.

Grossnickle, S.C.; Russell, J.H. 1991. Gas exchange processes of yellow-cedar (*Chamaecyparis nootkatensis* (D. Don) Spach) in response to environmental variables. Can. J. Bot. 69:2684-2691.

Grossnickle, S.C.; Russell, J.H. 1993. Water relations and gas exchange processes of yellow-cedar donor plants and cuttings in response to maturation. For. Ecol. Manage. 56:185-198.

Grossnickle, S.C.; Russell, J.H. 1996. Changes in shoot water relations parameters of yellow-cedar (*Chamaecyparis nootkatensis* D. Don) Spach) in response to environmental conditions. Can. J. Bot. 74:31-39.

Grossnickle, S.C.; Russell,J.H. 2006. Yellow-cedar and western redcedar ecophysiological response to fall, winter and early spring temperature conditions. Ann. of For. Sci. 63: 1-8.

Grossnickle, S.C.; Russell, J.H. 2010. Physiological variation among western redcedar (*Thuja plicata* Donn *ex* D. Don) populations in response to short-term drought. Ann. of For. Sci. 67:506-517.

Major, J.E. 1993. Influence of dormancy induction treatments on the photosynthetic response of field planted western hemlock and western redcedar seedlings. UBC MSc. Thesis.

Major, J.E.; Grossnickle, S.C.; Folk,R.S.; Arnott, J.T. 1994. Influence of nursery culture on western red cedar. I. Measurement of seedling attributes before fall and spring planting. New Forests, 8:211-229.

Russell, J.H. 1993. Genecology and genetic architecture in yellow-cedar. UBC PhD Thesis.

STEM WATER POTENTIAL OF WESTERN REDCEDAR AND DOUGLAS-FIR SEEDLINGS GROWING ACROSS A SOIL MOISTURE GRADIENT

Trevor Walter[1] and Gregory Ettl

ABSTRACT

Stem water potential of 2 year-old western redcedar (*Thuja plicata*) and Douglas-fir (*Pseudotsuga menziesii*) seedlings was measured across a range of volumetric water content. Western redcedar and Douglas-fir were planted in the winter of 2008 following a variable retention harvest of a 78 year-old Douglas-fir dominated stand at Pack Forest in the foothills of the western Cascades, WA. Stem water potential of 18 western redcedar and 18 Douglas-fir seedlings were measured on a hot day in August, 2009 (~32°C) across a gradient of soil water moisture: 3-33% volumetric water content. Seedlings were selected to represent the microsite variability in water availability which ranged from dry convexities to moist depressions. Branches from seedlings were clipped, placed in aluminum foil pouches, and stored in plastic bags with a moist towel in a cooler until water potential measurements could be taken (within an hour). A Scholander type pressure bomb was used to measure water potential predawn, and then at 9:30 AM, 1:00 PM (solar noon), 4:00 PM and 8:00 PM by clipping different branches off of each seedling throughout the course of the day.

Water potential readings were more negative for Douglas-fir than western redcedar across all soil moisture levels. Western redcedar showed its greatest water stress (-1.9 MPa) by 9:30 AM on dry sites, but water stress (-1.6 MPa) was delayed until solar noon and was less severe on wetter sites. Douglas-fir showed the greatest water stress (-2.0 to -2.7 MPa) at solar noon regardless of soil moisture, however seedlings with greater than 16% volumetric water content showed greater water stress (< -2.5 MPa), than seedlings from lower soil moisture sites. The results suggest differences in water stress response and a greater ability of western redcedar to tolerate moist soils than Douglas-fir.

---

[1] Center for Sustainable Forestry at Pack Forest, School of Forest Resources, College of the Environment, University of Washington, P.O. Box 352100, Seattle, WA 98195, ettl@uw.edu

FOLIAGE AND LIGHT-USE EFFICIENCIES OF WESTERN REDCEDAR (THUJA PLICATA) STANDS COMPARED TO WESTERN HEMLOCK (TSUGA HETEROPHYLLA)

Roderick W. Negrave[1]

ABSTRACT

Intensive silvicultural treatments have been suggested to increase forest productivity and for carbon sequestration in Coastal British Columbia. Better understanding of the effects of these treatments on growth processes will improve the ability to manage these treatments and increase ecological understanding of the species involved. This study examined the effects of fertilization, planting density and site light-capture, light-use efficiency and foliar efficiency in juvenile western redcedar (cedar) and western hemlock (hemlock) stands on northern Vancouver Island.

A factorial experiment was established in 1988 to examine the effects of: NPK fertilization versus non-fertilized; three establishment densities of 500 stems per ha (sph), 1500 sph and 2500 sph; the two species; and tree-size class. This design was replicated (4x) on two sites: Nutrient-poor cedar-hemlock (CH) and nutrient-medium hemlock-amabilis fir (*Abies amabilis*) (HA) sites. In 1997 and 2002, the experiment was measured for heights and diameters. Biomass estimation equations were developed through destructive sampling in 2002 and applied to plot data to produce estimates of total biomass and incremental biomass growth for each species. Photosynthetically-active light interception was assessed with hemispheric photography. Stand- and tree-level measures for growth efficiency were developed for foliage and intercepted light. Analysis was completed using PROC GLM in SAS ($p < 0.05$).

Fertilization did not improve foliar or light-use growth efficiency but increasing establishment density decreased these variables. Cedar had lower foliar growth efficiency than hemlock and this varied with tree size, tended to increase with tree size in cedar but decrease with size in hemlock. Light interception was increased by fertilization and increasing density. Growth increased exponentially with light interception. Results suggest that fertilization is a more efficient tool for increasing stand productivity compared to increasing density. If grown together, cedar will likely be at a disadvantage to hemlock during the early rotation and fertilization will amplify this disadvantage.

---

[1] Coast Forest Region, Ministry of Forests and Range, 2100 Labieux Rd., Nanaimo, BC, V9T 6E9

SECTION B

FOREST HEALTH

CLIMATE

GENETICS

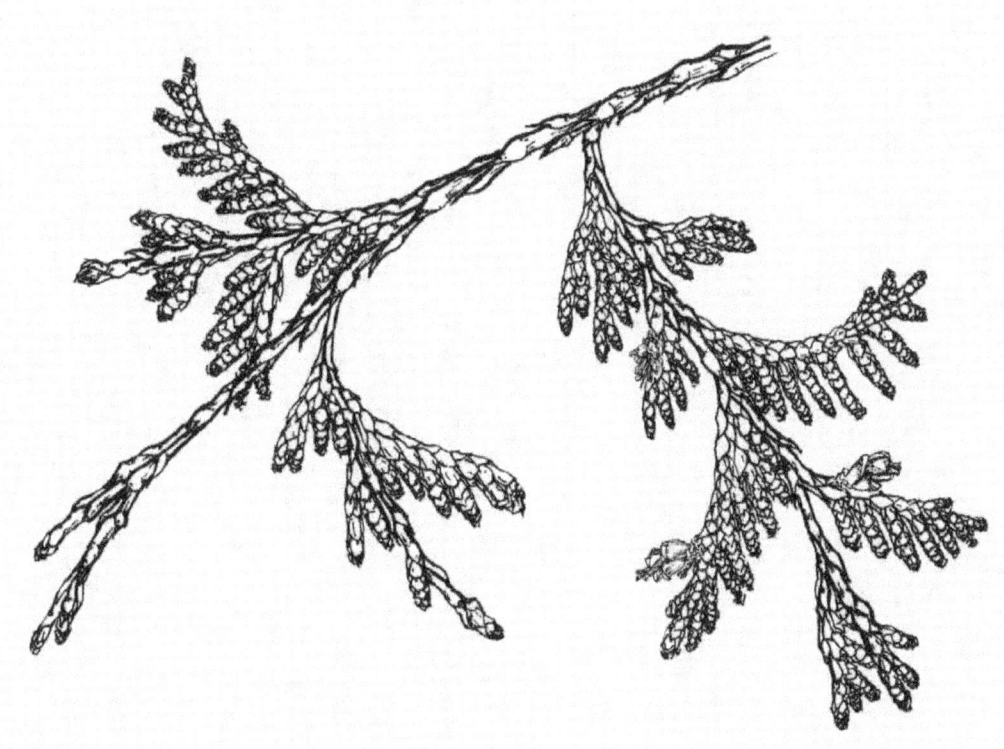

DETERMINING THE POTENTIAL TO RECONSTRUCT POPULATION DYNAMICS OF YELLOW-CEDAR IN DECLINING STANDS USING DENDROCHRONOLOGY

Amanda B. Stan[1], Thomas B. Maertens[2], Lori D. Daniels[3], and Stefan Zeglen[4]

ABSTRACT

Yellow-cedar (*Callitropsis nootkatensis,* syn *Chamaecyparis nootkatensis* (D. Don) Spach) forests of coastal British Columbia, Canada are experiencing decline in a manner similar to that observed in southeastern Alaska. In this pilot study, we use tree-ring data from live and standing dead yellow-cedar trees from four declining sites on the North Coast of British Columbia to assess some of the benefits and limitations of using tree rings to reconstruct population dynamics of yellow-cedar in declining stands. We found unique growth patterns between yellow-cedar trees from our sites and those from similar declining sites in nearby Alaska. Using outer-ring dates of increment cores, we were able to estimate time since death of decade to century old standing dead yellow-cedar trees, although the precision of the estimates was influenced by partial cambial mortality and erosion of outer rings. Our results provide valuable information for planning future studies that assess growth-climate relations of yellow-cedar and suggest potential for reconstructing long-term population dynamics of this species in declining stands.

KEYWORDS: dendrochronology, forest decline, *Chamaecyparis nootkatensis*, British Columbia.

INTRODUCTION

Widespread mortality of yellow-cedar (*Chamaecyparis nootkatensis* (D. Don) Spach), referred to as yellow-cedar decline, occurs on more than 250,000 ha of coastal forests in Alaska and British Columbia, Canada (Lamb and Wurtz 2009; Westfall and Ebata 2009). Past research in Alaska suggested that biotic agents were not the primary cause of death of yellow-cedar (Hennon and Shaw 1997). More recent hypotheses implicate factors related to climate change. In particular, increasing late-winter temperatures are leading to reduced snowpack and early dehardening of yellow-cedar, leaving this species susceptible to late-winter freeze events (Hennon et al. 2008).

Research on the population dynamics associated with the decline of yellow-cedar is needed to begin to understand how stands have changed, and potentially will change, in response to this phenomenon. In light of a shifting climate, this need is particularly pressing. Dendrochronology offers potential to assess the population dynamics of yellow-cedar and the decline phenomenon, as it can provide a means to reconstruct long-term trends in age structure, growth patterns, as well as recruitment and mortality rates.

In this pilot study, we explore the potential of dendrochronological techniques to reconstruct yellow-cedar population dynamics and decline. To do this, we use tree-ring data from live, asymptomatic and standing dead yellow-cedar trees from four declining sites on the North Coast of British Columbia. We compare our findings on crossdating quality, growth patterns, time since death, and partial cambial mortality of yellow-cedar to those of other studies in Alaska and British Columbia. Together, this information allows us to assess some of the

[1]Amanda B. Stan worked on this project while a postdoctoral researcher, [2]Thomas B. Maertens is a Ph.D. candidate, and [3]Lori D. Daniels is an Associate Professor, Department of Geography, University of British Columbia, 1984 West Mall, Vancouver, British Columbia V6T 1Z2, Canada
[4]Stefan Zeglen is a Forest Pathologist, Coast Forest Region, British Columbia Ministry of Forests and Range, 2100 Labieux Road. Nanaimo. British Columbia V9T 6E9. Canada

benefits and limitations of using tree rings to reconstruct population dynamics of yellow-cedar in declining stands, providing a foundation for future studies that aim to better understand causes and effects of decline.

METHODS

Field Procedures

We conducted this research at four sites near Prince Rupert, British Columbia (54° 19' N, 130° 20' W). Sites consist of concentrated patches of dying and dead yellow-cedar trees (Fig. 1) and appear to have similar characteristics as those associated with the yellow-cedar decline phenomenon in southeastern Alaska (Hennon et al. 2005). Across all four sites, mean annual temperature is 5.6°C, with a mean of 12.9°C in August and -0.7°C in January (very near the rain-snow temperature threshold), mean annual precipitation is 3793 mm, and mean annual growing season (May to September) precipitation is 982 mm (Wang et al. 2006). Site elevations range from 305 to 518 m a.s.l.

At each site, we entered patches of dying and dead trees and systematically traversed them to locate and core 20 yellow-cedar trees in each of two status classes: live, asymptomatic and standing dead. We visually assessed the crowns and boles of trees (diameter at breast height ≥ 10 cm) to separate healthy from declining and dead. Asymptomatic trees were those that had live and "healthy" crowns (i.e. green) and no obvious bole damage. Standing dead trees were assessed according to the six-class decay system for yellow-cedar described by Hennon et al. (1990).

From each tree, we extracted two increment cores at approximately 30 cm above the ground. In most instances, the second core was taken at a location ≥ 90° from the first core. However, for standing dead trees, we took the second core through the face of basal scars that likely formed prior to the death of other parts of the bole and did not appear to be the result of abrasion. This sampling approach was aimed at

capturing damage potentially associated with root death caused by freezing injury. By coring through these scars, we attempted to obtain data that maximized the difference in outer-ring dates between cores from the same tree to use in our analyses of partial cambial mortality.

Figure 1. Examples of declining yellow-cedar study sites near Prince Rupert, North Coast British Columbia, Canada.

Laboratory Procedures

We prepared all cores following the procedures of Stokes and Smiley (1968). Ring-width series from live, asymptomatic trees were first visually crossdated (Yamaguchi 1991) and then measured to the nearest 0.001 mm using a stereozoom microscope and a Velmex sliding-stage micrometer interfaced with MeasureJ2X software. We used the program COFECHA (Grissino-Mayer 2001) to detect crossdating errors and to calculate average mean sensitivity and average interseries correlation values, which we used to describe the crossdating quality of the ring-width series from each site. Ring-width series that could not be confidently crossdated were removed from the data set.

We used the program ARSTAN (version 41d for Windows XP; Cook 1985) to create a mean chronology for each site. First, we averaged the two ring-width series per asymptomatic tree, using only those years that were accurately dated and common to both series. Next, we detrended each resultant series by first fitting a negative exponential curve, line with a negative slope, or horizontal line, and subsequently fitting an 80-year cubic spline with a 50% frequency response. Finally, we created standard chronologies for the individual sites by averaging the index values of the series using a bi-weight robust mean (Cook et al. 1990).

We measured the ring widths of all standing dead trees and used COFECHA to statistically crossdate individual ring-width series against the corresponding set of site-specific, dated series from asymptomatic trees. After statistical crossdating, we visually examined the ring-width series from each standing dead tree and removed any that could not be accurately dated or that had broken or indiscernible outer rings. For each standing dead tree remaining in the data set, we first estimated its year of death using the most recent outer-ring date of the two ring-width series per tree and then calculated its time since death (i.e. 2007-year of death).

Data Analyses

We compared crossdating quality of the ring-width series from asymptomatic trees among the four sites and assessed growth patterns among the site chronologies. Growth patterns were examined both graphically, by comparing negative and positive marker rings (i.e. rings that differed from the mean tree-ring index by -/+ 1 SD or more) and suppressions (i.e. multi-year periods of below-average growth) among all chronologies, as well as quantitatively, by

calculating Pearson's (r) correlation coefficients between individual chronologies.

For standing dead trees, we combined individuals from all sites and used an ANOVA to test for differences in time since death among decay classes. Prior to analysis, time-since-death estimates were transformed using a natural logarithm. A Tukey's HSD test was subsequently used to contrast means among decay classes. To estimate the frequency and minimum duration of partial cambial mortality in yellow-cedar, we compared the outer-ring dates of the two ring-width series from the same standing dead tree. Finally, we calculated Spearman's (ρ) correlation coefficient to assess whether the difference in outer-ring dates between individual ring-width series from the same standing dead tree showed an increasing trend with increasing time since death.

RESULTS

Crossdating quality of the ring-width series from live, asymptomatic trees at each site was similar among all four sites. Average mean sensitivity values were 0.24 ± 0.01 (mean ± SD here and throughout the text). Average interseries correlation values were 0.48 ± 0.02.

Growth patterns of live, asymptomatic trees were similar among the four sites. The site chronologies ranged from 410 to 488 years. Between 1798 and 2006, the period in which all four chronologies had a minimum of 10 trees, there was an average of 32.0 ± 2.9 negative and 25.0 ± 1.7 positive marker rings (Fig. 2). During that same period, all four chronologies had negative marker rings in seven years: 1811, 1876, 1936, 1958, 1960, 1986, and 1987; three of the four chronologies had negative marker rings in an additional 16 years: 1810, 1812, 1835, 1856, 1873, 1875, 1877, 1887, 1894, 1896, 1917, 1918, 1920, 1926, 1972, and 1998 (Fig. 2). Between 1798 and 2006, periods of suppressed growth lasting three to eight years occurred in all four chronologies in the late 1800s through 1810s, 1870s, the late 1910s through the early 1920s, 1930s, 1950s, 1970s, and the late 1980s. Correlations between individual site chronologies ranged from 0.52 to 0.78 (p < 0.001) between 1798 and 2006.

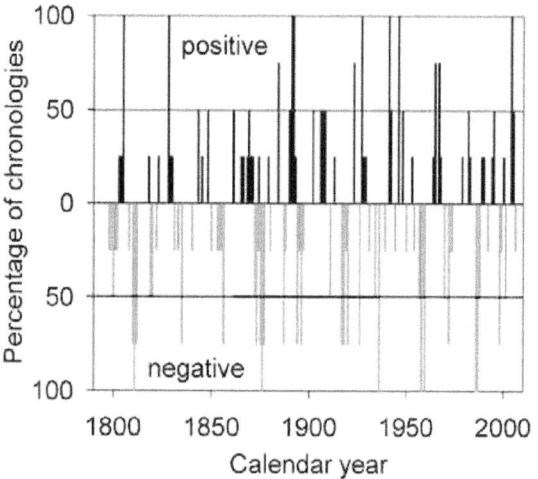

Figure 2. Percentage of ring-width chronologies (n = 4) with a negative or positive marker ring in each year from 1798-2006, i.e. the period in which all four chronologies had a minimum of 10 trees. Marker rings are those that depart from the mean tree-ring index by -/+1 SD or more.

We successfully crossdated 121 of 158 (77%) ring-width series from standing dead yellow-cedar and estimated the year of death of 70 of 79 (89%) trees. Of the 37 remaining ring-width series, eight were too suppressed to confidently crossdate and 29 had broken or indiscernible outer rings. Except for two trees with outer-ring dates of 1903 (decay class IV) and 1728 (decay class V), all trees had outer-ring dates between 1949 and 2006. Therefore, for 68 of the 70 trees assessed, time since death in 2007 ranged from 1 to 58 years.

Time since death increased significantly (F = 78.65, p < 0.001) with advanced stages of decay. Standing dead trees in decay classes I (n = 21), II (n = 25), and III (n = 20) died 4.71 ± 1.87, 12.56 ± 5.31, and 25.15 ± 9.87 years ago, respectively. Three trees in decay class IV (time since death = 40, 58, 104 years) and one tree in decay class V (time since death = 279 years) were not included in the analysis because of small sample sizes for those two classes.

The outer-ring dates of the two ring-width series from the same standing dead tree (n = 51) differed between 0 and 13 years. A total of 16% had the same outer-ring date. In contrast, 53% had dates that differed from 1 to 3 years, and 31% had dates that differed by more than 3 years. The difference in outer-ring dates between individual ring-width series from the same standing dead tree showed an increasing trend with increasing time since death (Spearman's ρ = 0.56, p < 0.001).

DISCUSSION

Crossdating quality of the ring-width series from live, asymptomatic trees at each of our four sites is comparable to the crossdating quality of all other known yellow-cedar ring-width series, which are from higher-elevation (> 1000 m a.s.l.), non-declining sites in southwestern British Columbia (Laroque and Smith 1999; Kellner et al. 2000; Parish 2005) and lower-elevation (< 300 m a.s.l.), non-declining and declining sites in southeastern Alaska (Beier et al. 2008). Our average mean sensitivity and interseries correlation values lie in the middle and upper end, respectively, of the range of all known values for yellow-cedar. Overall, these findings provide evidence of a moderately strong common signal and high-quality crossdating among the individual ring-width series at each of our four sites.

Common marker rings and periods of suppressed growth, as well as strong correlations, indicate coherency in growth patterns of yellow-cedar trees among our four sites. Interestingly, our chronologies from declining sites on the North Coast of British Columbia have negative marker rings in common with chronologies from declining sites in southeastern Alaska (i.e. 1926, 1936, 1986, 1987; Beier et al. 2008). Based on the resemblance of growth patterns between our yellow-cedar trees and those of trees in Alaska, similar growth-climate relations are plausible at declining yellow-cedar sites in British Columbia.

Our results demonstrate the feasibility of estimating time since death by means of directly assessing dead trees using dendrochronological techniques. For yellow-cedar trees in decay classes I to III, Hennon et al. (1990) found similar, although slightly more variable, time-since-death estimates as ours. In that study, the authors used an indirect approach, in which time-since-death estimates of trees in different decay classes were determined using dates of radial-growth releases of nearby living hemlock trees. Although slight, the lower variability in our results demonstrates the value of directly sampling standing dead trees to attain more precise time-since-death estimates of individuals in different decay classes.

While direct dendrochronological dating can sometimes provide more precise time-since-death estimates, this approach does have its shortcomings. Besides the fact that directly sampling standing dead trees may not be possible because of erosion of outer rings, even when it is, the correspondence of an outer-ring date to the actual death date of a tree is complicated by the potential for a tree to produce partial or no annual rings as it dies. In this study, a difference in outer-ring dates between individual ring-width series from the same standing dead tree suggests evidence of partial cambial mortality at our sites, with a gradual cessation of radial growth around the circumference of individual yellow-cedar trees that tends to happen over just a few years, rather than decades. Collecting multiple increment cores per tree provides an estimate of the minimum duration of mortality of yellow-cedar in declining stands that represents the degree of error when determining year of death using only a single core. However, because this estimate increases with time since death, it may represent error from erosion of rings over time as well as error from partial cambial mortality.

CONCLUSIONS
Our pilot study provides a foundation for additional research in declining stands. For example, by identifying unique growth patterns between our yellow-cedar chronologies and those from comparable declining sites in Alaska, our study informs others that aim to assess the extent to which yellow-cedar in British Columbia is vulnerable to damage from similar climatic stressors as those documented in Alaska (see Beier et al. 2008). Furthermore, our study demonstrates the value of dendrochronology for providing information on time since death and partial cambial mortality of yellow-cedar that will be useful for reconstructing various aspects of this species' population dynamics in declining stands. For example, estimating time since death of individual trees in different decay classes will facilitate reconstructing the frequency of yellow-cedar mortality through time and determining dead wood persistence in different classes. In addition, information on the frequency and duration of partial cambial mortality allows for a better understanding of tree decline and the use of less-intensive sampling procedures in the future. Future studies that assess growth-climate relations and reconstruct population dynamics of yellow-cedar in declining stands will provide managers with information essential to project changes to stands and ecosystem reorganization in coastal forests. For additional details on this study, please refer to Stan et al. (in press).

ACKNOWLEDGEMENTS
We thank Ron Diprose, Rachel Field, Harry Kope, Alex Marshall, Colin Nelson, and Mike Symons for assistance in the field, along with Kevin Johnstone, Jennifer Passmore, and Sonya Powell for assistance in the lab. Mike Grainger and the staff at the British Columbia Ministry of Forests and Range (BCMFR), North Coast Forest District, provided logistical support while in Prince Rupert. We are grateful to Colin Beier and Scott Sink for kindly supplying us their COFECHA outputs. The BCMFR provided funding for this project.

LITERATURE CITED
Beier, C.M.; Sink, S.E.; Hennon, P.E.; D'Amore, D.V.; Juday, G.P. 2008. Twentieth-century warming and the dendroclimatology of

declining yellow-cedar forests in southeastern Alaska. Can. J. For. Res. 38:1319-1334.

Cook, E.R. 1985. A time series analysis approach to tree-ring standardization. Ph.D. dissertation, University of Arizona, Tucson, AZ.

Cook, E.R.; Shiyatov, S; Mazepa, V. 1990. Estimation of the mean chronology. Pp 123-132 in: Cook, E.R.; Kairiukstis, L.A., eds. Methods of dendrochronology: applications in the environmental sciences. Kluwer Academic Publishers, Dordrecht, The Netherlands.

Grissino-Mayer, H.D. 2001. Evaluating crossdating accuracy: a manual and tutorial for the computer program COFECHA. Tree-Ring Res. 57:205-221.

Hennon, P.E.; D'Amore, D.V.; Wittwer, D.T.; Caouette, J.P. 2008. Yellow-cedar decline: conserving a climate-sensitive tree species as Alaska warms. Pp. 233-245 in: Deal, R.L., ed. Integrated restoration of forested ecosystems to achieve multiresource benefits: proceedings of the 2007 national siliviculture workshop. Gen. Tech. Rep. PNW-GTR-733. Portland, OR: USDA For. Serv., Pac. NW Res. Stn.

Hennon, P.E.; D'Amore, D.V.; Zeglen, S.; Grainger, M. 2005. Yellow-cedar decline in the North Coast Forest District of British Columbia. Res. Note. PNW-RN-549. Portland, OR: USDA For. Serv., Pac. NW Res. Stn. 16 p.

Hennon, P.E.; Shaw III, C.G. 1997. The enigma of yellow-cedar decline: what is killing these long-lived, defensive trees? J. For. 95:4-10.

Hennon, P.E.; Shaw III, C.G.; Hansen, E.M. 1990. Dating decline and mortality of *Chamaecyparis nootkatensis* in southeast Alaska. For. Sci. 36:502-515.

Kellner, A.M.E.; Laroque, C.P.; Smith, D.J.; Harestad, A.S. 2000. Chronological dating of high-elevation dead and dying trees on northern Vancouver Island, British Columbia. Northwest Sci. 74:242-247.

Lamb, M.; Wurtz, T., compilers 2009. Forest health conditions in Alaska – 2008. For. Heal. Protect. Rep. R10-PR-20. Juneau, AK: USDA For. Serv., Alaska Region 102 p.

Laroque, C.P.; Smith, D.J. 1999. Tree-ring analysis of yellow-cedar (*Chamaecyparis nootkatensis*) on Vancouver Island, British Columbia. Can. J. For. Res. 29:115-123.

Parish, R., 2005. Mount cain, Alaska yellow-cedar tree-ring record (CANA175). In: Grissino-Mayer, H.D.; Fritts, H.C., eds. International tree-ring data bank. IGBP PAGES/World Data Center-A for Paleoclimatology. NOAA/NGDC Paleoclimatology Program, Boulder, CO.

Stan, A.B.; Maertens, T.B., Daniels, L.D.; Zeglen, S. In press. Reconstructing population dynamics of yellow-cedar in declining stands: baseline information from tree rings. Tree-Ring Res.

Stokes, M.A.; Smiley, T.L. 1968. An introduction to tree-ring dating. University of Chicago Press, Chicago, IL.

Wang, T.; Hamann, A.; Spittlehouse, D.L.; Aitken, S.N. 2006. Development of scale-free climate data for western Canada for use in resource management. Int. J. Climatol. 26:383-397.

Westfall, J.; Ebata, T. 2009. 2008 Summary of Forest Health Conditions in British Columbia. Pest Management Rep. No. 15. Victoria, BC: BC Ministry of For. & Range, Forest Practices Branch 76 p.

Yamaguchi, D.K. 1991. A simple method for cross-dating increment cores from living trees. Can. J. For. Res. 21:414-416.

PHELLINUS WEIRII AND OTHER FUNGI CAUSING DECAY IN WESTERN REDCEDAR AND YELLOW-CEDAR

Rona N. Sturrock[1], Kevin W. Pellow[1], and Paul E. Hennon[2]

ABSTRACT

In the forests of western North America, western redcedar and yellow-cedar are two long-lived coniferous species that have the rather anomalous distinction of having wood that is very resistant to decay in service but also frequently having extensive decay, especially in old-growth trees. More than a dozen different species of Basidiomycetous decay fungi occur on living western redcedar and yellow-cedar. Despite the fungitoxic properties of the heartwood extractives in these two cedars, decay fungi can get established in trees just a few decades old and eventually cause significant cull or stem breakage. Decayed cedar stems that fail are also important agents of small-scale disturbance, altering the carbon budgets of coastal and inland forests. Research on how *Phellinus weirii,* one of the most important decay fungi occurring on living western redcedar, interacts with this cedar, is ongoing. Additional information is needed to identify the other major decay fungi in western redcedar and yellow-cedar and their infection biology. All such information will be useful to scientists producing carbon models and to professionals managing forests for timber and other resources.

KEYWORDS: Decay fungi, heart rots, root rots, butt rots, western redcedar, *Thuja plicata,* yellow-cedar, *Chamaecyparis nootkatensis, Phellinus weirii*

INTRODUCTION

In the forests of western North America, western redcedar (WRC; *Thuja plicata* Donn) occurs over a wide range of sites and elevations along the Pacific coast from California to southeast Alaska and along the interior wet belt from McGregor, British Columbia (BC) to western Montana and northern Idaho. Yellow-cedar (YC; *Callitropsis nootkatensis,* syn *Chamaecyparis nootkatensis* (D. Don) Spach) occurs predominantly at higher elevations along the Pacific coast from northern California to Prince William Sound in Alaska. In nature, both species reproduce sexually via seeds that mature in one year (WRC) or two years (YC) and also asexually by layering (Andersen 1959, Habeck 1968). These two long-lived coniferous species have the rather anomalous distinction of having wood that is very resistant to decay but also

frequently having extensive decay of live trees, especially in old-growth forests (van der Kamp 1975, 1988). Thus, these cedars have high rates of internal wood decay as live trees, but slow deterioration as dead trees. The trait of decay-resistant wood is a commercially valued property for these two species because of the long durability of wood in service. Individual WRC trees that were regenerated by layering are said to be more susceptible to fungal attack than those regenerated from seed (Klinka and Chourmouzis 2005).

More than a dozen different species of Basidiomycetous decay fungi have been identified on living western redcedar and yellow-cedar trees. Many of these species have several synonyms, a fact that has 1) likely

[1]Rona N. Sturrock is a research scientist, Pacific Forestry Centre, Canadian Forest Service, Natural Resources Canada, 506 W Burnside Road, Victoria, BC V8Z 1M5 Rona.Sturrock@nrcan.gc.ca
[1]Kevin W. Pellow is a research technician, Pacific Forestry Centre, Canadian Forest Service, Natural Resources Canada, 506 W Burnside Road, Victoria, BC V8Z 1M5
[2]Paul E. Hennon is a Research Forest Pathologist, Juneau Forestry Sciences Laboratory, Pacific Northwest Research Station, USDA Forest Service, 2770 Sherwood Lane, Suite 2A, Juneau AK 99801

created confusion about which decay organisms affect the two cedars and 2) made it challenging to find information on cedar decay in both historic and recent literature. The goal of this paper is to provide current information on the decay fungi affecting living WRC and YC trees.

Decay Fungi on Living Western Redcedar and Yellow-cedar

Decay fungi occurring on living WRC and YC trees cause either stem decay (= trunk or heart rots) or root and butt rot. The heart rots, which include *Physisporinus rivulosus* (Berk. & M.A. Curtis) Ryvarden, *Perenniporia subacida* (Peck) Donk, *Phellinidium ferrugineofuscum* (P. Karst.) Fiasson & Niemelä, *Porodaedalea pini* (Brot.) Murrill, *Ganoderma applanatum* (Pers.) Pat., *Fomitopsis pinicola* (Sw.) P. Karst, *Laetiporus conifericola* Burds. & Banik, and *Postia sericeomollis* (Romell) Jülich, tend to be spread by wind-disseminated spores that likely gain entry to living trees through wounds, fire scars, and branch stubs. The root and butt rot fungi may also spread by wind-disseminated spores but more frequently spread vegetatively on roots and/or through the soil. These fungi, which include *Armillaria solidipes* Peck, *Phellinus weirii* (Murrill) Gilb., *Heterobasidion occidentale* Otrosina & Garbelotto, *Onnia tomentosa* (Fr.) P. Karst., and *Phaeolus schweinitzii* (Fr.) Pat., frequently kill and cause decay of cedar roots as well as causing decay in heartwood, sapwood, and cambial tissues.

All of the decay fungi affecting western redcedar and yellow-cedar trees can be further categorized as causing either white rot or brown rot. White rot fungi digest all the components of wood tissue, including lignin, cellulose, and hemicellulose, and leave behind decayed wood that can be described as ranging from whitish to yellowish, spongy to stringy, and laminate to pitted. Brown rot fungi cannot digest lignin and so leave behind a distinctive brown cubical to brown crumbly wood decay which is composed of modified lignin. This material may be quite stable to further deterioration (Gilbertson and Ryvarden 1986) and thus would represent a sequestered form of carbon in the soil. Because most of the internal wood decay in live cedars is caused by white rot fungi, more of their carbon is likely to be released to the atmosphere as CO^2 through the complete deterioration of wood.

Although cedar trees are rarely killed by these decay fungi, infected trees may have extensive internal decay without any external signs of defect (Buckland 1946). More detailed information on each of these fungi and the diseases they cause can be found in publications such as Allen et al. (1996) and Sinclair and Lyon (2005). We thus present a list of fungi that cause wood decay of living western redcedar and yellow-cedar trees (Table 1). Currently, there is not enough information in the literature to identify with certainty which of these fungi are most important in particular regions, and which are minor species that are just occasionally found.

Little is known about the infection biology of the decay fungi affecting WRC and YC. It is thought that a succession of early colonizing fungal 'pioneers', which presumably enter trees through trunk scars or root wounds, detoxify heartwood extractives sufficiently to allow activity by wood-rotting fungi (van der Kamp 1986, Jin 1987, Jin et al. 1988). The principle fungitoxic extractives in WRC include alpha-, beta-, and gamma-thujaplicin, and beta-thujaplicinol (Rennerfelt 1948, Roff and Atkinson 1954), and plicatic acid (Stirling and Morris 2006, Stirling pers. comm. 2010). Biocidal extractives in YC (Barton 1976) include nootkatin, carvacrol, and other compounds (Rennerfelt and Nacht 1955, Kelsey et al. 2005). More research is needed on the suite of organisms involved in the decay processes in WRC and YC, including how and when they interact with heartwood compounds.

Phellinus weirii Research – An Update
Phellinus weirii sensu stricto is considered to be the most important white rot fungus causing decay in western redcedar, particularly in the inland forests of its natural range (Buckland 1946). This fungus also causes significant cull as a butt rot on yellow-cedar (Hennon 1991).

Table 1--A cast of characters: some of the principle decay fungi occurring on western redcedar (*Thuja plicata*) and yellow-cedar (*Chamaecyparis nootkatensis*). More research is needed to determine which of these fungi are important in particular regions and which are minor species just found occasionally.

Pathogen Disease Name	Synonyms	Decay Type	Western Redcedar	Yellow-cedar
Armillaria **spp.** Armillaria root rot	*Armillaria solidipes, A. ostoyae, A. obscura, A. mellea*	Root, White	√	√
Phellinus weirii laminated root rot	*Poria weirii, Fomitiporia weirii, Fuscoporia weirii, Inonotus weirii, Phellinidium weirii*	Root, White	√	√
Heterobasidion occidentale annosus root rot	*Heterobasidion annosum, Fomes annosus, Fomitopsis annosa, Polyporus annosus*	Root, White	√	
Onnia tomentosa Tomentosus root rot	*Inonotus tomentosus, Polyporus tomentosus, Coltrichia tomentosa*	Root, White	√	
Phaeolus schweinitzii schweinitzii butt rot	*Polyporus schweinitzii*	Root, Brown	√	
Physisporinus rivulosus white butt rot – white laminated rot	*Ceriporiopsis rivulosa, Polyporus rivulosus, Poria albipellucida, Poria rivulosa, Rigidoporus rivulosus*	Heart, White	√	
Perenniporia subacida stringy butt rot	*Poria subacida, Polyporus subacida, Poria fuscomarginata*	Heart, White	√	
Phellinidium ferrugineofuscum	*Phellinus ferrugineofuscus, Polyporus ferrugineofuscus*	Heart, White	√	
Porodaedalea pini red ring rot	*Phellinus pini, Fomes pini, Trametes pini*	Heart, White	√	√
Ganoderma applanatum white mottled rot	*Fomes applanatus, Polyporus applanatus*	Heart, White	√	
Fomitopsis pinicola brown crumbly rot	*Fomes pinicola*	Heart, Brown	√	√
Laetiporus conifericola brown cubical rot	*Polyporus sulphureus*	Heart, Brown	√	
Postia sericeomollis brown cubical & pocket rot	*Oligoporus sericeomollis, Polyporus sericeomollis, Poria asiatica, Poria sericeomollis, Tyromyces sericeomollis*	Heart, Brown	√	√

Phellinus weirii was recently confirmed to be a closely related but different fungal species from *P. sulphurascens* Pilát (Lim et al. 2005), which causes laminated root and butt rot of Douglas-fir and several other coniferous species (Thies and Sturrock 1995).

Research on how *P. weirii* and western redcedar interact is ongoing at the Pacific Forestry, Centre, Victoria, BC, Canada. Using a technique that we developed, we have inoculated *P. weirii* onto western redcedar roots in the field and have collected some preliminary data on the early stages of the infection process. To study *P. weirii's* genetics as well as perform other research on this fungus, single spores are required. Since sporocarp formation in *P. weirii* in the wild is not reliable and varies from year to year, depending on environmental conditions, we have developed a technique to induce formation of *P. weirii* fruiting bodies (Fig. 1), thus enabling the collection of single spores. Interestingly, although *P. weirii* is reported to fruit in the spring/mid-summer, we have observed fruiting in the fall as well, when conditions approximate those of the springtime.

We are also actively collecting *P. weirii* isolates from throughout western North America and thus far have over 25 isolates in long-term storage. Using molecular techniques, we have sequenced several genes from *P. weirii* isolates collected from western redcedar over a large geographic area. Results indicate regional differences between these isolates. Better, overall understanding of *P. weirii* behaviour and diversity will facilitate future management of this pathogen in North America's changing forests.

Figure 1-Sporophore of *P. weirii* induced to form on blocks of treated red alder (*Alnus rubra* Bong.). NRCAN, CFS photo.

IMPACTS AND OUTCOMES OF DECAY FUNGI

Decay fungi in general affect the quantity and quality of wood available for products. This issue led to research efforts in the 40s and 50s to document the amount of defect, or cull, in living conifers in the forests of the Pacific Northwest. One such study, conducted by Kimmey (1956), documented high rates of decay in live western redcedar in coastal Alaska. Most of the decay was apparently caused by two white rot fungi - *Physisporinus rivulosus* and *Phellinus weirii* sensu stricto - both of which do not typically form external indicators of defect.

Decay volumes in WRC are highly correlated with tree age. In BC, the total volume of accumulated decay in living trees is greater for WRC than for any other major conifer (Jin et al. 1988). Kimmey (1956) found the same pattern in coastal Alaska, where western redcedar had a higher rate of internal decay at early ages than did the associated western hemlock and Sitka spruce. Less is known about the leading fungi

that cause decay in living yellow-cedar, and the tree age – defect relationship.

The ecological roles of these wood decay fungi in old-growth forests have not received much attention. We have observed old, decayed western redcedar and yellow-cedar trees with boles that snapped to create canopy gaps (Fig. 2). Thus, decay fungi are probably important mortality agents of old cedar trees that create small-scale disturbance (Hennon 1995) in old-growth forests.

Despite the cultural, economic, and ecological importance of western redcedar and yellow-cedar, there is surprisingly little known about the fungi that cause so much defect in these live trees. More information is needed to identify the major decay fungi, resolve their infection biology, and determine at what tree and stand ages they become prevalent in different regions where the two cedars grow. Such information will be useful to scientists producing carbon models and to professionals managing forests for timber and other resources.

Figure 2-Stem breakage due to decay in western redcedar creates canopy gaps and adds woody debris to the forest floor. USDA, FS photo.

LITERATURE CITED

Allen, E.A.; Morrison, D.J.; Wallis, G.W. 1996. Common tree diseases of British Columbia. Victoria, BC: NRCAN, Can. For. Serv. 178 p.

Andersen, H.E. 1959. Silvical characteristics of Alaska-cedar (*Chamaecyparis nootkatensis*). Station Paper 11. Juneau, AK: USDA For. Serv., Alaska For. Res.Center. 10 p.

Barton, G.M. 1976. A review of yellow cedar (*Chamaecyparis nootkatensis* [D. Don] Spach) extractives and their importance to utilization. Wood and Fiber 8: 172-176.

Buckland, D.C. 1946. Investigations of decay in western red cedar in British Columbia. Can. J. For. Res. 18: 158-181.

Gilbertson, R.L.; Ryvarden, L. 1986. North American Polypores. Vol. 1. Fungiflora, Oslo. 433 p.

Habeck, J.R. 1968. Forest succession in the Glacier Park cedar-hemlock forests. Ecology 49: 872-880.

Hennon, P.E. 1991. Diseases, insects, and animal damage of yellow cypress. In: Lousier, J.D., ed. Yellow cypress: can we grow it? Can we sell it: Proceedings of a symposium. Nanaimo, BC: Richmond Inn, Richmond BC: 36-43.

Hennon, P.E. 1995. Are heart rot fungi major factors of disturbance in gap-dynamic forests? Northwest Science 69: 284-293.

Jin L. 1987. Detoxification of Thujaplicins in living western red cedar (*Thuja plicata* Donn.) PhD Thesis. University of British Columbia, Vancouver, British Columbia, Canada.

Jin, L.; van der Kamp, B.J.; Wilson, J. 1988. Biodegradation of thujaplicins in living western redcedar. Can. J. For. Res. 18: 782–786.

Kelsey, R.G.; Hennon, P.E.; Huso, M.; Karchesy, J.J. 2005. Changes in heartwood chemistry of dead yellow-cedar trees that remain standing for 80 years or more in Southeast Alaska. J. Chem. Ecol. 31: 2653-2669.

Kimmey, J.W. 1956. Cull factors for sitka spruce, western hemlock and western redcedar in southeast Alaska. Station Paper 6. Juneau, AK: USDA For. Serv., Alaska For. Res.Center. 31 p.

Klinka, K; Chourmouzis, C. 2005. Ecological and silvical characteristics of major tree species in British Columbia. In: Watts, S.B.; Tolland, L., eds. Forestry handbook for British Columbia. Vancouver, BC: Faculty of Forestry, University of British Columbia: 326-347.

Lim, Y.W.; Yeung, Y.C.A.; Sturrock, R.N.; Leal, I.; Breuil, C. 2005. Differentiating the two closely related species, *Phellinus weirii* and *P. sulphurascens*. Forest Pathology 35: 305-314.

Rennerfelt, E. 1948. Thujaplicin a fungicidal substance in the heartwood of *Thuja plicata*. Physiol. Plant 1: 245-254.

Rennerfelt, E.; Nacht, G. 1955. The fungicidal activity of some constituents from heartwood of conifers. Sven. Bot. Tidskr. 49: 419-432.

Roff, J.W.; Atkinson, P.M. 1954. Toxicity tests of a water-soluble phenolic fraction (thujaplicin-free) of western red cedar. Can. J. Bot 32: 308-309.

Sinclair, W.A.; Lyon, H.H. 2005. Diseases of trees and shrubs. New York: Cornell University Press. 660 p.

Stirling, R. 2010. Rod Stirling, Wood Chemist, Building Systems Department, FPInnovations Forintek, 2665 East Mall, Vancouver, BC, Canada V6T 1W5.

Stirling, R.; Morris, P.I. 2006. The influence of extractives in western redcedar's equilibrium moisture content. International Research Group on Wood Protection . Document No. IRG/WP/06-40331. 12 p.

Thies, W.G.; Sturrock, R.N. 1995. Laminated root rot in western North America. Gen. Tech. Rep. PNW-349. Portland, OR: USDA For. Serv., Pac. NW For. & Range Exp. Stn. 32 p.

van der Kamp, B.J. 1975. The distribution of microorganisms associated with decay of western red cedar. Can. J. For. Res. 5: 61-67.

van der Kamp, B.J. 1986. Effects of heartwood inhabiting fungi on thujaplicin content and decay resistance of western redcedar (*Thuja plicata* Donn.). Wood Fiber Sci. 18: 421-427.

van der Kamp, B.J. 1988. Pests of western redcedar. In: Smith, N.J. ed. Western red cedar—does it have a future: Proceedings of a conference. Vancouver, BC: Faculty of Forestry, University of British Columbia: 145–146.

TRAUMATIC RESIN DUCT FORMATION IN THE PHLOEM OF WESTERN REDCEDAR AND OTHER RESISTANCE MECHANISMS EFFECTIVE AGAINST ARMILLARIA ROOT DISEASE

Michelle R. Cleary[1]

ABSTRACT

Armillaria root disease is a significant forest health concern in the southern interior of British Columbia where the disease causes mortality in conifers and growth loss on trees that sustain non-lethal infections. One option to mitigate potential losses caused by *Armillaria ostoyae* is to plant conifer species that have a low susceptibility to killing by the fungus. A study of the pathological anatomy associated with different conifer species following infection by *A. ostoyae* revealed novel evidence of host reactions in western redcedar (*Thuja plicata*) characterized by traumatic resin ducts becoming included in the phloem. Other host reactions including necrophylactic periderm formation and barrier zone formation associated with compartmentalization of infected woody tissue impart increased resistance to the spread of *A. ostoyae* in host tissue. These results suggest that regenerating western redcedar on sites infested with Armillaria root disease may help alleviate some of the long-term impacts in second growth forests.

KEYWORDS: *Armillaria ostoyae*, western redcedar, resistance, host response, traumatic phloem resin ducts, necrophylactic periderm, British Columbia.

INTRODUCTION

Armillaria ostoyae (Romagn.) Herink is the primary pathogen causing Armillaria root disease of conifers in British Columbia. The fungus is widespread across the southern one-third of the province and is almost universally present and damaging in mid-elevation forests located in the Interior Cedar-Hemlock (ICH) biogeoclimatic zone (Cleary et al. 2008).

Much of the damage within this zone occurs in seral stages in plantations. The disease however goes unnoticed over time with only about one-quarter of trees with belowground infection showing aboveground symptoms of *Armillaria* (Morrison et al. 2000). In this zone, cumulative mortality in Douglas-fir (*Pseudotsuga menziesii* (Mirb) Franco) plantations can be as much as 20% by age 20-years and result in stands being serious understocked (Morrison and Pellow 1994).

Options to mitigate potential losses in new plantations include inoculum removal and planting species with low susceptibility to killing by *A. ostoyae*. Considering the latter however, there are no woody hosts that show complete resistance to the fungus.

In general, all conifer species less than about 15 years of age are highly susceptible to killing by *A. ostoyae* and some conifers will start to show greater resistance to the fungus with age (Morrison et al. 1991, Robinson and Morrison 2001). For example, western larch (*Larix occidentalis* Nutt.) becomes more tolerant of the fungus but only after it reaches about 20-25 years of age. Before this age, western larch suffers very high mortality rates that are as much or sometimes greater than that observed in Douglas-fir (M.Cleary pers comm). Otherwise, very little is known about resistance in most other conifers in British Columbia. Hence, the aim of this study was to identify other useful species that show effective resistance against *A. ostoyae*.

Western hemlock (*Tsuga heterophylla* (Raf.) Sarg.) and western redcedar (*Thuja plicata* Donn ex D. Don) are two species that are

[1] Michelle Cleary is a Forest Pathologist, BC Ministry of Forests and Range, Southern Interior Forest Region, 441 Columbia Street, Kamloops, BC, V2C 2T3, Canada.

commonly found intermixed with planted conifers throughout the ICH biogeoclimatic zone in the southern interior of BC. Both are listed as being highly susceptible to killing by the fungus, but there is some indirect evidence from other studies that suggests western redcedar may in fact be less susceptible to the disease (Delong 1996, Morrison et al. 1988, Morrison et al. 2000). Knowledge of effective resistance mechanisms operating in other species would enable forest manager to explore new silvicultural options with respect to species mixtures in areas where root disease is of concern.

One means of assessing resistance in different conifers is to look for specific resistance mechanisms operating in trees that are effective against the fungus. When trees become infected by *A. ostoyae*, defense mechanisms in the bark and in the wood on root systems will determine the outcome of a particular reaction as being either susceptible or resistant. Several studies have shown necrophylactic periderm (NP) to be involved in resistant reactions in woody plants in response to mechanical injury or pathogenic invasion (Blanchette and Biggs 1992, Wahlström and Johansson 1992, Robinson and Morrison 2001).

The overall objective of this study was to describe and compare host reactions to infection by *A. ostoyae* in the roots of western red cedar, western hemlock, and Douglas-fir; specifically necrophylactic periderm formation in the inner bark and barrier zone formation associated with the compartmentalization of infected woody tissue.

MATERIALS AND METHODS

Between 2002 and 2004, a series of geographically distinct field trials were implemented in ICH zone in the southern interior of BC to describe host response to infection by *A. ostoyae* on 20-30 year old Douglas-fir, western hemlock and western redcedar trees. In the field, root systems of trees were excavated and inoculated with *A. ostoyae* that was previously grown on woody segments in the lab and then sampled after a period of

weeks, months and 1 year post-inoculation. All roots were sectioned and examined for Armillaria lesions. Bark samples were collected, cryofixed and stored in liquid nitrogen. Woody samples showing compartmentalization were fixed in FAA and later sectioned on a rotary microtome to describe barrier zone anatomy.

In the lab, the cryofixed samples were sectioned in a cryostat maintained at -20°C and frozen sections were examined on a fluorescence microscope equipped with a freezing stage set at -35°C. Various histochemical staining techniques were used on thawed sections to detect lignin and suberin in some cells types. For each sample, host reactions and any anatomical changes in cells leading to the formation of these barriers in the bark and in the wood were described at the microscopic level and photographed.

RESULTS

Results showed noticeable differences between species in the ability to produce successful resistance reactions (either a NP in the bark or effective compartmentalization) to contain the fungus.

In Douglas-fir and western hemlock, NP formation was relatively infrequent or was formed initially but then breached by the fungus. Western redcedar responded more efficiently by forming a NP to contain infections in the bark. Other unique reactions induced in cedar included a hypersensitive-type response consisting of rhytidome formation in the vicinity of a site of initial penetration by the fungus. This successive periderm extends for some distance proximally and distally along the length of the root eventually joining the pre-existing periderm.

Also during this study, novel evidence of a host reaction in western redcedar involving traumatic phloem resin ducts (TPRD) was observed (Cleary and Holmes 2010). These resin ducts appeared as small, circular zone of tissue above the vascular cambium and under or adjacent to a a newly differentiated periderm.

A comparative study looking at host response to abiotic wounding versus fungal infection by *Armillaria* showed that the intensity of the response involving TPRD formation was higher in roots inoculated with *A. ostoyae* than in roots that were abiotically wounded (Cleary and Holmes 2010). Deeper injuries to the bark, particularly with those caused by *A. ostoyae*, affected the intensity of the response by increasing the longitudinal expansion of resin canal formation in roots several centimeters beyond the margin of a newly differentiated periderm.

Compartmentalization of *A. ostoyae* infections following cambial invasion was also more frequent on western redcedar roots compared to Douglas-fir and western hemlock. This is due in part to anatomical and biochemical differences between the cedar and the other conifers.

DISCUSSION
In many conifers, the formation of resin ducts in the phloem, xylem, or both, is normal whereas in others it is considered a non-specific host response to biotic or abiotic injury. Western redcedar trees form neither normal nor traumatic resin canals in the xylem (Cleary and Holmes 2010). Some reports exist describing traumatic resin duct formation in the phloem of species belonging to the Cupressaceae (namely Japanese cypress), however this study is the first to document the developmental anatomy and structure of traumatic resin canals in the phloem of western red cedar (Cleary and Holmes 2010). It is interesting that despite traumatic resin ducts being formed in the phloem, resinosus on the surface of the root was never observed. Precisely if or how oleoresin in cedar differs from that found in other conifers and the nature of the biochemical induction of resin ducts in the phloem with respect to its resistance against *A. ostoyae* warrants further investigation.

Overall, the frequency of resistance reactions in western redcedar was on average 3-4 times higher than in Douglas-fir and western hemlock enabling most roots to effectively limit the extent of cambial invasion and/or girdling in roots.

These results have practical implications with respect to reducing losses in new plantations. Planting western redcedar in higher proportions in mixtures with other conifers when regenerating sites infested with *A. ostoyae* can potentially reduced disease spread and tree mortality and help alleviate the long-term impacts of *Armillaria* to a more tolerable level.

ACKNOWLEDGEMENTS
Very special thanks to Ms. Rona Sturrock for presenting this work at the 'Tale of Two Cedars' conference on my behalf. Funding for this research was provided by Forest Investment and Innovation Ltd. (FII), Forest Investment Account – Forest Science Program, Natural Science and Engineering Research Council of Canada, IMAJO Cedar Management Fund, and the Canadian Forest Service – Pacific Forestry Centre. I gratefully acknowledge D. Morrison, G. Jensen, B. van der Kamp, and T. Holmes for their help with various aspects of the work as well as the BC Ministry of Forests and Range, Tolko Industries, and Pope and Talbot Ltd. for their support.

LITERATURE CITED
Blanchette, R.A. and Biggs, A.R. 1992. Defense mechanisms of woody plants against fungi. Springer-Verlag, New York. 458 pp.

Cleary, M.R. and T. Holmes. 2010. Formation of traumatic resin ducts in the phloem of western redcedar (*Thuja plicata*) roots following abiotic injury and pathogenic invasion by *Armillaria ostoyae*. IAWA Journal. [In press]

Cleary, M., van der Kamp, B. and Morrison, D. 2008. British Columbia's southern interior forests – Armillaria root disease stand establishment decision aid. BC Journal of Ecosystems and Management. 9:60-65. URL: http://www.forrex.org/publications/jem/ISS48/vol9_no2_art7.pdf

DeLong, D.L. 1997. A Retrospective Investigation of Advanced Western Redcedar Regeneration in the ICHwk1, ICHmw2, and ICHmw1 of the Nelson Forest Region – Experimental Project 1174. Res, Br., B.C. Min. For., Victoria, B.C. Work Pap. 25/1997.

Morrison, D.J., Pellow, K.W., Norris, D.J., and Nemec, A.F.L. 2000. Visible versus actual incidence of Armillaria root disease in juvenile coniferous stands in the southern interior of British Columbia. Canadian Journal of Forest Research 30:405-414. URL: http://article.pubs.nrc-nrc.gc.ca/ppv/RPViewDoc?_handler_=HandleIn itialGet&Journal=cjfr&volume=30&calyLang=f ra&articleFile=x99-222.pdf

Morrison, D.J., Williams, R.E., and Whitney, R.D. 1991. Infection, disease development, diagnosis, and detection. *In:* Armillaria root disease. *Edited by* C.G. Shaw, III, and G.A. Kile. U.S. Dep. Agric. For. Serv. Agric. Handb. 691. pp. 62-75.

Morrison, D.J., Wallis, G.W., Weir, L.C., 1988. Control of *Armillaria* and *Phellinus* root diseases: 20 year results from the Skimikin stump removal experiment. Pac. For. Res. Cent. Inf. Rep. BC-X-302, Can. For. Serv.

Morrison, D.J. and Pellow, K. 1994. Development of Armillaria root disease in a 25-year-old Douglas-fir plantation. *Eds:* M. Johansson and J. Stenlid. Swedish University of Agricultural Sciences, Uppsala, Sweden. pp. 560-571.

Robinson, R.M. and Morrison, D.J. 2001. Lesion formation in the roots of western larch (*Larix occidentalis* Nutt.) and Douglas-fir (*Pseudotsuga menziesii*) in response to infection by *Armillaria ostoyae* (Romagn.) Herink. For. Path. 31: 376-386.

Wahlström, K.T. and Johansson, M. 1992. Structural responses in bark to mechanical wounding and *Armillaria ostoyae* infection in seedlings of *Pinus sylvestris*. Eur. J. For. Path. 22:65-76.

A LANDSCAPE-LEVEL ANALYSIS OF YELLOW-CEDAR DECLINE IN COASTAL BRITISH COLUMBIA

Claire E. Wooton[1] and Brian Klinkenberg[1]

ABSTRACT

Yellow-cedar (*Chamaecyparis nootkatensis*) is currently undergoing a dramatic decline in western North America, with concentrated areas of decline located in southeast Alaska and coastal British Columbia. Recent research suggests that a shift in climate is responsible for the decline and a working hypothesis concerning the role of climate and biophysical factors has been proposed. In our research project we have investigated the spatial pattern of yellow-cedar decline in British Columbia at the landscape scale. Our study aims to assess whether we can identify any significant relations between landscape-level biophysical variables and areas of decline.

Our research questions are being addressed through a combination of remote sensing and GIS techniques. Sample points were distributed across the landscape according to a stratified sampling scheme and the presence/absence of decline at each point was determined using a forest cover dataset and aerial photograph interpretation. Spatial patterns of biophysical factors (e.g. elevation, slope, aspect) were derived from a 25 m digital elevation model of the province. In order to assess the strength of relations between the distribution of decline and the various environmental predictors, statistical and decision-tree models commonly used in predictive vegetation and species distribution modeling will be applied. Results from the optimal model will be presented, including maps of the probability of decline occurrence and binary presence/absence maps.

Studying how the pattern of decline observed on the landscape relates to biophysical factors will assist in elucidating possible mechanism(s) of decline. Using multiple models in the analysis will allow a thorough investigation of the associations between the biophysical variables and decline. Knowledge of the determinants of the spatial pattern of decline will improve predictability and provide critical information for conservation and resource management.

[1] Department of Geography, University of British Columbia, Vancouver, BC, V6T 1Z2, Canada, cwooton@geog.ubc.ca

BIOCLIMATIC ENVELOPES, FOREST DECLINE RISK FACTORS, AND MODELING SUITABLE HABITAT FOR YELLOW-CEDAR CONSERVATION AND MANAGEMENT

Paul Hennon[1], Dave D'Amore[2], Dustin Wittwer[3], John Caouette[4]

ASTRACT

Yellow-cedar (*Callitropsis nootkatensis, syn. Chamaecyparis nootkatensis*) has suffered an intensive mortality problem through the 1900s in coastal Alaska and adjacent British Columbia known as yellow-cedar decline. Our research has investigated the cause of death through a series of coordinated studies that evaluate climate, site factors, and cedar physiology. Details from some of these studies will be shared in various sessions of this symposium. The occurrence of yellow-cedar decline in Alaska is found on a subset of the distribution of yellow-cedar, suggesting zones of maladaptation. The cause yellow-cedar decline is complex, but can be reduced to two risk factors for landscape models – snow and soil drainage. We combine snow models using climate inputs with landscape models to identify portions of the landscape that are suitable and unsuitable to yellow-cedar as the climate warms. Examples of maladaptation and habitat suitability are given at several spatial scales. This partitioning of the landscape follows the bioclimate envelope concept as the basis for a regional conservation and management strategy. Management options for yellow-cedar in areas where it is maladapted (dead and dying) include salvage to recover valuable wood products. Utilizing dead yellow-cedar for wood products shifts some timber harvesting in other areas where it is thriving and serving conservation goals. More information is needed on successional trajectories in decline-impacted forests, whether or not salvage harvesting is conducted. Suitable current and future habitat for yellow-cedar includes drained soils that support deeper rooting and where snow persists past the last spring frost. Favoring yellow-cedar through artificial regeneration and thinning in these suitable areas will help maintain yellow-cedar in forested ecosystems of Alaska and British Columbia.

Key words: *Chamaecyparis nootkatensis*, yellow-cedar decline, climate, conservation strategy

INTRODUCTION

Yellow-cedar (*Chamaecyparis nootkatensis*) is an important tree along the Pacific coast. Our symposium highlighted the cultural, economic, and ecological values of this tree. Yellow-cedar has been dying on more than 250,000 hectares for the past 100 years in southeast Alaska and adjacent British Columbia. These patches of dead trees are conspicuous on the landscape as concentrations of long-dead, recently-dead, and dying trees. This forest problem is a leading example of a tree species negatively impacted by climate change. The goal of our research is to provide an understanding of the cause of yellow-cedar decline and to help develop a conservation and management strategy to ensure the long-term health of this valuable tree in Alaska's forest ecosystems.

THE BIOCLIMATIC ENVELOPE CONCEPT

The bioclimate envelope (or climate profile) concept is useful in interpreting yellow-cedar decline and in formulating an adaptive strategy for forest management. The distribution of trees is shaped primarily by climate. When climate

[1] Paul Hennon is research plant pathologist, and the corresponding author; [2] Dave D'Amore is research soil scientist, Forestry Sciences Laboratory, Pacific Northwest Research Station, 11305 Glacier Highway, Juneau, AK 99801. [3] Dustin Wittwer is aerial survey specialist, Forest Health Protection, 11305 Glacier Highway, Juneau, AK 99801. [4] John Caouette is statistician, The Nature Conservancy, Juneau, AK 99801

shifts relative to a tree's distribution, three spatial zones can be considered with respect to how well the tree is then adapted: "maladapted" and "stable" zones where the tree is growing,

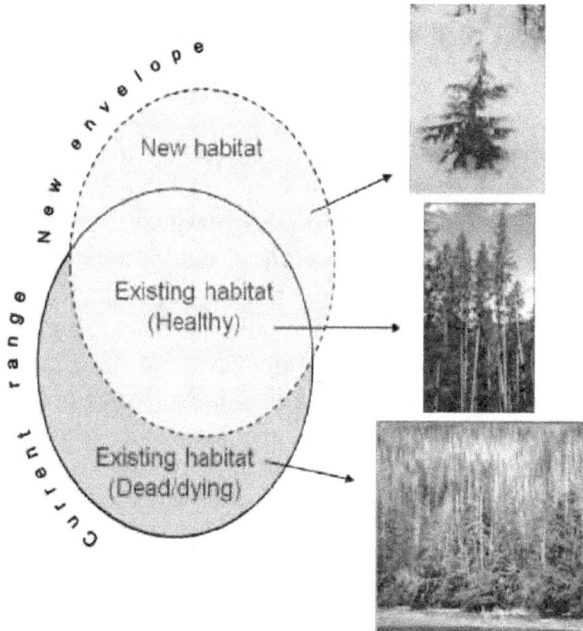

Figure 1-- Left: a shifting bioclimatic envelope creates three theoretical zones of climate adaptation for yellow-cedar: maladaptation where decline occurs, stability where the tree occurs but is not dying at an appreciable rate, and a migration zone where the climate has become suitable and is available for occupancy. Right: distribution of yellow-cedar decline (red) in Alaska represents the "maladapted zone", the surrounding occurrence of yellow-cedar (yellow) represents the "stable zone". The "migration zone" is not shown. The speckled areas on the outer west coast represent the possible refugia where yellow-cedar survived the Pleistocene Epoch; these were likely epicenters from which Holocene migration occurred.

and a "migration" zone that represents new potential habitat (Fig. 1). The broad-scale occurrence of yellow-cedar decline (Fig. 1) can be interpreted as this maladapted zone, which is surrounded by areas where yellow-cedar grows but is not dying at an appreciable rate (i.e., the stable zone). Not shown on this map are areas that have a suitable climate, but where the tree does not yet occur (i.e., migration zone). Note that the migration zone does not imply that the tree will actually migrate there within some time frame; it simply suggests that the climate has become suitable. This concept is dynamic through time, and with inputs of climate forecasting, can indicate predicted suitable habitat into the future.

FOREST DECLINE RISK FACTORS
After evaluating a number of potential biotic and abiotic factors associated with yellow-cedar decline (Hennon et al. 2008), we formed a working hypothesis around the one vulnerability of yellow-cedar—spring freezing injury. The cascading complex of factors that leads to fine root freezing injury in this scenario (Fig. 2) has become the framework for our research, with individual studies directed at testing each interaction of factors (Hennon et al. 2008).

Long-term climate or near-term weather events influence each of these steps. The cool, moist climate that developed in the late Holocene created the bog and forested wetland conditions that favored the abundance of yellow-cedar. Yellow-cedar was competitive on these wet sites through a unique ability to access nitrates with its habit of shallow fine roots (D'Amore et al. 2009). The open canopy conditions on boggy soils allow a more extreme microclimate: greater warming, which appears to trigger cedar dehardening in late winter, and the lack of thermal cover, allowing cold temperatures to penetrate more deeply into soil during cold

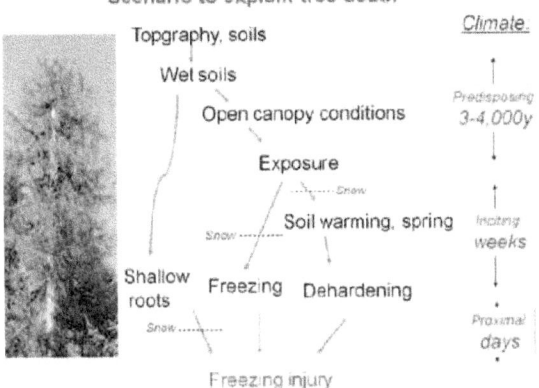

Figure 2 -- Shallow root freezing as the leading hypothesis to explain yellow-cedar decline, and the predisposing and inciting factors that lead to it.

weather (Hennon et al. 2010). Research on cold tolerance by demonstrates the vulnerability of yellow-cedar roots in early spring: soil temperatures below -5 °C are lethal (Schaberg et al. 2008).

The presence of snow buffers soil temperatures, disrupting the progression of events leading to tree injury. Analysis of weather station data confirms the trend of warmer winters and reduced snow, but persistent early spring freezing events throughout the 1900s (Beier et al. 2008); these are all conditions necessary for yellow-cedar decline. Comparing snow models to the distribution of yellow-cedar decline further reveals the controlling influence of snow in the health of yellow-cedar forests. We are finding that yellow-cedar is healthy wherever snow persists past the last cold period, or where yellow-cedar is deep-rooted on better drained soils.

The complex interaction of climate, site, and forest structure can be reduced to two simple risk factors the purpose of landscape risk

modeling for yellow-cedar decline: soil drainage and snow. These two risk factors play out at different spatial scales. Snow can be considered a broad- and mid-scale factor and modeled at the regional or small island spatial scale. Variation in soil drainage can be observed at every watershed in southeast Alaska; thus, it should be introduced into models at the fine spatial scale. Note that both risk factors, snow and soil drainage, are also important components in determining habitat features for live yellow-cedar.

A PROPOSED CONSERVATION – MANAGEMENT STRATEGY

Recommendations for the conservation or active management of yellow-cedar are based on current and future habitat suitability of this tree in the context of its vulnerability to climate. Partitioning the landscape into suitable and unsuitable areas is based on modeling risk factors and comparing those to the current distribution of the tree (Hennon *et al.* 2008). Snow modeling based on global circulation models helps predict habitat that will be suitable in the future. This highlights portions of the landscape where yellow-cedar is, or will be, dying, stable, and regenerating—an approach consistent with the shifting bioclimatic envelope concept (Hamann and Wang 2006).

Planting or thinning is often needed to ensure the initial regeneration and competitive status of yellow-cedar; thus, there is a role for active management (Hennon *et al.* 2009). These activities are directed at higher elevation or on well drained soils where snow or deeper rooting, respectively, protects yellow-cedar roots from lethal cold temperatures. Recent studies have also demonstrated that dead cedar forests represent a surprisingly valuable wood resource for salvage recovery (Hennon *et al.* 2007) because the tree's unique heartwood chemistry retains wood properties for up to a century after death (Kelsey *et al.* 2005). Salvage logging of dead cedar where it is now maladapted to climate can relieve pressure from other areas more suitable for long term conservation of yellow-cedar.

OPPORTUNITIES FOR COLLABORATIVE RESEARCH

Information gaps remain before a comprehensive conservation and management strategy can be fully implemented. These gaps in our knowledge represent opportunities to collaborate across international and discipline boundaries. Several examples are offered below.

Spatial and temporal aspects of yellow-cedar decline in British Columbia and Alaska should be contrasted. Research is underway in British Columbia to document the extent and timing of yellow-cedar decline. Recent findings reported in these proceedings suggest a continuation of decline occurring at higher elevation with decreasing latitude, as has been documented in Alaska. Integrating results from British Columbia and Alaska would cover a wide range of latitudes to strengthen this relationship. Research on the onset and development of decline in British Columbia should be compared to results on the epidemiology from Alaska.

Plant succession following intensive overstory yellow-cedar death needs to be documented in a variety of settings. The extent to which western redcedar benefits from yellow-cedar decline, and may provide similar ecosystem services, should be determined. Successional trajectories need to be assessed in forests that contain a variety of tree species (e.g., with and without western redcedar) and in different zones of productivity along the hydrology-soil drainage gradient. As above, this research should be conducted jointly between British Columbia and Alaska, or at least in a way that results could be compared.

Research on the yellow-cedar genetics is just beginning in Alaska but is more mature in British Columbia. The effect of yellow-cedar decline on the genetic structure of yellow-cedar populations has not been evaluated. Surviving yellow-cedar trees in stands impacted by decline have experienced intense selective pressure and thus may offer unique genetic material. Genetic conservation of yellow-cedar in the context of the widespread decline needs to be considered.

The silvics of yellow-cedar in young-growth forests need research attention and more experience from management, especially in Alaska. Deer browsing on regenerating yellow-cedar, and techniques to discourage it such as use of stock with high terpene concentrations, needs to be studied. The long-term ability of yellow-cedar to maintain its canopy status among competing tree species should be evaluated.

The unique way that cedars utilize calcium to alter nitrogen availability should be tested in the field. Selecting sites high in calcium, or fertilization with calcium on other sites, may provide a competitive advantage for yellow-cedar over most other trees.

Developing a conservation and management strategy in British Columbia and Alaska will require more landscape and climate modeling. Higher resolution distribution maps are needed for yellow-cedar. Ideally, these would show both occupied and unoccupied suitable habitat. Climate projections, with an emphasis on snow models, could be combined with the other forest decline risk factor, soil drainage, to produce a dynamic yellow-cedar decline risk map.

The various values of yellow-cedar justify these efforts by research and forest management. A multi-disciplinary approach with science and management partners from British Columbia and Alaska working together is necessary to develop and implement a conservation and management strategy for yellow-cedar.

LITERATURE CITED

Beier, C.M.; Sink, S.E.; Hennon, P.E.; D'Amore, D.V.; Juday, G.P. 2008. Twentieth-century warming and the dendroclimatology of declining yellow-cedar forests in southeastern Alaska. Canadian Journal of Forest Research. 38: 1319-1334.

D'Amore, D.V.; Hennon, P.E. 2006. Evaluation of soil saturation, soil chemistry, and early spring soil and air temperatures as risk factors in yellow-cedar decline. Global Change Biology. 12: 524-545.

D'Amore, D.V.; Hennon, P.E., Schaberg, P.G., Hawley, G. 2009. The adaptation to exploit nitrate in surface soils predisposes yellow-cedar to climate change-induced decline and enhances the survival of redcedar. Forest Ecology and Management. 258: 2261-2268.

Hamann, A.; Wang, T.L. 2006. Potential effects of climate change on tree spcies and ecosystem distribution in British Columbia. Ecology. 87: 2773-2786.

Hennon, P.E.; D'Amore, D.; Wittwer, D.; Caouette, J. 2008. Yellow-cedar decline: conserving a climate-sensitive tree species as Alaska warms. In: Deal. R., ed. Integrated restoration of forested ecosystems to achieve multiresource benefits: proceedings of the 2007 national silviculture workshop. Gen. Tech. Rep. PNW-GTR-733. Portland, OR: U.S. Department of Agriculture, Forest Service, Pacific Northwest Research Station: 233-245.

Hennon, P. McClellan, M.; Spores, S., Orlikowska, E. 2009. Survival and growth of planted yellow-cedar seedlings and rooted cuttings (stecklings) near Ketchikan, Alaska. Western Journal of Applied Forestry. 24(3): 144-150.

Hennon, P.; Woodward, B.; Lebow, P.K. 2007. Deterioration of wood from live and dead Alaska yellow-cedar in contact with soil. Forest Products Journal. 57(6): 23-30.

Kelsey, R.G.; Hennon, P.E.; Huso, M.; Karchesy, J.J. 2005. Changes in heartwood chemistry of dead yellow-cedar trees that remain standing for 80 years or more in southeast Alaska. Journal of Chemical Ecology. 31: 2653-2670.

Schaberg P.G.; Hennon P.E.; D'Amore, D.V.; Hawley, G.J; Borer, C.H. 2005. Seasonal differences in freezing tolerance of yellow-cedar and western hemlock trees at a site affected by yellow-cedar decline. Canadian Journal of Forest Research. 35: 2065-2070.

Schaberg, P.G.; Hennon, P.E.; D'Amore D.V.; Hawley, G. 2008. Influence of simulated snow cover on the cold tolerance and freezing injury of yellow-cedar seedlings. Global Change Biology. 14: 1282-1293.

MANAGING WESTERN REDCEDAR AND YELLOW-CEDAR IN A CHANGING ENVIRONMENT

Laura Gray[1] and Andreas Hamann

ABSTRACT

Human-aided movement of species populations in large scale reforestation programs could be a potent and cost effective climate change adaptation strategy. However, while there is broad consensus that the habitat of many species generally shifts north and to higher elevations, we usually do not know if this applies to a particular population and where exactly appropriate target habitat would be under uncertain future climates. In a case study of western redcedar (*Thuja plicata*) and yellow-cedar (*Chamaecyparis nootkatensis*) in western North America, we report results from bioclimate envelope modeling that predicts suitable habitat for locally adapted genotypes under 18 climate projections from general circulation models for the 2020s, 2050s and 2080s, as well as under observed climate trends. We generally find maintenance and expansion (both northward and at higher elevations) of potential suitable habitat, however the scale of potential range expansion is different for the two species. Our results suggest that population-specific recommendations for assisted migration can be made with reasonable confidence over a 10 to 20-year planning horizon, but model uncertainty does not allow for long-term planning, which means forest management will lag behind prescriptions that would be optimal under a continued directional climate trend.

[1] Department of Renewable Resources, Faculty of Agricultural, Life, and Environmental Sciences, University of Alberta, 751 General Services Building, Edmonton, AB, Canada, T6G 2H1

YELLOW-CEDAR AND WESTERN REDCEDAR ADAPTATION TO PRESENT AND FUTURE CLIMATES

John H. Russell and Jodie Krakowski[1]

ABSTRACT

Twelve range-wide yellow-cedar provenance trials and 23 western redcedar trials were assessed to quantify climatic influences on adaptive traits using regression analyses. Response variables were productivity (integrating height, survival and cold hardiness), and cedar leaf blight (CLB) infection on western redcedar. Climate change impacts by 2050 were modelled using the Canadian CGCM and the CSIRO models, B2 scenario. Range-wide productivity of yellow-cedar was weakly influenced by summer drought stress and growing season warmth (multiple $R^2 = 0.16$). Stronger adaptive patterns were apparent on the harshest sites when individual sites were analyzed. California populations of both species were always maladapted. Yellow-cedar population productivity was highest on warmer, wetter, and less snowy sites than the location of origin. Climatic limits on productivity may shift from winter temperatures to summer maximum temperatures and drought by 2050. Seed transfer can be broad on ecologically suitable sites. Western redcedar had moderately strong species-wide relationships with climate variables, and pronounced differences among regions. Warm wet conditions during the growing season were the strongest drivers of productivity. CLB increased with site moisture and winter warmth. Populations from warmer, wetter low-elevation coastal sites had lower CLB than predicted, inferring evolved resistance. Coastal sites may have increased productivity in future on summer-cool sites where moisture is not limiting, but also higher CLB risk. Broad latitudinal seed transfer in the maritime region within the elevation band of origin would optimize productivity and minimize risk of CLB (above or below 500 m), and submaritime populations can be transferred broadly. More populations and test sites in warmer climates are needed to fully characterize interior redcedar genecology.

KEYWORDS: Western redcedar, yellow-cedar, seed transfer, genecology, cedar leaf blight

INTRODUCTION

Yellow-cedar (*Callitropsis nootkatensis*) is primarily adapted to montane coastal sites with fluctuating water tables and winter snowpack. Western redcedar (*Thuja plicata*) typically occupies lower elevations and moist sites, overlapping with yellow-cedar, but its range extends broadly into interior wet forests. Studies have found no to weak clinal patterns for western redcedar in morphological and physiological traits (Cherry and Lester 1992; Fan et al. 2008; Grossnickle and Russell 2010), and no patterns in yellow-cedar seedlings (Russell 1998; Grossnickle and Russell 2010) despite significant population differences.

Phenotypic plasticity facilitates physiological adjustment to environmental changes in these indeterminate species (Russell 1998; El-Kassaby 1999). Many species with low population genotypic variation have phenotypic adaptive differences (e.g., Karhu et al. 1996). Coastal climates where western redcedar and yellow-cedar occur are relatively homogeneous and expected to have minimal changes due to future climate impacts (Spittlehouse 2008). The interior range of western redcedar encompasses wider climatic extremes due to topographic diversity and continentality and is expected to change substantially in the future.

[1] John Russell and Jodie Krakowski are Research Scientists, B.C. Ministry of Forests and Range, Research and Knowledge Management Branch, Cowichan Lake Research Station, Box 335, Mesachie Lake, B.C. V0R 2N0

Cedar leaf blight (CLB) causes foliar mortality in western redcedar and plantation failure in severe cases. Caused by the fungal pathogen *Didymascella thujina,* field studies show western redcedar populations from coastal low-elevation sites were most resistant (Russell et al. 2007). Determining climatic factors associated with CLB severity is key to developing site hazard and seedling deployment guidelines. Although prevalent along the coast, CLB has been completely overlooked in forest management, but will likely gain importance as forest health becomes a priority management objective.

Climatic models are largely in accord over the cedar species' ranges over the next 1-3 decades, after which they diverge considerably (Gray and Hamann, these proceedings). During the current management rotation, late- season drought is expected to become more severe in drier regions, earlier snowmelt will become more prevalent, and minimum and mean temperatures will increase. We explore the degree to which these factors influence the growth, survival, and health of western redcedar and yellow-cedar across their ranges.

Objective
Our first objective was to determine for each species the climatic factors which most influence adaptive traits. Our second objective was to determine the extent of local population adaptation to guide incorporating climatic adaptation into seed transfer for each species considering current and future climate predictions.

MATERIALS AND METHODS
Field trials
Seed for yellow-cedar trials was obtained from populations of three to 10 well-spaced trees from Alaska to California. Trials were established in 1990 and 1991 with one year old seedlings planted in randomized complete blocks. Each of the 12 sites (Fig. 1) tested 19-40 populations in 10 to 12 blocks and 5-tree row plots.

Western redcedar seed was collected from 10 to 50 trees per population range-wide, but primarily

within British Columbia. Field trials were established between 1991 and 1998 with one-year-old seedlings planted in randomized complete blocks with 9 to 26 populations in 10 to 44 blocks and single tree plots at each site (Fig. 1). Manual vegetation control was done as needed on all trials.

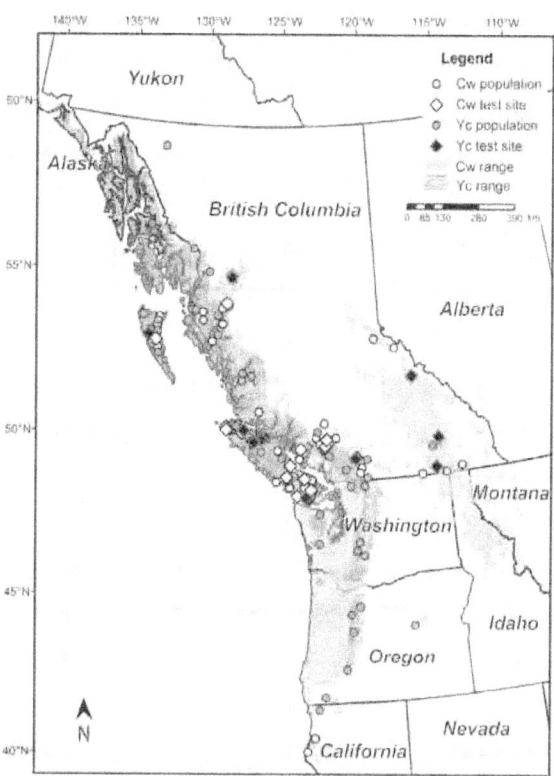

Figure 1 -- **Locations of tested provenances and field trials. Cw is western redcedar; Yc is yellow-cedar.**

Data analysis
Response variables assessed for both species were adaptability and height. Adaptability was scored as a binomial trait where dead or frost damaged trees scored 0 and healthy survivors scored 1. Height and adaptability were multiplied to yield a productivity index. Western redcedar CLB incidence was scored on a 0 to 6 scale indicating increased severity with a higher score. Individual western redcedar populations were analyzed for transfer functions, whereas response functions were based on grouping populations into 16 regions.

To standardize results across years and trial designs, each trial was analyzed separately using a linear mixed model to generate best linear unbiased predictions (BLUPs) for each quantitative response variable (ASReml ver. 2.0). Population-site BLUPs for height and adaptability were added to best linear unbiased estimates of site to facilitate intra-site comparisons.

Annual and seasonal regional climatic variables for each provenance origin and test site were estimated using ClimateWNA ver. 4.5.2 (Wang et al. 2010). Forward stepwise multiple linear regressions were used to identify for each species which combinations of climatic descriptors had the strongest influence on each response variable (SAS ver.9.1.3). To minimize the likelihood of spurious statistical relationships while capturing biologically significant differences α was set at 0.10. Well-adapted populations were considered those with average or better performance at a site, or across multiple sites (i.e., well-adapted to a climatic range).

Methodology of Rehfeldt et al. (1999) was used to develop transfer and response functions to test population adaptation to climatic variables. Univariate quadratic regressions were analyzed across all sites, and at each site. *Transfer distance* is the value of a geographic or climatic descriptor at the origin site minus the value at the test site. A *transfer function* is a regression with climatic transfer distance as the independent variable, and the response as the dependent variable. Local populations were deemed maladapted to a given climate variable when the local mean (performance at transfer distance of zero) fell outside the 80% confidence interval at the quadratic function vertex. This provides an estimate of the climatic distance between the local and optimum.

Response functions are regressions testing performance of a given population against a climate variable over multiple sites. Western redcedar populations were combined into 16 regional groups for response function analyses based on preliminary analyses supporting broad

adaptation patterns. Regional climate variables were the arithmetic mean of the maximum and minimum values of component populations.

Current climate normals and two climate models, the Canadian CGCM and the CSIRO model were selected to model climate in 2050 using the B2 scenario to provide predictive bound. The former model provides the best fit for the study area based on back-casting (Spittlehouse 2008) and the latter yielded the most divergent results. Population response patterns based on current climates were used to predict responses in 2050 with the assumption that this span is too short for evolutionary effects.

RESULTS AND DISCUSSION
Multiple regressions
Each species had only two significant climatic descriptors retained in the model for productivity. For yellow-cedar, 16.1% of variation in productivity was explained by maximum winter temperature and summer minimum temperature (cooler values were best). Western redcedar was more sensitive to climate with summer precipitation and maximum summer temperature explaining 29.1% of variation in productivity. CLB infection was associated with a complex set of environmental factors: summer precipitation accounted for 29%, while the best 2-variable combination of autumn precipitation and maximum summer temperature explained 38.5%. In total, a suite of 10 variables associated with warm, moist growing season conditions and warm winters accounted for up to 62.5% of CLB incidence.

Transfer functions
Yellow-cedar productivity had weak range-wide relationships with climatic factors (all $R^2 \leq 0.03$). Many local populations had better performance on on warmer, wetter, and less snowy sites than the location of origin. Productivity increased linearly as summer drought decreased, as the quadratic optimum was far beyond the range of habitat suitable for the species (Table 1). Future conditions predicted little change for yellow-cedar, except the CSIRO model showed slightly weaker influence of snow due to warming. Both

climate models indicated summer minimum temperatures would be less of an influence than currently.

Western redcedar productivity had significant relationships with a many climate descriptors $(0.42 \leq R^2 \leq 0.97)$, especially those associated with warm temperatures (Fig. 2). Populations were most productive on sites with a longer, wetter growing season, cooler summers, and warmer spring and fall than their locations of origin (Table 1), which corresponds in general to more southern climates. This may reflect adaptational lag from postglacial recolonization of its northern range from the south. Western redcedar productivity showed few range-wide differences from predictions based on current climate under expected future climates.

Under current conditions, significant amounts of variation in CLB were explained by almost all climatic variables $(0.03 \leq R^2 \leq 0.33)$, with maximum infection at temperate warm sites with wet, cool summers and mild winters. CLB incidence and severity may increase due to longer, milder growing seasons and warmer winters, since cold typically limits survival and spread of the pathogen. The CSIRO scenario $(0.05 \leq R^2 \leq 0.37)$ modelled warmer summers while the CGCM $(0.03 \leq R^2 \leq 0.36)$ predicted milder winters.

Individual sites expressed stronger relationships between yellow-cedar productivity and climatic indicators $(0.12 \leq R^2 \leq 0.52)$. Fall and winter maximum temperatures had the strongest influences, especially at environmentally stressful sites for this species. Western redcedar productivity at individual sites was most often

Table 1 -- Climatic transfer distances (0 is local) for optimizing yellow-cedar and redcedar productivity and CLB under current and 2050 conditions from 2 climate models with the B2 scenario. Blank cells show no significant relationship. Bold values show local maladaptation across a species' range. LP indicates linear patterns and thus no climatic optimum, or an optimum far beyond the climatic range of the species.

Variable[a]	Units	Yc productivity current	Yc productivity 2050 CGCM	Yc productivity 2050 CSIRO	Cw productivity current	Cw productivity 2050 CGCM	Cw productivity 2050 CSIRO	Cw CLB current	Cw CLB 2050 CGCM	Cw CLB 2050 CSIRO
MAT	°C				-11	-9	-7	2	4	4
MWMT	°C	-1	0.5	1.5	LP	LP	-8	7	8	7
MCMT	°C				-6	-4	-4	5	7	8
TD	°C				3	3	-4	-17	-14	-12
MAP	mm		LP	LP			-432	-2632	-2646	-2235
MSP	mm	LP	LP	LP	293	252	271	LP	LP	LP
AHM								13	11	13
SHM		LP	LP	LP	-1	6	7	66	67	67
PAS	mm	1058	LP	761.2		830	903			
EMT	°C					-7	0.4		42	30
TAV_wt	°C				-5	-6	-2	5	3	7
TAV_sp	°C				LP	-3	LP	1	3	
TAV_sm	°C				21	-10	-14	6	7	7
TAV_at	°C				-8	LP	-3	2	3	5
TMN_wt	°C				-6	-5	1	6	5	5
TMN_sp	°C				-5	-3	-3	2	10	
TMN_sm	°C		-0.4	-0.6	LP	LP	-7	1	17	20
TMN_at	°C	-3			-4	-2	-0.1	2		
TMX_wt	°C	-13	-12.9	-3.2	-5	-3	-7	3	8	10
TMX_sp	°C				24	-21	9	17	4	4
TMX_sm	°C				-4	-2	-1	24	3	4
TMX_at	°C	19	20.0		-72	-51	-24		4	5
PPT_wt	mm	1046	1154.2	1454.3			-754	-707	-472	-516
PPT_sp	mm							-691	-764	-697
PPT_sm	mm	427	435.8	479.3	164	158	159	LP	LP	LP
PPT_at	mm	1679	1567.7	LP				-1931	-2084	-1364

[a]MAT: mean annual temperature, MW(C)MT: mean temperature of warmest (coldest) month, TD: continentality, MWMT-MCMT, MA(S)P: mean annual (summer) precipitation, AHM: annual heat-moisture index, (MAT+10)/(MAP/1000), SHM: summer heat-moisture index, (MWMT)/(MSP/1000), PAS: precipitation as snow, EMT: extreme minimum temperature, TAV: average temperature, TMN: minimum temperature, TMX: maximum temperature, PPT: precipitation, wt: winter, sp: spring, sm: summer, at: autumn

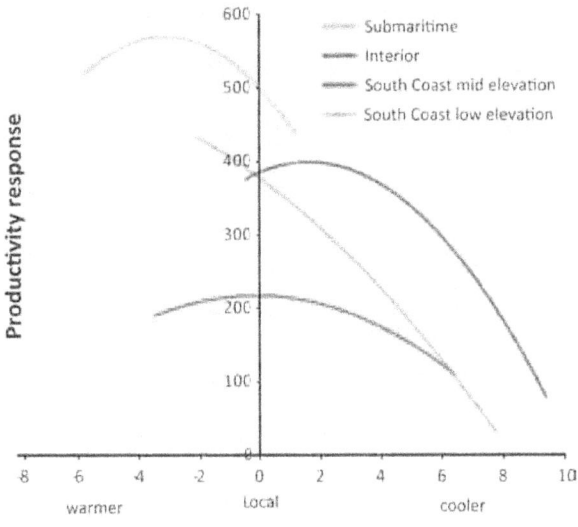

Figure 2 -- Transfer functions showing optimal productivity of select western redcedar populations across mean spring temperature range.

influenced by summer precipitation ($0.43 \leq R^2 \leq 0.93$), and summer drought index (SHM: see Table 1; $0.22 \leq R^2 \leq 0.94$). Individual site CLB was most strongly influenced by maximum summer temperature (warmest had least CLB; $0.46 \leq R^2 \leq 0.65$), continentality (more continental sites had least CLB: $0.28 \leq R^2 \leq 0.69$), and precipitation during the growing season (driest had least CLB).

Response functions

Yellow-cedar populations had the strongest responses on sites that it was most maladapted to due to cold temperature stress. Productivity of all populations that had significant patterns was most influenced by winter temperatures, which reflects the cold hardiness component of this response variable. Spring and autumn temperatures were also strong drivers, being correlated both with growing season length and early and late frost damage. There were no latitudinal patterns, and California populations had low survival at all test sites.

Twelve of the 16 western redcedar regional groups had significant relationships between productivity and growing season temperatures (warmer spring and fall, but cooler summers:

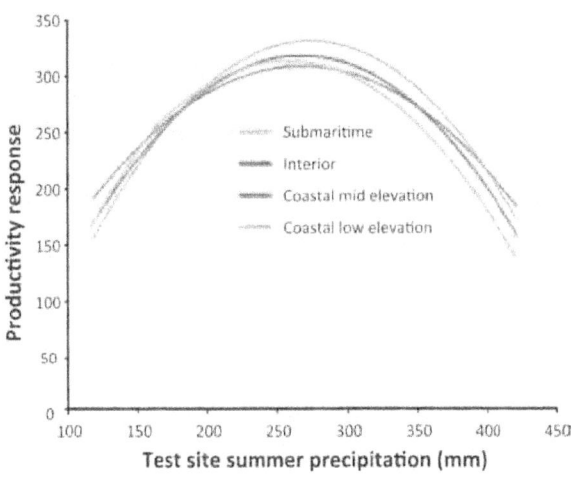

Figure 3 -- Response functions showing productivity versus test site summer precipitation of selected regionally grouped western redcedar populations.

$.40 \leq R^2 \leq 0.97$). Most regionally grouped populations, including those from the submaritime and high elevations, had significantly higher productivity at maritime test sites than continental sites. Populations from the coastal low elevation regions tended to outperform most others at a given site, except at the most continental and environmentally extreme sites (Fig. 3).

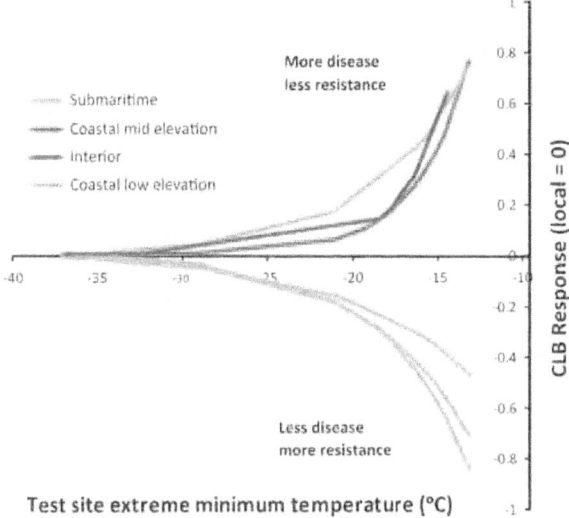

Figure 4 -- Select western redcedar population responses to extreme minimum temperature relative to site mean CLB severity.

Population CLB responses showed major divergence between coastal low elevation and other populations with warming winters (Fig. 4: $0.59 \leq R^2 \leq 0.96$). Populations from the maritime warmer regions with high CLB hazard had far less infection than average, indicating a potential coevolution of western redcedar with CLB. All other populations were more susceptible, with increasing infection severity on higher CLB incidence sites which were milder and wetter.

Seed transfer

Seed transfer of yellow-cedar can be broad on ecologically suitable sites, but more restricted on sites with heavy snowpack as population adaptation to snow varied. As long as western redcedar populations are kept within the elevation band of origin to minimize risk of CLB (above or below 500 m), broader latitudinal seed transfer than currently allowed ($\pm 3°$ for natural stand seed) along the coast appears acceptable. Submaritime populations can be transferred broadly, with highest western redcedar productivity on milder sites.

CONCLUSIONS

Yellow-cedar has very weak adaptive patterns associated with climate across its range, facilitating broad seed transfer. Productivity (combining height, survival, and frost hardiness) is most influenced by cool summer temperatures and summer moisture. Snowpack influences productivity primarily through frost damage, and likely by limiting early height growth. Western redcedar is much more sensitive to climate across its range. Productivity is highest on sites with long, wet growing seasons. Populations of both species have best productivity in climates that are warmer and with longer growing seasons than their locations of origin. CLB is most severe in coastal mild, cool sites with warm winters and wet summers; populations originating from above 500 m across the species range are highly susceptible, while coastal low elevation populations appear to have evolved resistance. CLB resistance as well as productivity should be considered when selecting western redcedar populations for reforestation.

LITERATURE CITED

Cherry, M.L.; Lester, D.T. 1992. Genetic variation in *Chamaecyparis nootkatensis* from coastal British Columbia. West. J. Appl. For. 7:25-29.

El-Kassaby, Y.A. 1999. Phenotypic plasticity in western redcedar. For. Genetics 6:235-240.

Fan, S.; Grossnickle, S.C.; Russell, J.H. 2008. Morphological and physiological variation in western redcedar (*Thuja plicata*) populations under contrasting soil water conditions. Trees 22:671-683.

Grossnickle, S.C.; Russell; J.H. 2010. Physiological variation among western redcedar (*Thuja plicata* Donn ex D. Don) populations in response to short-term drought. Ann. For. Sci. 67: 506-517.

Karhu, A.; Hurme, P.; Karjalainen, M.; Karvonen, P.; Kärkkäinen, K.; Neale, D.; Savolainen, O. 1996. Do molecular markers reflect patterns of differentiation in adaptive traits of conifers? Theor. Appl. Genet. 93:215-221.

Rehfeldt, G.E.; Ying, C.C.; Spittlehouse, D.L.; Hamilton Jr., D.A. 1999. Genetic responses to climate in *Pinus contorta*: niche breadth, climate change, and reforestation. Ecol. Monogr. 69:375-407.

Russell, J.H. 1998. Genecology of *Chamaecyparis nootkatensis*. Pp. 82–89 in: Coastally restricted forests. A.D. Laderman, ed. Oxford Univ. Press, Oxford, U.K.

Russell, J.H.; Kope, H.H.; Ades, P.; Collinson, H. 2007. Variation in cedar leaf blight (*Didymascella thujina*) resistance of western redcedar (*Thuja plicata*) Can. J. For. Res. 37:1978-1986.

Wang, T., A. Hamann, D. Spittlehouse. 2010. ClimateWNA v4.52: A program to generate climate normal, annual, seasonal and monthly data for genecology and climate change studies in Western North America (WNA) region. CFCG, Dept. For. Sci., UBC, Vancouver, B.C.

RATES AND CAUSES OF WESTERN REDCEDAR AND YELLOW-CEDAR MORTALITY IN OLD-GROWTH FORESTS OF MOUNT RAINER NATIONAL PARK

Andrew J. Larson[1] and Jerry F. Franklin[2]

ABSTRACT

We examined the rates and causes of mortality for *Thuja plicata* Donn ex. D. Don (western redcedar) and *Chamaecyparis nootkatensis* (D. Don) Spach (yellow cedar), and in contrast with co-occurring Pinaceae, using a three decade record of forest dynamics in old-growth forests of Mount Rainer National Park, WA, USA. All trees ≥15 cm dbh were tagged within 12, 1.00 ha permanent plots; trees were added to the study when they grew past the lower sampling size limit. Plots were censused every 4 to 10 years. Detailed observations of position, condition and causes of mortality were recorded for newly dead trees. The fates of 625 *C. nootkatensis* and 226 *T. plicata* were followed: a total of 58 *C. nootkatensis* and 13 *T. plicata* stems died during the study. Mortality rates of *T. plicata* and *C. nootkatensis* were exceptionally low, with average annual rates of 0.1% to 0.2% and 0.2% to 0.3%, respectively. Mechanical processes--uprooting, stem breakage and crushing by falling macrolitter--accounted for 69.2% of *T. plicata* mortalities; these same agents were responsible for 53.4% of *C. nootkatensis* mortalities. In contrast, a smaller proportion (43.4%) of co-occurring Pinaceae species were killed by mechanical processes, suggesting a family-level tradeoff characterized by lower susceptibility to biological mortality agents and greater tolerance of competitive stress for the Cupressaceae, and relatively greater resistance to mechanical mortality agents by Pinaceae in old-growth forests of the Pacific Northwest.

KEYWORDS: Old-growth, tree mortality, causes of mortality, permanent plots.

INTRODUCTION

Tree mortality directly regulates tree populations and forest community composition and structure, and mortality determines the upper bounds of tree size and age. In the old-growth forests of the Pacific Northwest, two Cupressaceae species (Figs. 1 & 2)—*Thuja plicata* Donn ex. D. Don and *Chamaecyparis nootkatensis* (D. Don) Spach—often attain greater ages than co-occurring Pinaceae. Empirical studies of rates and causes of tree mortality are the first step towards understanding how these two species attain great ages, and co-exist with typically more fecund Pinaceae.

Only direct long-term observations can reveal rates and causes of tree mortality in natural forests. Empirical documentation of the rates and causes of *T. plicata* and *C. nootkatensis* mortality in old-growth forests of the Pacific Northwest is limited to just two studies (Franklin and DeBell 1988, Edmonds et al. 1993), each from a single site. Consequently, mortality rates and causes for these species remain poorly understood in old-growth forests.

In this paper we report stem mortality rates for several populations of *T. plicata* and *C. nootkatensis* studied over a three decade period at Mount Rainer National Park, in the western Washington Cascade Range, USA. We also report proximate causes of mortality for *T. plicata* and *C. nootkatensis*, and contrast these causes of mortality with those of co-occurring Pinaceae.

[1] Andrew J. Larson, Assistant Professor of Forest Ecology, The University of Montana, College of Forestry and Conservation, Department of Forest Management, Missoula, MT 59812-0596. E-mail: andrew.larson@cfc.umt.edu
[2] Jerry F. Franklin, Professor of Ecosystem Analysis, University of Washington, School of Forest Resources, Box 352100, Seattle, WA 98195-2100. E-mail: jff@uw.edu

METHODS

Study Forests and Field Procedures

Twelve, 1.00 ha permanent forest study plots were established in 1977 and 1978 in old-growth conifer forests in Mount Rainer National Park, WA, USA, an ecological reserve. The study sites represent the *Tsuga heterophylla* and *Abies amabilis* Zones (Franklin and Dyrness 1988), the dominant lower and middle elevation forests of the western Cascade Range. Detailed descriptions of the physical and biological characteristics of the study sites are available online (http://www.fsl.orst.edu/lter/pubs/webdocs/permplot.cfm); additional details on the plant associations characteristic of each study plot is presented in Franklin et al. (1988).

In each plot all live trees ≥15 cm dbh (diameter at breast height, 1.4 m above ground level) were measured for diameter to the nearest 0.1 cm, identified to species and individually tagged. Plots were censused every 4 to 10 years, most recently in 2007 or 2008.

Detailed information about tree position, condition and cause of mortality was recorded for newly dead trees at each census (excepting the first census when only the initial population of live trees was inventoried). Because proximate cause of mortality for intact standing dead trees can be difficult to assign when census intervals exceed 1 year field observations were summarized in three classes of proximate cause of mortality which can be unequivocally distinguished: biological/competitive stress (i.e., standing dead trees), mechanical mortality (uprooting and stem breakage), and crushing by falling trees or tree parts.

Data Reduction and Statistical Analysis

The annual mortality rate, m, was calculated as:

$$m = 1 - \left[1 - \left(M_1 / N_0 \right) \right]^{1/t} \qquad (1)$$

where N_0 is the number of trees alive at the previous census, M_1 is the number of trees dying between the previous and current census, and t

is the time between censuses in years (Sheil et al. 1995, Lutz and Halpern 2006).

The null hypothesis of independence of family (Cupressaceae vs. Pinaceae) and frequency of mortality was evaluated with the randomization method. For each plot, simulations ($n = 10000$) in which the observed number of trees dying in the ith census interval were randomly selected (without replacement) from the empirical live tree list at the beginning of the ith census interval: variation due to census interval is accounted for in the simulations. Each simulation was summarized with the chi-square statistic. All $n = 10000$ simulation results were compiled into null distributions to which the observed chi-square statistic for the plot of interest, to which the chi-square statistic for the empirical data was compared using the randomization test (Roff 2006) with α = 0.05.

RESULTS

Stem Mortality Rates

The fates of 625 *C. nootkatensis* and 226 *T. plicata* were followed: a total of 58 *C. nootkatensis* and 13 *T. plicata* stems died during the study.

Sufficient numbers of *T. plicata* and *C. nootkatensis* occurred in $n = 4$ plots (AB08, AG05, TO04, TO01) and $n = 3$ plots (AE10, AR07, AM16), respectively, to calculate annualized mortality rates. Mortality rates of both species were exceptionally low. Annual mortality rates of *T. plicata* for all site X census combinations ranged from 0.0% to 0.8%; annual mortality rates for *C. nootkatensis* across all site X census combinations ranged from 0.0% to 0.5%. Mean annual mortality rates (average of rates for individual census intervals within sites) for *T. plicata* ranged from 0.1% to 0.2%; mean annual mortality rates for *C. nootkatensis* ranged from 0.2% to 0.3%.

Randomization tests did not support rejection ($P > 0.1$) of the null hypothesis of independence of family (Cupressaceae vs. co-occurring Pinaceae) and frequency of mortality for any of the 4 plots hosting populations of *T. plicata* or the 3 plots with *C. nootkatensis* populations.

Causes of Mortality

T. plicata and *C. nootkatensis* were more likely to be killed by stem breakage than species belonging to Pinaceae (Fig. 3). Mechanical processes--uprooting, stem breakage and crushing by falling macrolitter--accounted for 69.2% of *T. plicata* mortalities; these same agents were responsible for 53.4% of *C. nootkatensis* mortalities. In contrast, a smaller proportion of co-occurring Pinaceae species were killed by mechanical processes, suggesting that lower susceptibility to biological mortality agents and greater tolerance of competitive stress may explain the low observed rates of *T. plicata* and *C. nootkatensis* mortality. This difference was complemented by a relatively lower proportion of standing deaths for *T. plicata* and *C. nootkatensis* relative to Pinaceae.

DISCUSSION

The low annual stem mortality rates for *T. plicata* and *C. nootkatensis* are exceptional, lower even than the 0.29% yr^{-1} reported for *Sequoia sempervirens* $\geq$10 cm dbh (Busing and Fujimori 2002). The results presented here, together with the other published data for *Thuja* and *Chamaecyparis*, indicate that very low mortality rates are characteristic of these species in old-growth forests of the Pacific Northwest. Franklin and DeBell (1988) reported mortality 0.52% yr^{-1} for *Thuja* during a 36-year period in the southwest Washington Cascades; no *Thuja* died and *Chamaecyparis* died at a rate of 0.68% yr^{-1} in the western Olympics (Edmonds et al. 1993).

The divergent patterns of mortality causes for Cupressaceae and Pinaceae suggest a potential family-level tradeoff in demographic strategies. The mortality cause differences observed here— lower susceptibility to biological mortality agents and greater tolerance of competitive stress for the Cupressaceae, and relatively greater resistance to mechanical mortality agents by Pinaceae—may correspond to differing strategies of resource allocation to

secondary defense compounds and wood physical properties. The small number of Cupressaceae dying during this study limits the strength of this inference; this interpretation should be regarded as a hypothesis to be tested with additional observations.

Improved understanding of the quantitative life history of tree species, including rates and causes of mortality, will require substantial investment—beyond current levels—in long-term research and monitoring of larger tree populations across a wider range of environmental and geographic gradients. Only n = 58 *C. nootkatensis* and n = 13 *T. plicata* died during this three decade study (which included fully 360 hectare-years of observations); continued observations and additional study sites are necessary to understand mortality across the population size structure and environmental gradients. The importance of the data from long-term demographic studies cannot be overstated: such data constitute the primary means of testing predictions from basic ecological theory (e.g., Condit et al. 2006) and for developing forecasts for tree population structure in future climate scenarios (e.g., van Mantgem et al. 2009).

ACKNOWLEDGEMENTS

Many field workers contributed to this study three-decade study of tree mortality. The most recent census was only possible with help from Dan Underwood and his students at Peninsula College, the Lewis & Clark College Outdoors program, and James Freund and his field crews from the University of Washington. Fieldwork and data storage and management was made possible through funding and in king support provided by the National Science Foundation, the USFS PNW Research Station, the Wind River Canopy Crane Research Facility, Oregon State University, the University of Washington and the H.J. Andrews Experimental Forest LTER program. Permission to conduct this research within Mount Rainer National Park is gratefully acknowledged.

LITERATURE CITED

Busing, R.T.; and Fujimori, T. 2002. Dynamics of composition and structure in an old *Sequoia sempervirens* forest. Journal of Vegetation Science 13: 785-792.

Condit, R.; and 39 others. 2006. The importance of demographic niches to tree diversity. Science 313: 98-101.

Edmonds, R.L.; Thomas, T.B.; and Maybury, K.P. 1993. Tree population dynamics, growth and mortality in old-growth forests in the western Olympic Mountains, Washington. Canadian Journal of Forest Research 23: 512-519.

Franklin, J.F.; and Dyrness, C.T. 1988. Natural vegetation of Oregon and Washington. Oregon State University Press, Corvallis, Oregon, USA.

Franklin, J.F.; and D.S. DeBell. 1988. Thirty-six years of tree population change in an old-growth *Pseudotsuga-Tsuga* forest. Canadian Journal of Forest Research 18:633-639.

Franklin, J.F.; W.H. Moir; M.A. Hemstrom; S.E. Greene; and B.G. Smith. 1988. The forest communities of Mount Rainer National Park. Scientific Monograph Series No. 19. USDI National Park Service, Washington, D.C.

Lutz, J.A.; and Halpern, C.B. 2006. Tree mortality during early forest development: A long-term study of rates, causes, and consequences. Ecological Monographs 76: 257-275.

Roff, D.A., 2006. Introduction to computer-intensive methods of data analysis in biology. Cambridge University Press. Cambridge, UK.

Sheil, D.; Burslem, D.F.R.P.; and Alder, D. 1995. The interpretation and misinterpretation of mortality rate measures. Journal of Ecology 83: 331-333.

van Mantgem, P. J.; Stephenson, N.L.; Bryne, J.C.; Daniels, L.D.; Franklin, J.F.; Fulé, P.Z.; Harmon, M.E.; Larson, A.J.; Smith, J.M.; Taylor, A.H.; and Veblen, T.T. 2009. Widespread increase of tree mortality rates in the western United States. Science 323: 521-524.

Figure 1 (above left). Large *Thuja plicata* individuals in Mount Rainer National Park, Washington, USA. Figure 2 (above right). *T. plicata* often attain greater age and size than co-occurring Pinaceae (primarily *Abies amabilis* and *Tsuga heterophylla* in the western Washington Cascade Range). Figure 3 (below). Proximate causes of mortality for *Chamaecyparis nootkatensis*, *T. plicata* and Pinaceae species in old-growth forests of Mount Rainer National Park.

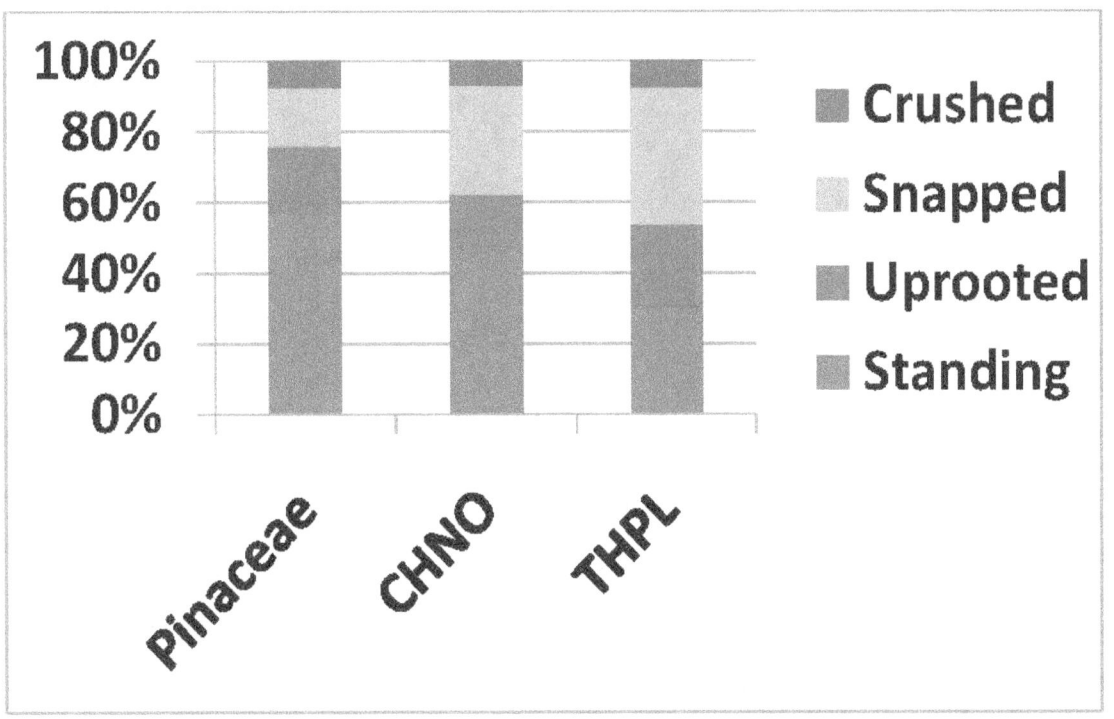

COMPARISONS OF THE COLD TOLERANCE AND ROOTING DEPTH OF YELLOW-CEDAR, WESTERN REDCEDAR, WESTERN HEMLOCK, MOUNTAIN HEMLOCK AND SITKA SPRUCE GROWING TOGETHER IN KETCHIKAN, ALASKA

Paul G. Schaberg[1], Paul E. Hennon[2], David V. D'Amore[2], Joshua M. Halman[3] and Gary W.T.F. Hawley[3]

ABSTRACT

It has been proposed that yellow-cedar decline is initiated by the freezing injury of roots when soils freeze during times of low snow cover. To explain the unique susceptibility of yellow-cedar to this damage, yellow-cedar roots would need to be 1) less cold tolerant, and/or 2) more concentrated in upper soil horizons than co-occurring tree species that are not declining. We measured the root cold tolerance and used ratios of foliar cations as an assay of rooting depth of five species growing together in one forest in Ketchikan, Alaska. Species evaluated were yellow-cedar (*Chamaecyparis nootkatensis*), western redcedar (*Thuja plicata*), western hemlock (*Tsuga heterophylla*), mountain hemlock (*Tsuga mertensiana*), and Sitka spruce (*Picea sitchensis*). Roots were collected in November 2007 and January, March and May 2008 to assess relative hardiness levels in fall through spring. Foliage was collected in January 2008. Yellow-cedar and redcedar roots were less cold tolerant than roots of other species on all dates. Yellow-cedar roots were slightly less cold tolerant than redcedar roots in November and January. Yellow- and redcedar foliage had significantly different concentrations of Ca (higher), Al (lower), Mn (lower), and ratios of Ca:Al and Ca:Mn (both higher) than foliage from other species. Yellow-cedar had higher foliar concentrations of Ca, and higher ratios of Ca:Al and Ca:Mn than did redcedar. Because concentrations of Ca are greatest in the upper soil horizons, whereas concentrations of Al and Mn are greater in the deeper soil horizons, the higher foliar concentrations of Ca, and ratios of Ca:Al and Ca:Mn, may indicate that the roots of yellow-cedar preferentially occupy higher soil horizons than the other species tested. Limited cold tolerance and shallow rooting may both contribute to the unique sensitivity of this species to freezing injury and decline.

[1] Forest Service, US Department of Agriculture, Northern Research Station, South Burlington, VT 05403, pschaberg@fs.fed.us
[2] Forest Service, US Department of Agriculture, Pacific Northwest Research Station, Juneau, AK 99801, phennon@fs.fed.us and ddamore@fs.fed.us
[3] The University of Vermont, Rubenstein School of Environment and Natural resources, Burlington, VT 05405, Joshua.Halman@uvm.edu and Gary.Hawley@uvm.edu

GENETIC PERSPECTIVES ON THE COLONIZATION HISTORY AND POPULATION STRUCTURE OF WESTERN REDCEDAR (*THUJA PLICATA*, CUPRESSACEAE)

Stacey Lee Thompson[1], Alison Dawn Scott[1], Lisa O'Connell[2], Kermit Ritland[2]

ABSTRACT

As knowledge of historical migration in response to climatic change allows insight into the dynamic nature of range shifts, patterns of post-glacial colonization were evaluated for the western redcedar (*Thuja plicata*). We sampled and genotyped 620 trees from 23 populations across its range, including disjunct coastal and interior mesic sites. Genetic variation at eight hypervariable microsatellite loci (mean alleles/locus = 10.30, mean expected heterozygosity = 0.755) was much higher than previous studies involving other markers, and inbreeding coefficients were predominantly positive (mean = 0.110). The two southernmost populations showed the greatest genetic distances, while remaining populations clustered into three distinct geographic groups, comprising northern/coastal, central, and southern/interior populations, respectively. Genetic diversity decreased with latitude, while genetic and geographic distances were strongly correlated ($r = 0.788$). Our findings are consistent with independent routes of relatively recent colonization from one major refugium, located south of the glacial maximum, rather than ancient vicariant events. Regional bottlenecks, detected in the south of the range, may have resulted from local extinctions as the range of western redcedar advanced northward. Combined with inbreeding and the evolution of inbreeding tolerance, this may have promoted homozygosity for most classes of genetic markers as observed in other studies of this species. The high heterozygosity for these microsatellite markers imply that there should be significant heritabilities for traits of concern for tree breeding programs, while the observed population clusters broadly delimit seed zones for reforestation.

[1] Department of Biological Sciences, California State University, Los Angeles, 5151 State University Drive, Los Angeles CA 90032, *staceylee.thompson@calstatela.edu* and ascott3@calstatela.edu
[2] Department of Forest Sciences, University of British Columbia, Vancouver BC V6T 1Z4 kermit.ritland@ubc.ca

CORRELATES OF CLONALITY IN WESTERN REDCEDAR (*THUJA PLICATA*)

Alison Scott[1], Jesse Granados, Stacey Lee Thompson

ABSTRACT

Asexuality has several evolutionary implications, including the reduction of genetic diversity, the creation of spatial genetic structure, the promotion of realized inbreeding through mating among clone-mates, and the ultimate pace of adaptation. Western redcedar, a cornerstone of Pacific Northwest cultures, growing from California to Alaska, can reproduce both sexually and asexually through vegetative clones. Understanding environmental correlates of clonality in redcedar populations is critical, as the lack of recombination that accompanies asexuality could mean that certain natural stands may be less able to adapt to environmental change. To evaluate clonal reproduction in redcedar populations, we are genotyping seven highly polymorphic microsatellite loci in conjunction with spatial and climatic data. Foliage was sampled from ~60 trees in each of five natural populations that transect the coastal British Columbian range. In addition, spatial data were recorded and cores were taken from a subset of trees. Preliminary screening data from a test panel of 13 trees demonstrate the hypervariable nature of these loci (from 4-11 alleles per locus; observed heterozygosities from 0.538-0.846 per population). This high level of polymorphism across loci will allow us to genetically identify clones and determine the frequency of clonal reproduction. Field data indicate that sampling sites varied in stand density and age, moisture regime, temperature, and biogeoclimatic ecosystem. The integration of these data will allow us to better understand clonality in the species and how it correlates to environmental variability, which will be useful in maintaining genetic diversity when replanting of forested areas in British Columbia and to predict the impacts of a changing climate.

---

[1] Department of Biological Sciences, California State University Los Angeles, Los Angeles, CA, ascott3@calstatela.edu

LOCAL AND RANGEWIDE GENETIC STRUCTURE OF YELLOW CEDAR

Kermit Ritland[1], Terry Pape[1], Stacey Lee Thompson[2]

ABSTRACT

We describe two studies that document genetic structure at both local and regional scales in yellow cedar (*Callitropsis nootkatensis*). Based upon isozymes, the proportion of diversity among populations was considerable (G_{st} =0.139), and three major geographical groups were evident: (1) Vancouver Island – mid-north coast British Columbia (B.C.); (2) south coast B.C. – Washington state; (3) southeast Alaska. This may indicate the presence of multiple refugia during ice-age range contractions. The average inbreeding coefficient of adult trees was 0.18 suggesting considerable selfing (ca. 30%). In a second investigation into the effects of clonality on inbreeding and relatedness at small spatial scales, 485 trees from nine populations were mapped to x-y coordinates and genotyped for 5 highly informative microsatellite loci (11-15 alleles per locus, ca. 75% heterozygosity). In accordance with expectations, substantial clonality was found. A "three-gene" analysis showed that clonality actually promotes inbreeding and spatial structure in most populations, probably through limited dispersal of outcrossed offspring and subsequent sib mating within cohorts derived from the same clone. Overall, the levels of geographic structure and selfing that we found in yellow cedar are quite high for a conifer (although other Cupressoideae species have comparable levels). Our results have implications for population conservation and breeding of yellow cedar.

[1] Department of Forest Sciences, University of British Columbia
[2] Department of Biology, California State University, Los Angeles

DEVELOPMENT OF MARKERS FOR UNGULATE BROWSING RESISTANCE IN WESTERN REDCEDAR (*THUJA PLICATA* DONN EX D. DON)

Adam Foster[1], Leanne Mortimer[1], Dawn Hall[2], Regine Gries[1], Gerhard Gries[1], Aine Plant[1], Jörg Bohlmann[2], John Russell[3], and Jim Mattsson[1]

ABSTRACT

Reforestation with *Thuja plicata* is severely hampered by extensive ungulate browsing of seedlings. High foliar monoterpenoid content correlates with reduced browsing, providing a target for resistance breeding. The most abundant terpenoids in *T. plicata* foliage are the monoterpenes α- and β-thujone, both of which strongly deter ungulate browsing. Here we present work towards the development of alternative markers, morphological and genetic, that may improve accuracy and possibly also reduce the cost and time to predict monoterpene content in breeding populations. *T. plicata* foliage contains glands that presumably stores resin. We found that monoterpenes are almost entirely stored in resin glands, suggesting that the foliar amount of glands may correlate with foliar monoterpene content. We have found initial evidence in support of this hypothesis and are currently expanding the analysis. The genetic basis of monoterpenoid biosynthesis in *T. plicata* is unknown; however it is suspected that the monoterpene sabinene is the precursor of thujone biosynthesis. With the aim of identifying a *T. plicata* sabinene synthase, we sequenced a large number of expressed messenger RNA sequences from leaf foliage and compared the sequences to known monoterpene encoding genes. We identified several putative monoterpene synthase genes, one of which is expressed over 100-fold higher in foliage than the other genes. Expression of this gene is localized to the epithelium of foliar resin glands. *In vitro* enzyme assays showed that the corresponding protein converts geranyl pyrophosphate almost entirely into sabinene. In line with its expression in gland epithelium, the expression of this gene is very low in breeding lines lacking resin glands and high in breeding lines with large and many resin glands. In summary, we are well underway towards developing both morphological and genetic markers for foliar monoterpene content and indirectly also for ungulate browsing resistance.

[1] Department of Biological Sciences, Simon Fraser University, Burnaby, B.C.
[2] Michael Smith Laboratories, University of British Columbia, Vancouver, B.C.
[3] Cowichan Lake Research Station, Ministry of Forests and Range, Research and Knowledge Management Branch, Mesachie Lake, B.C. V0R 2N0

SECTION C

WOOD

SILVICULTURE AND MANAGEMENT

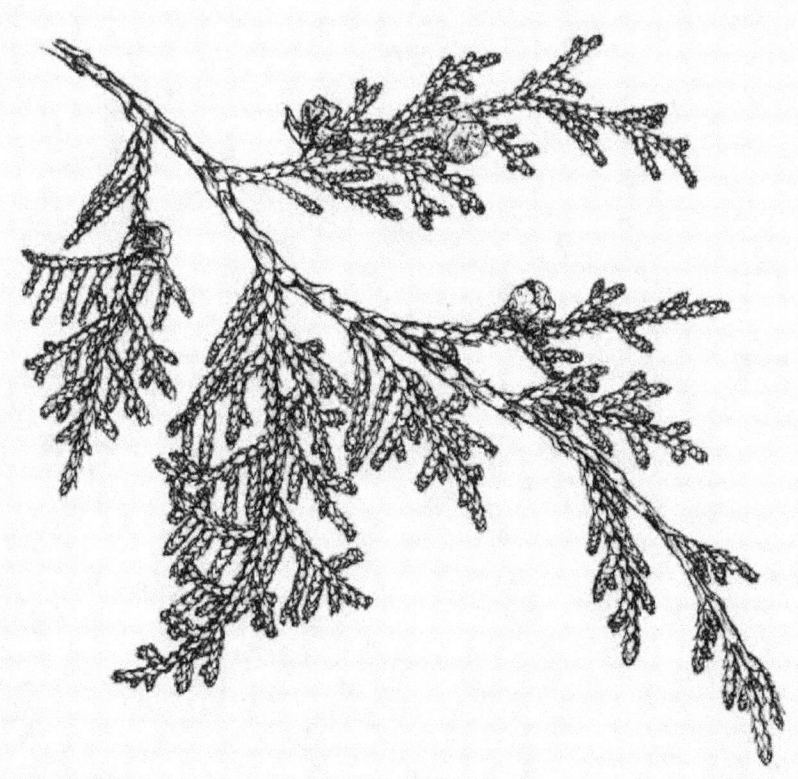

VARIATION IN WESTERN REDCEDAR HEARTWOOD EXTRACTIVES

John H. Russell[1] and Bob Daniels[2]

ABSTRACT

Western redcedar heartwood contains the extractives α-thujaplicin (α-th), ß- thujaplicin (ß-th), γ-thujaplicin (γ-th) and ß- thujaplicinol (ß-thl) which are natural fungicides and are believed to be responsible for much of the woods natural resistance to fungal attack. Lignans such as plicatic acid (PA) and thujaplicatin methyl ether (TME), while much less toxic to fungi, are more abundant than the thujaplicins giving it the potential to play an important role in protecting the tree from decay. In this study four age classes of heartwood were sampled at breast height for extractives using high performance liquid chromatography: old-growth (OG; >200 years old), second growth (SG; five populations 50-115 years old), young trees (YT; 25-year-old clonal trials) and juvenile trees (JT; 10-year-old progeny trials). All of the extractives increased with age except α-th which decreased relative to the other thujaplicins. Genetic parameters for individual extractives were significant, as were the positive genetic correlations among these compounds. Development of western redcedar durable breeds that incorporate important fitness traits for future climates, including cold-hardiness, growth, heartwood durability, deer browse resistance and cedar leaf blight resistance is discussed.

KEYWORDS: Western redcedar, heartwood extractives, phenotypic variation, age, breeding

INTRODUCTION

Western redcedar is prized for its natural durability and is used in many exterior applications such as fencing, decking, roofing and siding. Traditionally, these products have come from old growth heartwood. The inevitable decrease of old growth stands available for harvesting raises the questions of second growth heartwood durability and the feasibility of the western redcedar coastal tree breeding program in British Columbia to develop durable phenotypes for inclusion in seed orchards. Harvesting pressures have resulted in an extensive regeneration program including the establishment of seed orchards for coastal British Columbia. Up to 10 million seedlings are planted annually in British Columbia, with over 80% of the seed coming from managed orchards.

The heartwood contains tropolones including α-thujaplicin, ß-thujaplicin, γ-thujaplicin and ß-thujaplicinol, which are all excellent natural fungicides and are believed to be responsible for much of the heartwood's natural resistance to fungal attack (Maclean and Gardner 1956). Lignans such as plicatic acid, while much less toxic to fungi, can be up to ten times as abundant as the thujaplicins, indicating they may play an important role in protecting the tree from decay. The toxicity of ß-thujaplicin and γ-thujaplicin have been compared to that of pentachlorophenol, while plicatic acid has been compared to zinc chloride, which is only one tenth as effective as pentachlorophenol (Sterling *et al.* 2007) The roles of thujaplicatin methyl ether, thujic acid and methyl thujate in decay resistance are not yet known but they may also have some effects.

In this study, we explore the effects of age, population and individual tree variation on expression of heartwood extractives in western redcedar.

[1] Cowichan Lake Research Station, B.C. Ministry of Forests and Range, Box 335, Mesachie Lake, BC, Canada V0R 2N0 John.Russell@gov.bc.ca
[2] FP Innovations, Vancouver, BC, Canada

MATERIALS AND METHODS

Heartwood was collected from four different age classes: old growth, second growth, saplings, and juvenile trees. All material was collected from breast height (except juvenile trees as described below) and separated into inner and outer heartwood to minimize within-tree variation.

Individual old growth trees: Six trees varying in age from 200-360 years old were selected from British Columbia coastal low elevation sites. Trees were felled and discs taken at breast height.

Second growth populations: Six to seven trees were selected from each of four populations; two from coastal and two from interior British Columbia. Discs at breast height were taken on all trees.

Young clonal trial: Five-mm cores were taken at breast height from 2-4 copies each of 100 clones. The trial, located on south Vancouver Island, was a randomized complete block design with single tree plots. Trees were 20 years old at time of sampling.

Juvenile progeny trial: Discs were taken at the base of ten-year-old trees from an open-pollinated progeny trial. Samples were taken from 30 families with eight trees per family. The trial, located on south Vancouver Island, was a completely randomized block design.

Extractives

A suite of known and unknown extractives were isolated using high performance liquid chromatography with a gradient elution (Daniels and Russell 2007). Volume weighted averages for each compound were calculated for inner and outer heartwood separately, assuming the tree was perfectly cylindrical. All extractive values are expressed as $\mu g/cm^3$ of heartwood.

Data analysis

Simple statistics including means, variances and standard errors were estimated using SAS ver. 9.1.3. Genetic analyses including heritabilities and correlations were done with ASREML ver

2.0. Data analyses reported here focused on the known fungicidal compounds from the tropolone (α-, β-, and γ-thujaplicin), and lignin (plicatic acid) groups.

RESULTS

Age Effects

There was a significant increase in the amount of α-thujaplicin compared to the other tropolones and plicatic acid at age 10 ($P<0.05$), but this was not evident at age 20. There were no significant differences among all four compounds at age 20; however, plicatic acid dramatically increased in the second growth trees and was seven-fold higher than the total thujaplicin concentration in old growth trees (Fig. 1). β- and γ-thujaplicin had similar in concentrations in second growth and old growth trees, and both were significantly greater than α-thujaplicin ($P<0.05$) which decreased dramatically in old growth trees (Fig. 2).

Population effects

Interior British Columbia populations had significantly less α- and β-thujaplicin than coastal populations ($P<0.05$). Plicatic acid and γ-thujaplicin concentrations were similar between the two geographic areas.

Genetic parameters

Coefficients of clonal variation were high, varying from 40% (α-thujaplicin) to 189% (plicatic acid). Estimations of coefficients of additive variation from the 10-year-old progeny trial were 69%, 86% and 159% for α-, β-, and γ-thujaplicin, respectively. There was no detectable plicatic acid in the juvenile trees. Clonal mean repeatabilities varied from 0.62 (α-thujaplicin) to 0.75 (γ-thujaplicin), and narrow-sense heritabilities were 0.55, 0.24 and 0.24 for α-, β-, and γ-thujaplicin, respectively.

α-thujaplicin had significant positive genetic correlations ($P<0.05$) with β-thujaplicin (0.56), γ-thujaplicin (0.66), and plicatic acid (0.48). There was a non-significant but positive genetic correlation between β- and γ-thujaplicin (0.34). Plicatic acid had a significant positive genetic correlation with α-thujaplicin (0.48) and γ-

thujaplicin (0.49), but was there was no significant correlation with ß-thujaplicin. All of the extractives had positive genetic correlations with growth; the correlations for plicatic acid (0.42) and α-thujaplicin (0.44) were statistically significant (P<0.05).

IMPLICATIONS FOR BREEDING

Incorporating wood durability in the western redcedar breeding program is certainly feasible. Wood extractives that have fungicidal properties – lignans and tropolones – are present in 20-year-old heartwood at significant concentrations and have high additive coefficients of variation and narrow-sense heritibilities. There are also favorable genetic correlations among the important extractives, as well as between extractive concentrations and growth.

Managing the western redcedar gene resource for the future under a changing climate needs to address a number of challenges: growth and environmental related stress responses, ungulate damage, cedar leaf blight, as well as wood fungal rots. Ensuring a sustainable supply of durable products from future forests is the most economically important one; however, the other challenges cannot be ignored. If western redcedar forests are to remain adaptable in the long term, they must have positive growth responses to environmental stresses, as well as exhibit cold and drought tolerance. Deer browse and elk grazing pressures currently carry an annual economic cost of over $25 million just in seedling protection alone, and this pressure will most likely increase in the future, given an increasing trend in ungulate populations in redcedar habitat. As climate warms, favorable conditions for cedar leaf blight, a serious pathogen that causes decreased growth and mortality, will increase along the moist coastal areas of British Columbia and the Pacific Northwest. A gene resource management strategy that addresses these challenges is a necessity to ensure healthy future forests.

There are currently over 1000 parent trees in the western redcedar breeding program for the Maritime low elevation Seed Planning Zone (under 600 metres). Approximately 350 of these have been characterized for wood extractives. These same parent trees have also been progeny tested yielding breeding values for growth and cedar leaf blight. In addition, each parent tree has been characterized for foliar monoterpenes, an important secondary chemical in deterring deer browse. Genetic correlations among these traits have been near zero or moderately positive, allowing the selection of these traits through independent culling for future breeding populations.

LITERATURE CITED

Daniels, B.; Russell, J.H. 2007. Analysis of western redcedar (*Thuja plicata* Donn) heartwood components by HPLC as a possible screening tool for trees with enhanced natural durability. J. Chrom. Sci. 45(5):281-285.

Maclean, H.; Gardner, J.A.F. 1956. Distribution of fungicidal extractives (thujaplicin and water-soluble phenols) in western red cedar heartwood. Forest Products Journal, 6(12):510-16.

Stirling, R.; Daniels, C.R.; Clark, J.E.; Morris, P.I. 2007. Methods for Determining the Role of Extractives in the Natural Durability of Western Red Cedar Heartwood. International Research Group on Wood Protection. Document No. IRG/WP/07-20356. 12p.

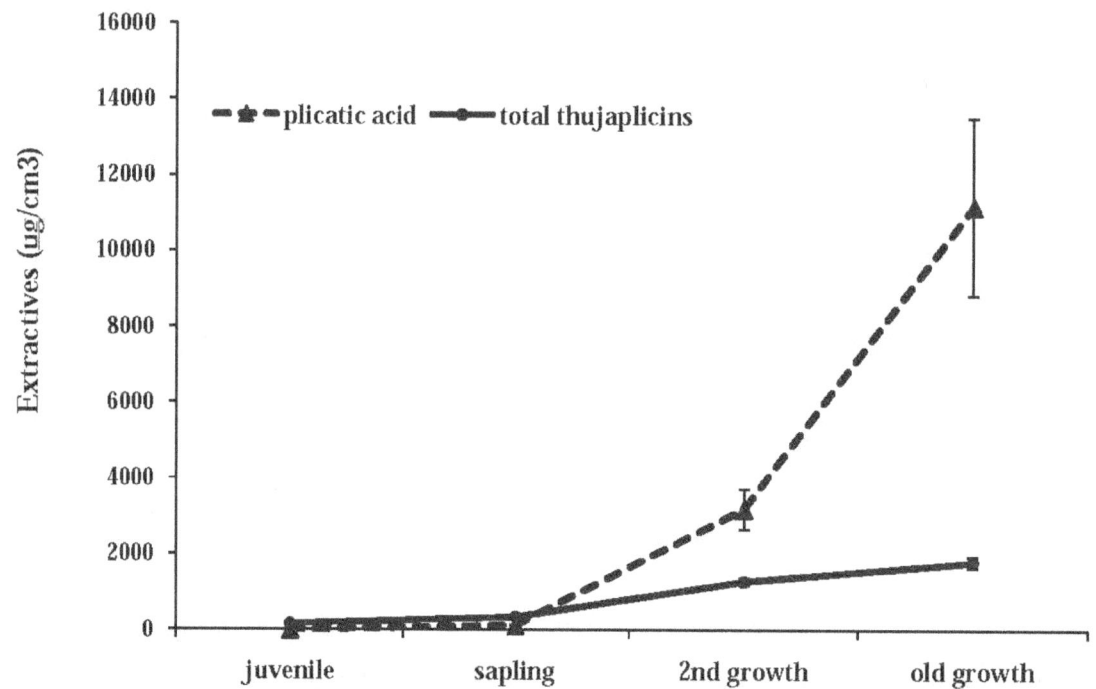

Figure 1 -- Average plicatic acid and total thujaplicin concentrations across four age classes

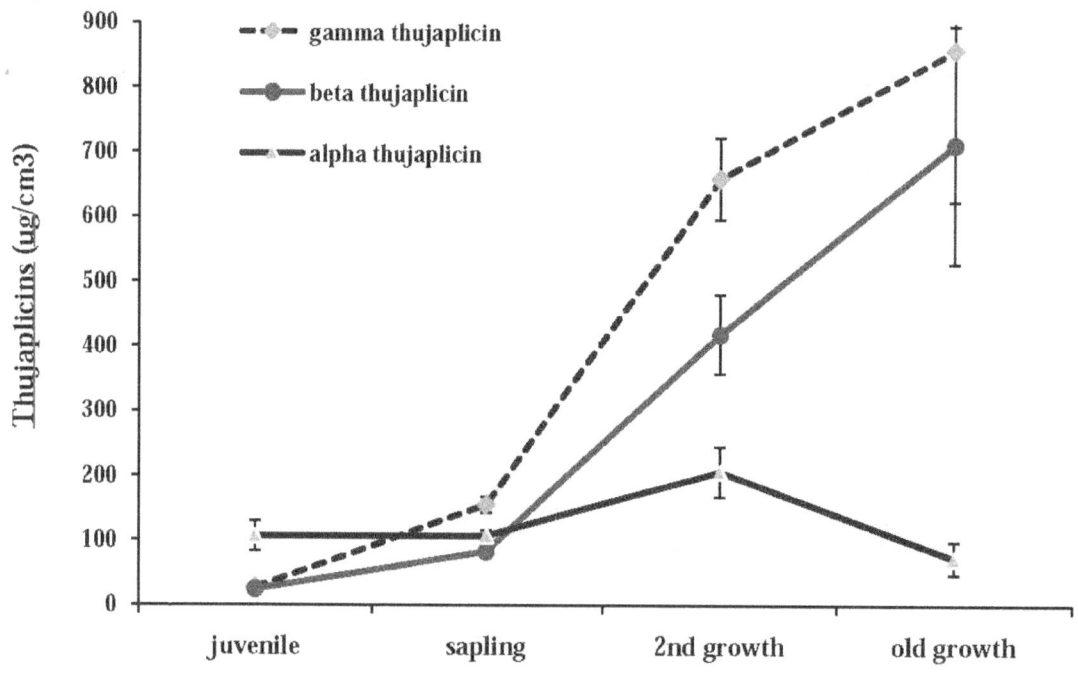

Figure 2 -- Average α-, ß-, and γ-thujaplicin concentrations across four age classes

REDUCING DEPLETION OF WESTERN REDCEDAR EXTRACTIVES FROM WOOD IN SERVICE

Rod Stirling[1] and Paul I. Morris[1]

ABSTRACT

The natural durability of western redcedar depends on the presence of heartwood extractives. The depletion of these extractives by leaching or biological detoxification increases the wood's susceptibility to decay. One potential way of reducing extractives leaching is to reduce their mobility by fixing them to the wood. This could potentially reduce losses from leaching, reduce extractive staining, and enhance the service life of western redcedar products used in exposed applications.

Twelve experimental fixative treatments were evaluated for their ability to prevent leaching in a laboratory test. A zirconium-based tannin-stain-blocking additive and several cationic polymers were found to significantly reduce the leaching of extractives, particularly plicatic acid. In a soil-block decay test some of the cationic polymers were associated with improved decay resistance of leached western redcedar heartwood samples, and no significant change in the durability of pine sapwood. This suggested that decay resistance was achieved through increased extractive retention, not inherent fungitoxic properties. Above-ground field tests have recently been initiated to evaluate the ability of the more effective fixative treatments to enhance service life and reduce extractive staining.

KEYWORDS: durability, extractives, fixatives, leaching, western redcedar

INTRODUCTION

One of western redcedar's (*Thuja plicata* Donn ex D.Don) most important attributes is the natural durability derived from its unique set of heartwood extractives. The concentration of these extractives varies, with the highest concentration found in the outer heartwood and lower down the trunk (MacLean and Gardner 1956). The heartwood of second growth trees tends to have higher concentrations than the same age rings on old growth trees due to extractive detoxification in these older trees (Jin et al. 1988). However, the outer heartwood of old growth trees is laid down by older trees and therefore contains even higher concentrations than second growth trees (Nault 1988). As a result there is a perception in the marketplace that second growth western redcedar (WRC) may not be as durable as old growth WRC. Recent laboratory (Freitag and Morrell 2001) and field tests (Laks et al. 2009) suggest heartwood from second-growth long-rotation managed forests may be, on average, as durable as old growth. However, without selection of planting stock for durability (Daniels and Russell 2007), the best of the second growth will not be as durable as the best of the old growth due to shorter harvest rotations. Decay of old growth takes a considerable length of time and only proceeds rapidly after the loss of the extractives through biodegradation in the standing tree (Jin et al. 1988) or depletion in service (Johnson and Cserjesi 1980) likely due to leaching as well as biodegradation (Chedgy et al. 2007). The durability of heartwood with initially low extractives content may be enhanced by treatments designed to reduce the loss of extractives.

Properly selected, applied, and maintained coatings can slow the loss of extractives by leaching from wood in service (Stirling et al. 2006). However, extractives remain mobile

[1] Wood Chemist and Group Leader, respectively. FPInnovations 2665 East Mall, Vancouver, BC V6T 1W5
rod.stirling@fpinnovations.ca

beneath the coating and can cause staining if an effective stain-blocking primer is not used. An alternative approach is to use a fixative agent to bind extractives to the wood and reduce their leaching. Fixative agents are used in the textile industry to bind functional chemicals to fabric, in the cosmetics industry to bind chemicals to hair and skin, and in the pulp and paper industry to bind fines to the sheet. Fixative treatments may also contribute to reduced extractive bleed and reduced extractive stain-lines caused by wetting at one end and drying further along the board.

The present work describes the evaluation of fixatives agents for their ability to reduce extractive leaching, enhance resistance to decay fungi, and enhance service life of WRC products used in above-ground applications.

MATERIALS AND METHODS

Second-growth WRC heartwood was obtained from the Malcolm Knapp Research Forest in Maple Ridge, BC. Straw-colored outer heartwood with no visible signs of fungal colonization was milled to provide test blocks of dimensions 19 x 19 x 19 mm. Ponderosa pine sapwood test blocks were prepared in parallel for use as a reference in soil block decay testing. WRC blocks were prepared for testing using eighteen replicates for each fixative agent, plus eighteen blocks for use as unleached controls in soil block testing.

Test blocks were conditioned for 48 hours in a forced-draught oven at 60°C, weighed and then subjected to a vacuum/pressure impregnation with the fixative solution. The schedule was a 15-minute vacuum at 26 inches of mercury followed by 30 minutes of pressure at 415 kPa (60 psi) and no final vacuum. Blocks remained submerged for a further 30 minutes, after which excess solution was wiped off and the blocks weighed. Blocks were then conditioned for 48 hours at 60°C in a forced-draught oven prior to weighing, with the exception of the CCA-treated blocks which were stored at 60°C in sealed bags prior to conditioning. In addition to the chemical treatments, a set of water-treated

control blocks, as well as a set of control blocks with no treatment, were prepared.

All blocks were leached following the AWPA Standard E11 with the exception that more than four blocks were placed in an appropriately-sized container. Blocks were placed in containers, grouped by concentration, immersed in water (50 mL per block) and a vacuum of 26 inches of mercury was pulled for 15 minutes followed by 30 minutes of pressure at 415 kPa (60 psi) and no final vacuum. The blocks remained immersed for a further 30 minutes. The restraining weights were removed from the waterlogged blocks and the water changed. Leach water was changed daily for a two-week period excluding weekends, using 50 ml/block. Samples of the leachate water were taken on a daily basis, excluding weekends, for extractive analysis. Leached blocks were then conditioning at 60°C in a forced-draught oven for 48 hours and weighed.

Ten untreated, randomly selected WRC blocks were used to provide an extractives baseline. The blocks were cut and ground to pass through a number 20 mesh, and extracted and analyzed by HPLC according to the method outlined by Daniels and Russell (2007). Leachates were analyzed by HPLC based on the methods of Daniels and Russell (2007) using an external standard method.

Sixteen leached and unleached WRC and ponderosa pine blocks from each treatment group were selected for soil-block testing. These blocks were sterilized by electron beam and put in a soil-block test with the brown rot fungus *Coniophora puteana* (Schum. ex Fr.) Karst., Ftk 9G, and the white rot fungus *Irpex lacteus* (Fr.) Fr., Ftk 103B, based on AWPA standard E10. For each treatment group six blocks were exposed to each fungus and four blocks were left uninoculated as check blocks. The test method followed was generally as described in the AWPA E10-06 Standard for laboratory soil block testing (AWPA 2006). Cylindrical glass jars were half-filled with soil adjusted to approximately 50% moisture content. The soil was topped with two 3 x 29 x 35 mm ponderosa pine sapwood feeder strips, the jar was closed, and the assembly sterilized by autoclaving. After cooling on a clean air bench, each jar was inoculated with one of the test fungi grown on 1.5% malt, 2.0% agar (Difco). White-rot infected jars were incubated for four and one half weeks at 25°C and 80% relative humidity, while brown-rot infected jars were incubated for three and one half weeks before the irradiated blocks were aseptically placed, two per jar, on top of the feeder strips. Jar assemblies were then incubated for a further 12 weeks (brown rot), or 24 weeks (white rot). At the end of the incubation period, blocks were removed from jars, cleaned of any adhering mycelium, and weighed. Blocks were then conditioned at 60°C in a forced-draught oven and reweighed. Mass losses were corrected using non-inoculated treated check block results to compensate for any non-fungal mass loss or gains. Decay was confirmed by a visual inspection of the test blocks.

RESULTS AND DISCUSSION

The average extractives content of each of the test blocks were consistent with previous analyses of WRC heartwood (Daniels and Russell 2007). Though some methyl thujate was detected in the extracted wood blocks, none was detected in the leachates so this extractive was not considered further.

The concentration in the leachates decreased rapidly during the first week and leveled off in the second week. The percentages of total extractives leached from each fixative treatment, relative to the untreated, unleached control group are shown (Fig. 1).

Plicatic acid, the most abundant extractive, was also leached in the greatest quantity. The leaching of plicatic acid was most strongly affected by treatment type. The treatments most effective at reducing leaching were CCA (treatment O), which was included as a reference since it was suspected to have fixation properties, and the tannin stain blocking additive (treatment L). Both of these are metal-

based systems that likely reduced leachability through coordination with plicatic acid's pyrocatechol group (Barton and MacDonald 1971). It should be noted that treatment L was applied in much higher solution strength (as per manufacturer's instructions) than the other compounds tested, so its efficacy may not be as good on an equivalent mass basis. Most of the cationic polymers tested (treatments H to K) performed well, reducing leaching by at least 50%. The anionic nature of plicatic acid suggests that it could be bound well by cationic polymers. Some of the remaining treatments reduced extractive loss slightly but did not perform much better than the water-repellent coating (treatment N).

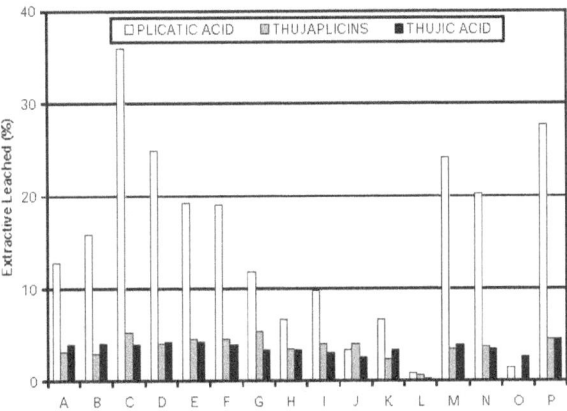

Figure 1 -- Concentration of extractives leached relative to abundance in untreated, unleached WRC

Improved retention of plicatic acid is important as it has been implicated in WRC's natural durability, both as a biocide (Roff and Atkinson 1954) and as a radical scavenger and metal chelator (Stirling et al. 2007). Water-soluble phenolics, of which plicatic acid is the most abundant in WRC heartwood, have also been associated with lower equilibrium moisture content (Stirling and Morris 2006) and are some of the last extractives to be lost from WRC shakes and shingles (Stirling 2010).

The leaching of the thujaplicins was less affected by treatment, though the metal-based systems (treatments L and O) were particularly effective in reducing the amount of thujaplicins detected in the leachates. This is not surprising as the thujaplicins are well known metal chelators (MacLean and Gardner 1956).

Mass losses for the pine blocks were high for the blocks treated with the polymeric fixatives (G – K), as well as the untreated control suggesting that the fixatives themselves were not directly toxic to *C. puteana* (Fig. 2). Fixative L, which contained zirconium compounds and was treated to a much higher retention than the polymeric fixatives, had a reduced mass loss that could indicate toxicity to *C. puteana*. As expected the CCA reference showed no mass loss in either the pine or WRC blocks, leached or unleached.

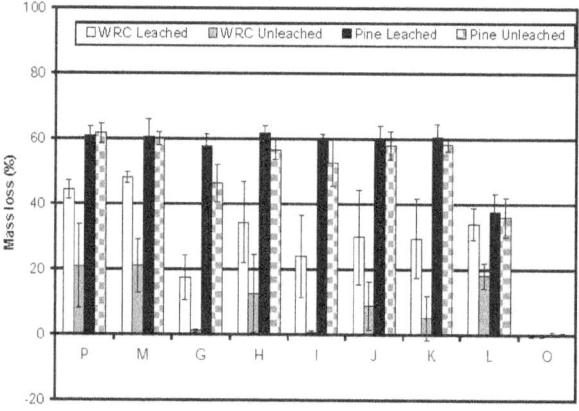

Figure 2 -- Mass loss from *Coniophora puteana* in leached and unleached WRC and ponderosa pine blocks treated with selected fixative agents.

Untreated, unleached WRC blocks had a mass loss of 21% with *C. puteana* which would correspond to a rating of "resistant" (which is the book rating for WRC) in ASTM D2017-05, since untreated pine hit the target of 60% mass loss. Treatments G, I, J and K all had mass losses less than 10%, which would correspond to a "highly resistant" wood. Untreated, leached WRC blocks had a mass loss of 44%, only slightly lower than leached pine. Leached WRC blocks treated with fixatives G and I had mass losses of 17 and 24% respectively. Although these treatments did not completely prevent decay (like CCA) they were able to keep mass

loss down to the same level as untreated unleached WRC. Such treatments could be useful in ensuring a more uniform durability in WRC and extending service life in applications where untreated WRC is used. These treatments may be even more effective in above-ground uses where spore germination, rather than mycelial attack is the main mode of infection.

There were no significant mass losses from untreated WRC blocks exposed to *I. lacteus* (data not shown). Data from this test can therefore not be used to evaluate fixative efficacy in WRC. However, *I. lacteus* did cause significant mass loss in the ponderosa pine blocks, indicating that untreated WRC is resistant to this fungus. Treatments G, H, I and L showed reduced mass loss in ponderosa pine samples, indicating some potential toxic effects towards *I. lacteus*.

Field tests have been initiated to evaluate the performance of selected cationic polymers. Above-ground tests were set up to evaluate resistance to decay, and extractive staining.

CONCLUSION
Pressure-treatment of WRC with CCA or a zirconium-based tannin blocking stain additive reduced the leaching of all quantified extractives.

Several cationic polymers were identified which reduced extractive leaching from WRC, largely by reducing the loss of plicatic acid. These polymers were also associated with reduced mass loss in a soil-block test.

ACKNOWLEDGMENTS
FPInnovations would like to thank its industry members, Natural Resources Canada (Canadian Forest Service); the Provinces of British Columbia, Alberta, Saskatchewan, Manitoba, Ontario, Quebec, Nova Scotia, New Brunswick, as well as Newfoundland and Labrador and the Government of Yukon for their guidance and financial support for this research.

Thanks to Lisa McCuaig for conducting the leaching test, and Jean Clark for conducting the soil-block test.

LITERATURE CITED

American Society for Testing and Materials. 2005. ASTM D2017-05 Standard Test Method of Accelerated Laboratory Test of Natural Decay Resistance of Woods. ASTM, West Conshohocken, PA. 5p.

American Wood-Preservers' Association, 2005. AWPA E10-01. Standard Method of Testing Wood Preservatives by Laboratory Soil-Block Cultures. AWPA. Selma, AL. 11p.

Barton, G.M.; MacDonald, B.F. 1971. The Chemistry and Utilization of Western Red Cedar. Can. For. Serv., Dept. Fish and For., For. Prod. Lab., Vancouver, BC. Publ. No. 1023. 31p.

Chedgy, R.J.; Morris, P.I.; Lim, Y.W.; Breuil, C. 2007. Black stain of Western red cedar (Thuja plicata) by *Aureobasidium pullulans*: the role of weathering. Wood Fiber Sci. 39(3): 472-481.

Daniels, C.R.; Russell, J.H. 2007. Analysis of western red cedar (*Thuja plicata* Donn.) heartwood components by HPLC as a possible screening tool for trees with enhanced natural durability. J. Chromatographic Sci. 45: 281-285.

Freitag, C.M.; Morrell, J.J. 2001. Durability of a changing western redcedar resource. Wood Fiber Sci. 33(1): 69-75.

Jin, L.; van der Kamp, B.J.; Wilson, J.; Swan, E.P. 1988. Biodegradation of thujaplicins in living western red cedar. Can. J. For. Res. 18: 782-786.

Johnson, E.L.; Cserjesi, A.J. 1980. Weathering effect of thujaplicin concentration in western red cedar shakes. For. Prod. J. 30(6): 52-53.

Laks, P.; Morris, P.I.; Larkin, G.M.; Ingram, J.K. 2008. Field tests of naturally durable North American wood species. Int. Res. Group Wood Protect. Document No. IRG/WP/08-10675. 11p.

MacLean, H.; Gardner, J.A.F. 1956. Distribution of fungicidal extractives (thujaplicin and water-soluble phenolics) in western red cedar heartwood. For. Prod. J. 6(12): 510-516.

Nault, J.R. 1988. Radial distribution of thujaplicins in old-growth and second-growth western red cedar (*Thuja plicata* Donn.). Wood Sci. Technol. 22(1): 73-80.

Roff, J.W.; Atkinson, J.M. 1954. Toxicity tests of a water-soluble phenolic fraction (thujaplicin-free) of western red cedar. Can. J. Botany. 32(1): 308-309.

Stirling, R.; Morris, P.I. 2006. The Influence of Extractives on Western Redcedar's Equilibrium Moisture Content. Int. Res. Group Wood Protect. Document No. IRG/WP/06-40331. 12p.

Stirling, R. 2010. Residual extractives in western red cedar shakes and shingles after long-term field testing. For. Prod. J. In press.

Stirling, R.; Morse, B.; Morris, P.I. 2006. The Effects of Various Coatings on Western Red Cedar Extractive Retention. Proc. Can. Wood Preserv. Assoc. 27: 14p.

Stirling, R.; Daniels, C.R.; Clark, J.E.; Morris, P.I. 2007. Methods for Determining the Role of Extractives in the Natural Durability of Western Red Cedar Heartwood. Int. Res. Group Wood Protect. Document No. IRG/WP/07-20356. 12p.

Table 1 -- Fixative agents

Treatment	Description	Concentration (in water)
A	Imidized poly (isobutylene-co-maleic anhydride) copolymer, personal care product fixative	5% + 0.2% triethanolamine
B	Sodium polyvinylpyrrolidone, personal care product fixative	3%
C	Anionic sodium polystyrene sulfonate, personal care product fixative	3%
D	Modified corn starch, personal care product fixative	3%
E	Acetyltriethyl citrate, personal care product fixative	5%
F	Polyvinylpyrrolidone, personal care product fixative	3%
G	Cationic polyethylene polyamine resin, dye fixative	2%
H	Polymerized quaternary ammonium salt, dye fixative	3%
I	Cationic polyethylene polyamine resin, dye fixative	2%
J	Polyethyleneimine, pulp and paper cationic retention aid	3%
K	Modified polyethyleneimine, pulp and paper cationic retention aid	3%
L	Zirconium compounds in acetic acid solution, tannin stain blocking additive	18%
M	Distilled water (control)	-
N	Water-repellent coating (reference)	Brush applied
O	Chromated copper arsenate (CCA, reference)	0.4%
P	Untreated (control)	-

DURABILITY OF SECOND GROWTH VERSUS OLD GROWTH CEDAR LUMBER

Paul I. Morris[1], P. Laks[2], G. Larkin[2] and J.K. Ingram[1]

ABSTRACT

As harvesting shifts towards more second growth, questions increasingly asked about naturally-durable-heartwood species include:

"Is the lumber we are buying now as durable as the material we used to get?"

"What is the effect on service life of sapwood faces on lumber?"

And, in new markets: "Is yellow cedar really as durable as western red cedar?"

There were plenty of textbook references and anecdotal evidence but little or no hard data on which to answer such questions. This paper reports on a collaborative field experiment designed to provide such answers, and develop basic data on the naturally durable species of northern North America. Old growth and second growth lumber of a range of species, with and without sapwood was installed in above-ground and ground-contact field tests in Maple Ridge, BC; Petawawa, Ontario; Gainesville, Florida; and Hilo, Hawaii. Ground-contact tests at all four sites and above ground tests in Florida and Hawaii were evaluated annually. Only the data on western red cedar and yellow cedar are reported here.

Contrary to expectations based on some previous work, second growth from long-rotation managed forests decayed at the same rates as old growth material in ground contact. While the sapwood parts clearly decayed faster than the heartwood the effect of small amounts of sapwood on the mean decay rating was negligible for old and second growth western red cedar, or old growth yellow cedar <u>in ground contact</u>. The exception was second growth yellow cedar where material with sapwood decayed faster at all four test sites. Yellow cedar and western red cedar showed similar decay rates in ground contact as expected from their textbook durability ratings. Above ground, only the Hawaii site showed some degree of separation among the various groups, thus it is too soon to draw firm conclusions.

[1] FPInnovations – Forintek Division, 2665 East Mall, Vancouver, BC, V6T 1W5 Canada, Paul.Morris@FPInnovations.ca (correspondending author at <u>Paul.Morris@FPInnovations.ca</u>)

[2] Michigan Technological University, 1400 Townsend Drive, Houghton, MI 49930-1295 USA

MODELLING THE CROWN PROFILE AND BRANCH SIZE OF WESTERN REDCEDAR (*THUJA PLICATA* DONN) IN COASTAL BRITISH COLUMBIA.

Roberta Parish[1] and James W. Goudie

ABSTRACT

Western redcedar (WRC, *Thuja plicata* Donn) is one of the most valuable timber species harvested in British Columbia. Despite its high timber, cultural and non-timber value, little modelling work has been done on the coast of British Columbia for this species. WRC often regenerates under the canopy in mixed stands, and emerges as dominant species when others have dropped out. As part of a project to expand the Tree and Stand Simulator (TASS) to complex stands containing multiple species and age classes, we began a two-year WRC sampling effort in 2009. Following modified protocols used with other species, we destructively sample 30 trees from three age classes (30, 60 and 90+ years) in each year. We measure crown characteristics (height growth, branch distributions, branch angle, branch size, and foliage biomass and leaf area) and bole attributes (ring growth, relative density and other ring variables). In this paper we report preliminary models predicting the crown profile, branching, and knot size characteristics of WRC from the first year's data. These models will enhance TASS and other models in predicting the rate of crown growth, site occupancy and the wood quality characteristics of WRC, thereby improving forecasts of multiple stand values.

[1] BC Ministry of Forests and Range Research Branch, P.O. Box 9519 Stn. Prov. Gov., Victoria, BC Canada V8W9C2. Roberta.Parish@gov.bc.ca, Jim.goudie@gov.bc.ca

WESTERN REDCEDAR OF THE ROCKY MOUNTAINS: ECOLOGY AND MANAGEMENT

Russell T. Graham[1] and Theresa B. Jain

ABSTRACT

Western redcedar is a major component of the moist forests of the northern Rocky Mountains. As a late seral species it can be extremely long-lived (e.g., 1,000 years) with its major associates being western white pine, ponderosa pine, lodgepole pine, Douglas-fir, western larch, grand fir, and western hemlock. Very lush, robust, and complex forest structures and compositions often exist in these mixed conifer forests. The species has the ability to thrive and be climax in the wettest environments (wetter than western hemlock) and it is also the climax tree species on upland (drier than western hemlock) sites. As such, two potential vegetation classifications are determined by the regeneration and development of western redcedar. It has the ability to persist in the understory of early and mid-seral species for decades and when weather, fire, insects, or other disturbances thin the overstory, western redcedar can release and grow relatively well and in other situations trees succumb to diseases, sun- scald, and other damaging agents. Currently and historically, the species produced high value products such as shakes, siding, rails, and by far one of the most valuable products, utility poles. Nevertheless, the management of stands containing western redcedar has had mixed success, because of uncertainty in how it responds to weedings, cleanings, and thinnings. More often than not, western redcedar management is secondary to managing the early and mid-seral pines, western larch, and Douglas-fir. Even aged silvicultural systems have been used to manage stands containing western redcedar with limited success, however uneven-aged systems show promise.

[1] Forest Service, Rocky Mountain Research Station, 1221 South Main, Moscow, ID, 83843; 208.883.2325, rtgraham@fs.fed.us

COMPARISON OF WESTERN REDCEDAR AND YELLOW-CEDAR GROWTH UNDER DIFFERENT SILVICULTURAL TREATMENTS

W.J. (Bill) Beese[1] and Dillon Chrimes[2]

ABSTRACT

Western redcedar (*Thuja plicata* Donn ex D. Don) and yellow-cedar (*Callitropsis nootkatensis* (D. Don) Oerst.) are two of the highest valued native trees on the Pacific coast. On Vancouver Island, their natural ranges overlap between roughly 600m and 800m elevation; consequently, their relative performance under different silvicultural systems and treatments is of management interest. We present 15- to 20-year results from two studies comparing the growth of redcedar and yellow-cedar and associated species in replicated experiments. The first study compared growth among low-severity and high-severity prescribed burns and unburned controls. Both cedars were planted in mixtures with Douglas-fir (*Pseudotsuga menziesii* (Mirb.) Franco) in randomized rows. The second study (MASS: Montane Alternative Silvicultural Systems) compared growth among clearcut (69 ha), patch cut (1.5 ha), dispersed retention (25 trees per ha) and shelterwood (25% basal area retention) silvicultural systems. Both cedars were planted in pure plots and were compared to Douglas-fir, western hemlock (*Tsuga heterophylla* (Raf.) Sarg.) and amabilis (Pacific silver) fir (*Abies amabilis* Douglas ex J. Forbes).

On the fire study, both cedars had their best 20-year height growth on burned sites, where competition from ericaceous shrubs (*Gautheria shallon* Pursh, and several *Vaccinium* species) was reduced compared to unburned sites. Survival of both cedars was also improved with burning. Redcedar height and volume were equal to or greater than yellow-cedar on all treatments; this likely reflects the fact that the study areas (450m to 600m) are below the natural range of yellow-cedar in that area. Yellow-cedar survival, however, was typically better than redcedar. Foliar nitrogen was higher for yellow-cedar than redcedar across all treatments. Douglas-fir growth performance was greater on burned sites and exceeded both cedars in all treatments.

At the MASS study, 15-year conifer growth did not differ among the clearcut, green tree and patch cut treatments. Growth in the shelterwood was typically slower than in the other silvicultural systems. Although this was the trend for yellow-cedar and redcedar, differences in growth were not significant for yellow-cedar, and were only significant for some growth parameters for redcedar. Yellow-cedar out-performed redcedar in the shelterwood, but growth was similar for these two species in the clearcut. Douglas-fir and western hemlock had better growth in all treatments than both cedars. In some cases, growth of the cedars exceeded that of amabilis fir.

These studies showed that both cedars grow best in open environments and respond positively to prescribed burning. Low levels of retention are not likely to have significant impacts on growth for either redcedar or yellow-cedar. Because of slower relative growth of cedars compared to commonly associated conifers, mixed regeneration must be planned carefully. The high value of both cedars for products and for wildlife habitat makes them highly desirable species despite slow growth rates.

KEYWORDS: Silvicultural systems, prescribed burning, western redcedar, yellow-cedar.

[1] W.J. (Bill) Beese is a forest ecologist, Vancouver Island University, Forestry Department, 900 Fifth Street, Nanaimo, BC, V9R 5S5, Email: bill.beese@viu.ca
[2] Dillon Chrimes has a PhD from the Swedish University of Agricultural Sciences, Department of Silviculture, Umea, Sweden and currently resides in Victoria, BC.

GROWTH OF WESTERN REDCEDAR AND YELLOW-CEDAR

Constance A. Harrington[1] and Peter J. Gould[2]

ABSTRACT

Western redcedar (*Thuja plicata*) and yellow-cedar (*Callitropsis nootkatensis*, syn *Chamaecyparis nootkatensis*) are important tree species in both ecological and economic terms but relatively little information has been available on their growth rates under different stand and site conditions. We took a "data-centric" approach to ask: (1) which environmental variables are most related to site index (for redcedar), (2) what are the limits to growth (size-density relationships) for both species, and (3) how is growth related to stand conditions and site quality? Data was analyzed for over 50,000 trees on more than 3,000 plots throughout the range of both species. A wide range in tree age and stand type was sampled. Results include a classification tree predicting site index for redcedar using climate variables, maximum size-density relationships for both species, and a model for redcedar diameter growth using site and stand variables. Less data was available for yellow-cedar than redcedar but where comparisons across species were possible it appears that although maximum growth rates appear to be lower for yellow-cedar than redcedar, both species respond similarly to stand density.

KEYWORDS: redcedar, yellow-cedar, site index, height growth, diameter growth, size-density relationships

INTRODUCTION

Western redcedar and yellow-cedar are important species in northwestern North America but relatively little information is available on their growth rates (Klinka and Brisco 2009). We know that both species are tolerant of shade, have wide ecological amplitude, and are indeterminate in height growth (have no overwintered bud) (Minore 1990, Harris 1990). Some information is available for redcedar on within-season height growth (Walters and Sooes 1963) and diameter growth (Reukema 1965), and a density management diagram has been available (Smith 1989 and Farnden 1996 in Klinka and Brisco 2009) but most past analyses have used small data sets which have been limited geographically. In addition, very little information has been available for redcedar on topics such as effects of climate on site quality or the effects of stand and site variables on height and diameter growth and almost no quantitative information is available for yellow-cedar. For this project, we surveyed the literature, pulled together our own data sets and contacted several organizations to develop a data set of research and inventory plots where these species were present. We required measurements on fixed-area plots using standard protocols. Plots which had been remeasured were especially useful as they could be utilized to develop or evaluate growth functions, however, plots with only one measurement were also useful for a subset of our analyses. We compiled a data set with 3420 plots with 73,406 trees for redcedar (75% of the plots were remeasured) and 739 plots with 5897 trees for yellow-cedar (46% of the plots were remeasured). Although the two species occupy different ecological niches, we were hopeful that due to their shade tolerance and growth habits they might respond similarly for growth modeling. If so, this would allow us to develop information for redcedar based on a large data set and use it to guide stand management for both species.

METHODS

We analyzed climate variables associated with redcedar site index using a regression tree approach (De'ath and Fabricius 2000). There

[1,2] Pacific Northwest Research Station, 3625 93rd Ave SW, Olympia, WA 98512-9193, USA. [1]Email: charrington@fs.fed.us

were 1606 observations from a wide geographic area. Climate variables used were from Crookston (2010) which included 15 variables that characterize monthly or seasonal temperature or precipitation; variables included monthly means, minimums, and maximum values as well variables related to time periods such as the frost free period. The classification tree was created using the "tree" package in R software for statistical computing (Ripley 2009).

Density management diagrams (first proposed by Reineke 1933) are used by many foresters to look at tradeoffs between number of trees and tree size (QMD or stem volume) and information taken from these diagrams is used in growth models to predict mortality and regulate stand density (Drew and Flewelling 1979). We developed maximum size-density relationships for both species by selecting plots where either redcedar or yellow-cedar was at least 50% of the basal area. We used this threshold for selecting plots to avoid reducing our data set too substantially. We plotted quadratic mean diameter (QMD) and number of trees per ha (in most cases only trees ≥ 2.5 cm DBH were measured) on a log-log scale. We fit the maximum density line to these points for redcedar using frontier analysis and compared the results to those for western hemlock (*Tsuga heterophylla*) and Douglas-fir (*Pseudotsuga menziesii*) by Weiskittel et al. 2009. Maximum Stand Density Index (Max SDI = number of trees on the line where QMD= 25 cm) was determined as first proposed by Reineke (1933). The Max SDI value and slope of the maximum density line were compared to the previous values for redcedar developed by Smith (1989) and Farnden (1996) (in Klinka and Brisco 2009) and recent values published for Douglas-fir and western hemlock (Weiskittel 2009), two common tree associates. We had to convert the earlier redcedar analyses from tree volume to QMD. We also plotted values over time for remeasured plots which experienced mortality in the BC Ministry of Forests and Range data set. In addition, the redcedar line was compared to the plot information available for yellow-cedar. We did not fit a separate line for yellow-cedar as we had insufficient remeasurement data to verify a separate line would be warranted.

ORGANON is a growth and yield model developed by David Hann and others at Oregon State University (http://www.cof.orst.edu/cof/fr/research/organon/). It models tree diameter growth as a function of tree diameter, basal area (BA), basal area in trees larger than the subject tree (BAL), crown ratio, and site index. Very few of our plots had crown data and only a subset had site index (SI) values. We predicted site index for our plots using the regression tree. We developed a model using an ORGANON-type growth equation (i.e., using the same equation form as in ORGANON) based on tree diameter, BA, and BAL, and SI.

We did not model height growth but we did evaluate height increments for redcedar from remeasured plots by plotting them on the same scale as the commonly used site index curves for redcedar (Kurucz 1985). We determined the percentage of the plots which had height increments close to (± 25%), greater than (>25%) and less than (<25%) the predicted slope for that age and site index. This was done for two large datasets: the BC Ministry of Forests permanent sample plot network and the Continuous Vegetation Survey plots from national forests in WA and OR. There were very few plots with remeasured heights for yellow-cedar so this comparison was only possible for redcedar.

We also determined years from 0.1 m to breast height (1.3 m) from stem analysis data from 10 trees from each of the 19 naturally regenerated sites in BC, WA and OR sampled by Radwan and Harrington (1986) and compared those field values to the ones that would be predicted from the equations in Mitchell and Polsson 1988).

RESULTS AND DISCUSSION
The most important climate variables in the regression classification for redcedar site index were: mean maximum temperature in the warmest month, minimum temperature in the

coldest month, day of year to accumulate 100 degree days > 5°C (a measure of how mild the winter is), and growing season precipitation (Fig. 1b). These variables separated site index values into 6 classes. Looking at the plots spatially (Fig. 1a,c), we can see the sites with the lowest site index are mostly in southeast AK (which is not too surprising). However, the regression tree does provide interesting insights into the geographic separation of sites with moderate or high values for site quality. The greatest site index values were predicted for areas in OR, WA and southern BC that are moderately warm (winter and summer) and have relatively high growing season precipitation. Coastal sites in northwest Oregon, western WA, and BC appear to be limited in productivity by summer temperatures when compared to sites further inland.

Comparisons of height growth increments against Kurucz (1985) site index curves indicated an interesting difference between the 2 redcedar data sets (Fig. 2a,b). The BC data was relatively balanced in terms of the breakdown of percentage of plots with greater (21%) and lower (28%) slopes for the height increments than would be predicted for that age and site quality. On the other hand, in the OR-WA data set, the breakdown in percentage of plots (slopes of height increments compared to the SI curves) was 69% of plots with greater slopes and 15% with lower values. Since the curves under-predict growth for the majority of the OR and WA sites, this could indicate that the curves under predict height growth in warm environments and a future research topic could be the development of new curves for redcedar across a wider range of environments.

The number of years to breast height for redcedar varied within sites (Fig. 3) but did not differ across our range of sampled site index (mean= 4.7 years). This compares to the mean value of 9.5 years as calculated from the equation in Mitchell and Polsson (1988); the M&P equation values differ by SI but the range is quite small. We assume the highest values in Figure 3 would represent trees which were

damaged by browsing or other factors early in their life. The lowest values shown on the graph indicate that early height growth can be quite good under favorable conditions.

We developed an ORGANON-type equation for predicting diameter growth of redcedar and compared it to an existing model for Douglas-fir. We used moderate SI values for Douglas-fir (37 m) and redcedar (25 m). With these SI values, the models predict similar growth rates for redcedar and Douglas-fir (Fig.4a) when they are grown with minimal competition. Although the two species are well matched in this example, their growth rates could differ substantially if the SI for either species was changed. However, in all the comparisons we made growth rates are reduced much more sharply for Douglas-fir than redcedar when basal area is increased (Fig.4b). This trend was especially pronounced when BAL increased (Fig. 4c) as diameter growth of redcedar was predicted to be considerably greater than that of Douglas-fir in dense stands and when trees are in poor competitive positions. There was not enough remeasured plot data to fit a similar type of growth equation for yellow-cedar. On plots where both cedars were present (at least 2 of each species) and mean diameter for the 2 species was ± 10 cm, mean growth of yellow-cedar was about 25 to 30% slower than that of redcedar (but relative growth rates were variable, see Fig. 4). In the absence of more data for yellow-cedar, models developed for yellow-cedar could be adjusted downward by 0.3 or could be adjusted based on local information.

The maximum size-density relationship we developed for redcedar (n = 1688 plots) had a maximum density line with a lower slope (-1.29 vs -1.77) and a higher Max SDI (2170 vs 1780) than that previously developed by Smith (1989), but our model was similar to more recent information (Farnden, 1996 as presented in Klinka and Brisco, 2009 had slope = -1.44, Max SDI = 2046) (Fig. 5a). We had a wider range in diameters and larger sample size than was available to Smith. Max SDI was higher than that reported for Douglas-fir (1462) and western hemlock (1582) (Weiskittel 2009). Reineke (1933) proposed a slope of -1.605; our slope of -1.29 is significantly lower (95% confidence intervals = -1.34 to -1.24). The high Max SDI and lower slope may reflect the ability of this shade-tolerant species to grow in multilayered stands. Remeasured data from the BCMF data set fit the maximum size- density line very well (Fig. 5b). The data cloud for yellow-cedar appeared to fit the line developed for redcedar (Fig. 5c) and values associated with the redcedar line would probably be adequate for yellow-cedar until more data is available to fit a separate line for each species.

CONCLUSIONS

In summary, redcedar productivity is quite sensitive to climate variables with the best sites having warm summers, mild winters, and high summer precipitation; thus, the factors which limit growth differ geographically. Redcedar and yellow-cedar have shared characteristics such as the capacity to develop very high stand densities and good survival in the understory. Although the species differ in their ecological niches, they appear to respond similarly in terms of stand density-tree size relationships. Most of our data was from natural stands and many of these stands were unmanaged. We recognize that management activities can have a major impact on tree growth (e.g., use of genetically improved stock, control of browsing, fertilization); however, until more data is available (e.g., genetic multipliers for growth models, juvenile height growth curves for managed stands), incorporation of our results into growth models and silvicultural guidelines should result in better management of these neglected species. The limited data available for yellow-cedar means managers will need to use relationships developed for redcedar or use knowledge based on local stand conditions.

ACKNOWLEDGEMENTS

We thank the following for their assistance: Tara Barrett, PNW Research Station, for assistance in processing FIA data (FIA = USFS Forest Inventory & Analysis program); Jim Menlove, Rocky Mountain Research Station, for providing FIA plot data for Idaho and Montana; Ron Planden, Forest Analysis & Inventory Branch, BC Ministry of Forests and Range, for providing data from the BC permanent sample plot network; Jane Reid, PNW Research Station, for providing FIA plot data for Alaska; Robin Lesher and Cindy McCain, US Forest Service, for providing data from Region 6 Ecology plots; and Bob Brown, USDA Forest Service Region 6, for help with accessing the CVS data.

Figure Captions

Figure 1 -- Regression tree to predict redcedar SI based on climate variables. The regression tree (b) divided the observations into two "cold" groups (a) and four "warm" groups (c).

Figure 2 -- Height growth increments of dominant and codominant trees from the BC and OR WA CVS datasets compared with the expected height trajectories from Kurucz (1978) site index curves. Height increments with slopes that are 25% greater than the site index curve (a) and 25% less than the site index curve (b) are color-coded by data source.

Figure 3 -- The average number of years to reach breast height across a range of site index for redcedar. Each grey point represents a single tree; the blue bars show the mean for each stand that was sampled.

Figure 4 -- Comparison of new diameter-growth model for redcedar (red lines) with an equation used in ORGANON for Douglas-fir (blue lines). Diameter-growth rates were predicted to be about the same for both species when they are open-grown (a). Predicted growth was compared for stand basal areas of 10, 40, and 80 m^2/ha and for trees in superior competitive positions (b; 75% of basal area in smaller trees) and inferior positions (c; 75% of basal area in larger trees).

Figure 5 -- Fit of a maximum stand density line for redcedar (red) compared with lines presented by Smith (1989) and Farnden (1996).

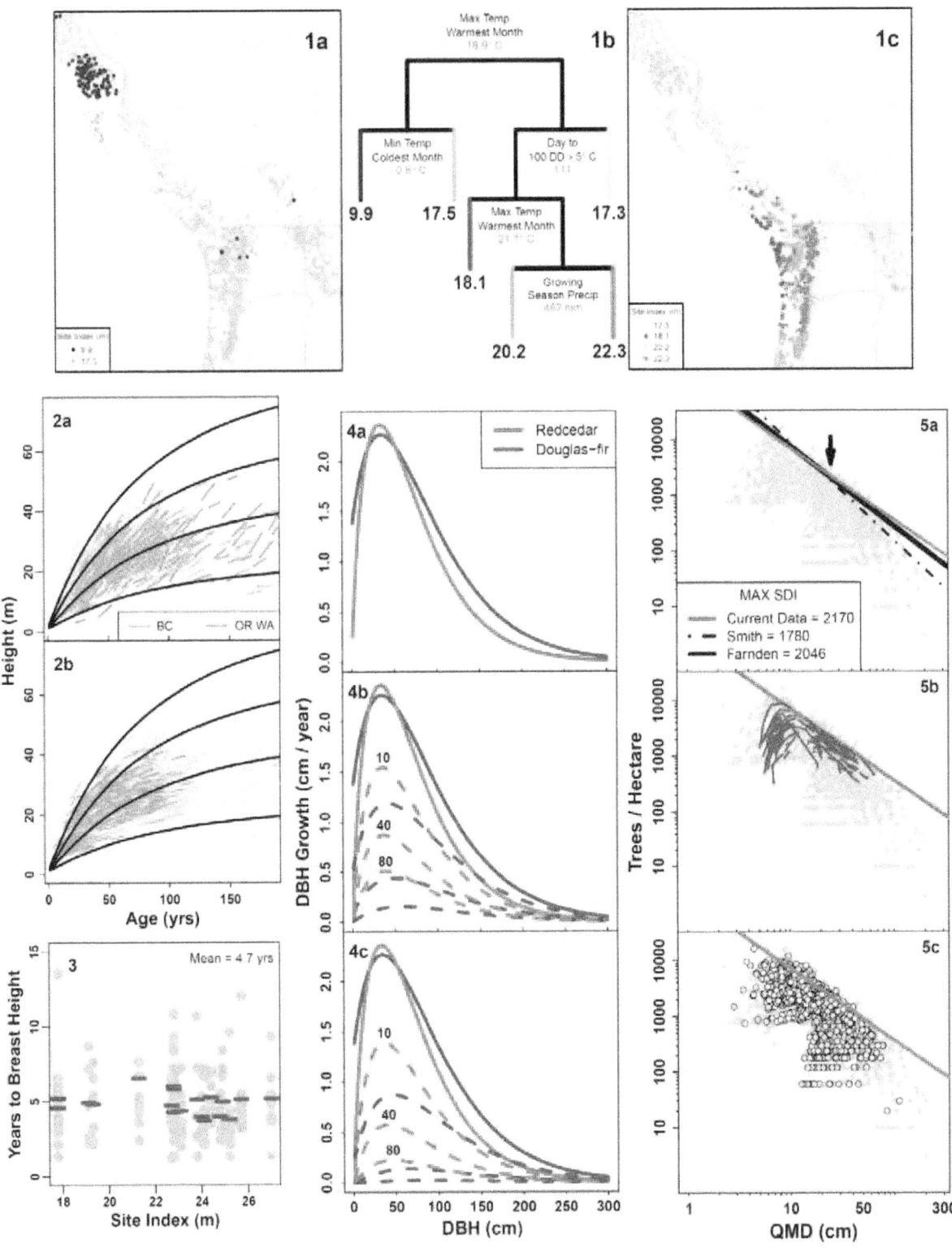

101

LITERATURE CITED

Crookston, N. L. 2010. Current climate data for western North America. http://forest.moscowfsl.wsu.edu/climate/current Climate.html (last accessed April 8, 2010).

De'ath, G.; Fabricius, K.E. 2000. Classification and regression trees: a powerful yet simple technique for ecological data analysis. Ecology 81:3178-3192.

Drew, T.J.; Flewelling, J.W. 1979. Stand density management: an alternative approach and its application to Douglas-fir plantations. For. Sci. 25: 518-532.

Farnden, C. 1996. Stand density management diagrams for western redcedar. Silviculture Br.,B.C. Min. For. Data Source: TASS-generated managed stand yield tables contained in the computer program WINTIPSY Version 1.3. B.C. Min. For., Forest Productivity and Decision Support Section, Victoria, B.C.

Harris, A.S. 1990. *Chamaecyparis nootkatensis* (D.Don) Spach, Alaska-cedar. Pp 97-102 in: Burns, R.M.; Honkala, B.H., tech. coords. Silvics of North America, Vol.1, Conifers. USDA For. Serv. Agric. Handbk 654. Wash. D.C.

Klinka, K.; Brisco, D. 2009. Silvics and silviculture of coastal western redcedar, B.C. Min. For.& Rang, For. Sci. Prog., Spec Rep. Ser. 11. Victoria, B.C. 105 p.

Kurucz, J.F. 1978. Preliminary, polymorphic site index curves for western redcedar – Thuja plicata Donn – in coastal British Columbia. MacMillan Bloedel Forest Research Note 3. 40 p.

Minore, D. 1990. *Thuja plicata* Donn ex.D.Don, western redcedar. Pp 590-66 in: Burns, R.M.; Honkala, B.H., tech. coords. Silvics of North America, Vol.1, Conifers. USDA For. Serv. Agric. Handbk 654. Wash. D.C.

Mitchell, K.J.; Polsson, K.R. 1988. Site index curves and tables for British Columbia: Coast ppecies. FRDA Report 37.

Radwan, M.A.; Harrington C.A. 1986. Foliar chemical concentrations, growth, and site productivity relations in western red cedar. Can. J. For. Res. 16: 1069-1075.

Reineke, L.H. 1933. Perfecting a stand-density index for even-aged forests. J. Agric. Res. 46: 627–638.

Reukema, D.L. 1965. Seasonal progress of radial growth of Douglas-fir, western redcedar and red alder. USFS Res. Pap. PNW-26. 14 p.

Ripley, B. 2009. Tree: Classification and regression trees. R package version 1.0-27. http://CRAN.R-project.org/package=tree (last accessed April 8, 2010).

Smith, N.J. 1989. A stand-density control diagram for western red cedar, *Thuja plicata*. For. Ecol. Mangmt. 27: 235-244.

Walters. J.; Soos J. 1963. Shoot growth patterns of some British Columbia conifers. For. Sci. 9:83-85.

Weiskittel, A. R; Gould, P.J; Temesgen, H. 2009. Sources of variation in the self-thinning boundary line for three species with varying levels of shade tolerance. Forest Science 55:84-93.

EFFECTS OF PRUNING SEVERITY ON THE GROWTH OF WESTERN REDCEDAR AFTER 12 YEARS

Louise E. de Montigny[1], Roderick W. Negrave[2] and Peter K. Ott[3]

ABSTRACT

It is assumed that pruning of western redcedar (*Thuja plicata* Donn ex D. Don.) may increase the proportion of high-value, knot-free wood and improve stem form characteristics. A pruning trial was initiated in a 14-year-old western redcedar stand on northern Vancouver Island in 1993 to investigate the effects of pruning severity on tree growth, taper, epicormic branching, and occlusion of pruning scars. The treatments consisted of an unpruned control and crown removal of 20, 30, 40, 50 and 60% of the total tree height. At the time of pruning, average tree height was 4.5–5.1 m. Initial tree size had a larger effect on growth than the pruning treatments after 12 years. Moderate pruning, up to 50% crown removal, did not reduce tree growth. Pruning only reduced taper at the highest severity (60% removal). The frequency and length of epicormic branches were not significant after 12 years of growth. Branch stub occlusion is not readily apparent in young trees. The financial returns of pruning western redcedar can be improved through the use of green-foliage pruning for floral boughs or the production of cedar oil.

KEYWORDS: Western redcedar, silviculture, pruning, epicormic branching, branch occlusion.

INTRODUCTION

Western redcedar (*Thuja plicata* Donn ex D. Don.) is an important commercial species in British Columbia (B.C.), Washington, and Oregon. The wood has low density and strength, but is aesthetically pleasing and has superior dimensional stability, durability, and insulating properties. The wood is highly desirable for decorative and specialty products, many of which require high-value clear wood that is currently obtainable only from large, old-growth logs. Second growth western redcedar ("cedar") is commonly an understorey component of mixed stands with red alder (*Alnus rubra* Bong.), western hemlock (*Tsuga heterophylla* [Raf.] Sarg.), and/or Douglas-fir (*Pseudotsuga menziesii* [Mirb.] Franco) (Stubblefield and Oliver 1978). Cedar grows slowly under these conditions, with large living or dead branches, high stem taper, and fluting (Oliver et al. 1987).

Trees in this environment take several hundred years to develop the high-quality wood characteristics of old-growth cedar. In contrast, cedar grown in even-aged, single-species stands at relatively close spacing can grow rapidly and produce trees of desirable form much sooner (Oliver et al. 1987). Cedar plantations have been established on over 150,000 hectares on northern Vancouver Island and the mid-Coast of B.C. A well-designed intensive silviculture program may produce the wood quality characteristics of old-growth cedar in younger trees. For example, ensuring adequate spacing when trees are planted and pruned, and stand fertilization could improve rates of cedar growth and production of knot-free wood with better stem form and taper. There are still many unknowns: the growth response of cedar to pruning, its susceptibility to epicormic branching, rates of branch stub occlusion,

[1] Louise de Montigny PhD, R.P.F. is Research Leader for Silvicultural Systems and Forest Dynamics, Research, Innovation and Knowledge Management Branch, B.C. Ministry of Forests and Range. P.O. Box 9519 Stn. Prov. Govt., Victoria, B.C. V8W 9C2
[2] Roderick Negrave PhD, PAg, RPF is Research Team Leader, Research, Innovation and Knowledge Management Branch, B.C. Ministry of Forests and Range, 2100 Labieux Road, Nanaimo, B.C. V9T 6E9.
[3] Peter Ott is a statistician, Research, Innovation and Knowledge Management Branch, B.C. Ministry of Forests and Range. P.O. Box 9519 Stn. Prov. Govt. Victoria, B.C. V8W 9C2.

the susceptibility of pruned trees to disease, and the effects of pruning on wood quality.

A pruning experiment was initiated in 1993 to examine the effects of pruning severity on 12-year-old plantation cedar. Objectives of this study were to compare height and diameter growth, taper, the rate of occlusion of pruned branch stubs and epicormic branch development among pruning treatments.

METHODS

The study site is located near Port Hardy, B.C. (50°38'08" N, 127°17'54"), in Western Forest Products Ltd. Tree Farm License 25. The study area is classified as mesic, in the submontane variant of the very wet maritime subzone within the Coastal Western Hemlock biogeoclimatic zone (CWHvm1/01 cedar—salal phase). The understorey is predominantly salal (*Gaultheria shallon* Pursh.) and deer fern (*Blechnum spicant* [L.] Roth.), with pockets of *Vaccinium* species. Soils are Humo-Ferric Podzols (Spodosols), often with a Duric horizon or other root- and water-restricting layers. The area receives approximately 1900 mm of precipitation annually, most of which falls as rain so there is typically no growing season soil moisture deficit. Average daily mean temperature ranges from 3.3°C in January to 14.1°C in August.

The site was logged and broadcast burned in 1980 and planted the following spring with 2-year-old container-grown cedar at 1030 stems per ha. In December 1986, the stand was broadcast fertilized with urea and ammonium phosphate to deliver 225 kg/ha of N and 75 kg/ha of P.

Prior to plot layout, a reconnaissance survey was done to identify site differences and ensure homogeneity of treatment units. A randomized complete block design (RBCD) was used for this study, comprised of six pruning severity treatments and two blocks. Within each block, treatments were randomly assigned to a treatment unit that contained a single 0.1-ha core measurement plot with a surrounding 0.1-

ha buffer. There were 75–100 measurement trees in each core plot. The treatments consisted of an unpruned control and crown removal of 20, 30, 40, 50, and 60% of the total tree height from the crown base, which was virtually equivalent to the tree base in this plantation. Pruning treatments were applied in the winter of 1993–94. Heights were measured immediately before pruning to determine the height of foliage to remove using pruners and loppers. Immediately post-pruning and in 1995, 1997, 2001, and 2005, we measured tree height, diameter at 1.3 m (or breast) height (DBH), pruning height, categorical measures of the number of epicormic branches (0, 1–10, 11–20, and > 20) and maximum vigour (length) of the epicormic branches (< 4 cm, 5–10 cm, and > 11 cm), estimated branch stub occlusion, and assessed tree damage and condition classes. We also measured height to crown base in 1994 and diameter at 30 cm in 2006.

We used a mixed-effects model to determine the significance of treatment and temporal differences on cedar height and DBH. We used Proc Mixed (SAS Institute Inc. 2004) to fit the following analysis of variance (ANOVA) model:

$$Y_{ijkl} = \mu + B_i + P_j + (BP)_{ij} + S_{k(ij)} + T_l + (BT)_{il} + (PT)_{jl} + (BPT)_{ijl} + (ST)_{kl(ij)}$$

where Y_{ijkl} is the response of the kth tree nested in both the ith block and j^{th} treatment level, measured at year l. The parameter μ denotes the overall experimental mean. Parameters B_i, P_j, $S_{k(ij)}$, and T_l represent the effects of block, pruning treatment, tree (nested within block and treatment), and year of measurement, respectively. The trees measured within each plot represent subsamples within the randomized complete block design, and year was analyzed as a repeated measures effect (e.g., a split-plot factor). All factors and interactions except P_j, T_l, and $(PT)_{jl}$ were considered random, and were considered independent from one another, each with a normal distribution with zero mean and a unique variance component. The correlation between residuals from a tree measured at year t_l and t_{l+m}

was modelled as $\rho^{|t_j - t_{j+m}|}$, where $|\rho| < 1$. Custom contrasts were used to compare treatment levels with the control for each year. Comparisons of each mean with the control were adjusted using a simple Bonferroni-type correction (i.e., the level of significance was changed to $\alpha \div 5$). Where there was a significant treatment × year (PT) interaction, simple main-effect tests were used to separately compare treatments for each year.

A yearly observation data point was eliminated if the height or DBH at the previous growth period was larger. Pearson and Studentized residuals were graphically examined for outliers, severe departures from normality, and heteroscedasticity. After removing a handful of obvious outliers, the residuals appeared to meet model assumptions for all dependent variables. A significance level of $\alpha = 0.05$ was used for all tests unless otherwise indicated.

For epicormic branching, wound occlusion, and tree condition, data were summarized for these variables in each treatment by year of measurement without performing any formal statistical tests.

RESULTS

Height to Crown Base
Total tree height averaged 4.5–5 m prior to pruning treatments. The height to crown base in the unpruned control was 40 cm, or about 10% of the total height. Pruning treatments increased the height to crown base by about 0.5 m with every 10% increase in pruning severity: from about 1.0 m for the 20% crown removal treatment to 3.0 m for the 60% removal treatment (Table 1). The variability in the total tree height by plot led to a range of heights to crown base within treatments, such that any height to crown value was not exclusive to any one treatment.

Diameters
No significant difference developed for DBH between the control and the pruning treatments until 8–12 years after pruning (Table 1). By twelve years after pruning, only the 60% removal treatment was significantly smaller than the control. The estimate of the residual correlation parameter ρ was close to 1 (i.e., 0.98–0.99) and highly significant in both cases, indicating that the DBH of the tree at the start of measurements strongly influenced the DBH of the tree after 12 years.

For diameter at 0.3 m, measured at year 12, none of the treatments were significantly different from the control, although the 60% removal treatment was the smallest (p = 0.1006).

Height
At the time of pruning, there were no significant differences in heights among treatments (Table 1). None of the pruning treatments were significantly smaller than the control 12 years after pruning, but the 50% removal pruning treatment was significantly taller than the control. The estimate of ρ was 0.99 (highly significant), indicating that the initial tree height strongly influenced the height of the tree after 12 years.

Branch Stub Occlusion
One year after pruning, branch stubs were open on nearly 100% of trees in all pruning treatments. After 12 years, the branch stubs had occluded (healed over) in all pruning treatments, except that bark did not appear to grow over the wounds, but remained dimpled where the branch had been. It is unclear whether this will affect wood quality.

Epicormic Branch Number and Vigour
Epicormic branching increased with pruning severity (Table 2). After two years, trees that received moderate to severe pruning treatments (40–60% crown removal) tended to have more epicormic branches than lightly pruned (20–30% removal) trees. In the first two years, most epicormic branches were > 4 cm and their number and vigour tended to be slightly higher on the south side of the tree than the north side. There were generally ten or fewer epicormic branches per sample side (data not shown).

Table 1: Least-squares means (standard errors) and analysis for height, DBH, and volume at 0, 4, 8, and 12 years after pruning; branch length at crown base and height to crown base at 0 and 12 years after pruning; and diameter at 30 cm.

| | Years since pruning | Crown removal treatment (%)[a] | | | | | | p-value | NDF[b] | DDF[c] |
		Control	20	30	40	50	60			
DBH (cm)	0	7.49 (0.76)	6.63 (0.79)	8.82 (0.79)	7.85 (0.76)	8.50 (0.76)	7.26 (0.76)	0.379	5	15
	4	9.82 (0.76)	8.87 (0.76)	11.67 (0.76)	9.84 (0.76)	10.50 (0.76)	8.30 (0.76)	0.080	5	15
	8	11.52 (0.76)	10.46 (0.76)	13.79 (0.76)	11.79 (0.76)	12.64 (0.76)	9.75 (0.76)	0.022	5	15
	12	13.03 (0.76)	11.80 (0.76)	15.58 (0.76)	13.38 (0.76)	14.51 (0.76)	11.05 * (0.76)	0.008	5	15
Height (m)	0	4.81 (0.24)	4.57 (0.24)	5.01 (0.24)	5.08 (0.24)	5.15 (0.24)	4.76 (0.24)	0.536	5	15
	4	6.17 (0.24)	6.01 (0.24)	6.76 (0.24)	6.65 (0.24)	6.83 (0.24)	5.96 (0.24)	0.064	5	15
	8	7.04 (0.24)	6.74 (0.24)	7.83 (0.24)	7.55 (0.24)	7.78 (0.24)	6.64 (0.24)	0.008	5	15
	12	7.86 (0.24)	7.48 (0.24)	8.70 (0.24)	8.43 (0.24)	8.78 * (0.24)	7.41 (0.24)	0.002	5	15
HCB[d] (m)	0	0.40 * (0.05)	0.92 * (0.05)	1.51 * (0.05)	2.04 * (0.05)	2.59 * (0.06)	2.85 * (0.07)	0.0001	5	5
D@30[e] (cm)	12	17.7 (1.12)	15.5 (1.12)	20.0 (1.12)	18.0 (1.12)	19.3 (1.11)	14.4 (1.13)	0.089	5	5

[a] Treatment levels with an asterisk are statistically significant from the control at $\alpha = 0.05 \div 5 = 0.01$

[b] NDF – numerator degrees of freedom for F-test

[c] DDF – denominator degrees of freedom for F-test. Tests of simple main effects from the full model (equation 1) will have more degrees of freedom (15) than tests based on a separate reduced model for each year (5)

[d] HCB – height to crown base

[e] D@30 – diameter at 30 cm

Twelve years after pruning, the proportion of trees that had developed epicormic branches increased to about 20–35% of lightly-pruned trees; approximately 45–55% of moderate-severity pruned trees, and 73% of severely pruned trees. Trees that developed new epicormic branches had 1–10 per tree (Table 2). The number of trees with 11–20 epicormic branches per tree decreased, suggesting this was likely due to mortality of these branches over the 12-year period. Twelve years after pruning, the proportion of trees with epicormic branches > 11 cm increased with pruning severity (Table 2) from 6–9% in light pruning, 19–42% in the moderately severe pruning treatments, and 60% in the severe pruning treatments.

DISCUSSION

Pruning may improve the growth and yield of western redcedar for several reasons: improved height growth, better stem form, and reduced knot size and number. Pruning did not significantly reduce height growth, which is consistent with other studies that found moderate pruning did not negatively impact height growth (reviewed by Maguire and Petruncio 1995); however our results suggest that cedar growth may be even less sensitive to pruning than other species. In our study, only the 60% treatment resulted in a mean DBH that was significantly smaller than the control. Other pruning studies found that one-third to one-half of live crown length can be removed before DBH is negatively affected (Gallagher 1984; Pentruncio 1994; de Montigny and Stearns-Smith 2001a, 2001b). Although not significantly different, the average DBH of trees in the 30% removal treatment was larger than that of the control, likely because the pruned height was roughly equivalent to breast height (1.5 vs. 1.3 cm, respectively), and because growth along the stem is largely controlled by relative proximity to the photosynthate source (Smith 1962). Several authors have suggested that pruning results in a reallocation of radial growth along the stem resulting in less taper (Larson 1965; Maguire and Petruncio 1995). A more detailed analysis of changes in stem form and volume

Table 2: Proportion of trees across treatments in categories for occurrence (count of) epicormic branches per tree and vigour (length) of the longest epicormic branch per tree.

Crown Removal (%)	Epicormic Occurence (number per tree)	Vigour (length of epicormic branches)							
		1995				2006			
		< 4 cm	5–10 cm	> 11 cm	Total	< 4 cm	5–10 cm	> 11 cm	Total
20	0	n/a	n/a	n/a	83.06	n/a	n/a	n/a	65.03
	1–10	9.84	1.09	0.55	11.48	4.92	20.22	9.29	34.43
	11–20	2.73	1.64	1.09	5.46	0.00	0.00	0.55	0.55
30	0	n/a	n/a	n/a	80.32	n/a	n/a	n/a	80.85
	1–10	13.83	0.53	0.00	14.36	3.19	9.57	6.38	19.15
	11–20	3.72	0.53	1.06	5.32	0.00	0.00	0.00	0.00
40	0	n/a	n/a	n/a	44.89	n/a	n/a	n/a	53.41
	1–10	37.50	0.00	2.27	39.77	2.84	24.43	18.75	46.02
	11–20	13.07	1.70	0.57	15.34	0.00	0.00	0.57	0.57
50	0	n/a	n/a	n/a	33.51	n/a	n/a	n/a	42.55
	1–10	38.83	2.13	0.53	41.49	1.06	12.77	42.02	55.85
	11–20	21.81	3.19	0.00	25.00	0.00	0.00	1.60	1.60
60	0	n/a	n/a	n/a	25.90	n/a	n/a	n/a	23.49
	1–10	34.94	4.22	0.00	39.16	0.60	12.65	59.64	72.89
	11–20	27.11	6.63	1.20	34.94	0.00	0.60	3.01	3.61

should be undertaken in future studies.

Pruning can stimulate the growth of epicormic branches from dormant buds under the bark and from new buds that form in callus tissues as they respond to changes in heat, light, and/or in stem tissue hormonal balances (Collier and Turnblom 2001). Epicormic branching has been noted in other conifer species (Hingston 1990; Collier and Turnblom 2001; Waring and O'Hara 2005). These studies typically find that the more severe the pruning, the more epicormic shoots develop, but they tend to die as residual crowns expand after pruning. Our results support that finding; after 12 years, the majority of trees have 0 to 10 epicormic branches per tree. The impacts of this epicormic branching on wood quality will be investigated using destructive sampling methods at a later date.

Occlusion of branch stubs is important because it is only after the branch stub has occluded that clear, high-value wood is produced by the tree. Any delay in occlusion reduces the volume of the clear wood and allows pathogens to enter. In cedar, the rate of occlusion was difficult to judge based on external appearances because the bark did not grow over the wound, even after twelve years. Since the pruned cedar trees remain healthy with no visible signs of decay, it indicates that the wound has likely occluded. Destructive sampling will allow a better

evaluation of the branch stub occlusion below the cambium.

Pruning as a silviculture investment has been shown to provide reasonable economic return only in stands with relatively high site indices that maintained rapid diameter growth over short rotations (Fight et al. 1987). This is typically not the case with cedar, which requires a long rotation age to achieve high quality, knot-free wood. However, the high initial investment for pruning could be offset by selling the pruned green foliage material for floral boughs or essential oil production, especially if entrepreneurs prune them at no cost to forest licensees. Such a situation has been documented by Western Forest Products Inc. in Tree Farm License 6 near Port McNeill (Western Forest Products 2003), where a local entrepreneur has pruned large areas of plantation-grown cedar for green foliage and has added almost $1.5 million to the community through cedar oil production. A well-designed intensive silviculture program that utilizes the foliage as a non-timber forest product may result in high-value cedar plantations with attractive financial returns.

CONCLUSION
Pruning may be a viable treatment to increase the value of wood produced in western redcedar plantations. We found that initial tree size had a

greater effect than pruning treatment on growth 12 years after pruning. Pruning up to 50% of the tree height in young cedar did not affect total height or DBH. Excessive epicormic branching and the inability of pruned branch stubs to occlude do not appear to be a concern at this time if pruning severity is kept below about 50% of tree height. Continued measurement over a longer term and destructive sampling are necessary before conclusions can be made about the effects of pruning on wood quality. Despite long rotations and potentially high investment costs, the financial returns of pruning cedar can be improved entrepreneurs can prune the green foliage for non-timber forest products such as cedar leaf oil or floral boughs.

ACKNOWLEDGEMENTS

Funding came from the Forest Investment Account–Forest Science Program, the B.C. Ministry of Forests and Range, and Western Forest Products Ltd.

LITERATURE CITED

Collier, R.; E. Turnblom. 2001. Epicormic branching on pruned coastal Douglas-fir. W. J. Appl. For. 16(2):80-86.

de Montigny, L.; S. Stearns-Smith. 2001a. Pruning density and severity in coastal western hemlock: 4-year results. B.C. Min. For., Res. Br. Ext. Note 51. Victoria, B.C.

de Montigny, L.; S. Stearns-Smith. 2001b. Thinning and pruning coastal Douglas-fir near Chilliwack, B.C.: 8-year results. B.C. Min. For., Res. Br. Ext. Note 56. Victoria, B.C.

Fight, R.D.; J.M. Cahill; T.D.Fahey; T.A. Snellgrove. 1987. Financial analysis of pruning coast Douglas-fir. Res. Pap.PNW-RP-390. Portland, OR: USDA For. Serv. Pac NW Res. Stn.

Gallagher, G. 1984. To prune or not to prune? FWS Res. Br., Res. Note 2/84. Bray, Ireland. 4p.

Hingston, R.A. 1990. Chemical control of epicormic shoots on 4 year old Pinus radiata *D.Don* Aus. For. 53(1):3-6.

Larson, P.R. 1965. Stem form of young Larix as influenced by wind and pruning. For. Sci. 11:413-424.

Maguire, D.A.; M.D. Petruncio. 1995. Pruning and growth of western Cascade species: Douglas-fir, western hemlock and Sitka spruce. P. 179-215 in Hanley D.P. ed.. Proceedings, Forest pruning and wood quality of western North American conifers. For. Res. U. Wash. Seattle, WA. 403 p.

Oliver, C.D.; M.N. Nystrom; D.S. DeBell. 1987. Coastal stand silvicultural potential for western redcedar. P. 39-46 in N.J.Smith (ed). Proceedings, Western redcedar—does it have a future? Faculty of Forestry, Univ. B.C., Vancouver, B.C.

Petruncio, M. 1994. Effects of pruning on growth of western hemlock (Tsuga heterophylla) and Sitka spruce (Picea sitchensis) in southeast Alaska. PhD dissertation, Univ. Wash, Seattle, WA. 160 p.

SAS Institute Inc. 2004. The SAS system: SAS OnlineDoc® Version 9.1.3. Cary, N.C.

Smith, D.M. 1962. The practice of silviculture. 7th ed. John Wiley and Sons. New York, N.Y. 578 p.

Stubblefield, G.W.; C.D. Oliver. 1978. Silvicultural implications of the reconstuction of mixed alder/conifer stands. P. 307-320 in W.A. Atkinson, et al. (eds.). Utilization and management of red alder. Gen. Tech. Rep. GTR-PNW-70. Portland OR: USDA For. Serv., Pac NW Res. Stn.

Waring, K.M.; K. L. O'Hara. 2005. Ten-year growth and epicormic sprouting response of western larch to pruning in western Montana. J. Appl. For. 20(4):228-232.

Western Forest Products Ltd. 2003. Tree Farm Licence 6, 2003 Annual Report. Vancouver, B.C. http://www.westernforest.com/fstew/download/TFL6-AR-2003.pdf

GROWTH OF WESTERN REDCEDAR WITH DOUGLAS-FIR IN YOUNG PLANTATIONS IN WESTERN OREGON

Doug Mainwaring[1] and Doug Maguire[2]

ABSTRACT

Basal area and height growth of western redcedar growing with Douglas-fir in 19-24-year-old operational plantations in western Oregon were measured four years after plot establishment. Plantations were established in stands infected with *Phellinus sulphurascens*, and contained mixes of planted western redcedar and natural Douglas-fir.

Basal area and height growth of redcedar was determined by initial tree size and competitive position, with significant reductions in growth resulting from overtopping Douglas-fir. Where dense stands have resulted in significant stand differentiation, reductions in redcedar growth are significant. Relative to pure redcedar, individual tree basal area growth was reduced 30% for 20-year-old redcedar growing with as few as 125 Douglas-fir per ha. Depending on tree size, basal area growth was reduced 40-80% when redcedar was mixed with 500 Douglas-fir per ha. Reductions in height growth were significantly less, amounting to only 8% in the presence of 125 Douglas-fir/ha and 8-80% with 500 Douglas-fir/ha, depending on tree size. Four-yr mortality of redcedar decreased with size and increased with competitive position, reaching nearly 50% for 5 cm trees growing in a stand with $20m^2$/ha of Douglas-fir.

Where surrounding stands are nearly pure Douglas-fir, current stand trajectories imply that the number of naturally regenerating Douglas-fir must be controlled if redcedar is to remain a major overstory component to ameliorate *Phellinus sulphurascens*.

KEYWORDS: western redcedar, Douglas-fir, mixed species, western Oregon

INTRODUCTION

In the last fifteen years, land managers in western Oregon have shown an increasing interest in growing and managing western redcedar. Although this change is primarily the result of high redcedar log prices relative to Douglas-fir (*Pseudotsuga menziesii* (Mirb.) Franco), the onset of a Swiss needle cast epidemic in Oregon Coast Range forests has also contributed. Swiss needle cast (SNC) is caused by a foliar fungus which causes premature needle abscission of Douglas-fir (Hansen et al. 2000). Resulting growth losses in SNC-infected 10-30 yr old Coast Range plantations were estimated to average 23% in 1996 and were 52% in the most severely impacted plantations (Maguire et al. 2002). In stands where disease intensity is especially high, Douglas-fir is not considered a good candidate for reforestation (Filip et al. 2000). Managers have instead planted non-susceptible alternative species such as western hemlock (*Tsuga heterophylla* (Raf.) Sarg.), Sitka spruce (*Picea sitchensis* (Bong.) Carr.), and western redcedar (*Thuja plicata* Donn ex D. Don).

Although high log prices make western redcedar the preferred species for new plantations where SNC presents a risk, managers have found establishment difficult and expensive, primarily due to deer and elk browse (M. Gourley, Pers. Comm.). The high cost of protecting seedlings

---

[1] Doug Mainwaring is a Faculty Research Assistant, Oregon State University College of Forestry, 204 Peavy Hall, Corvallis, Ore., 97331.

[2] Doug Maguire is a Professor and Director of the Center for Intensive Planted-forest Silviculture, Oregon State University College of Forestry, 204 Peavy Hall, Corvallis, Ore., 97331.

with barriers and high rates of seedling mortality have motivated managers to plant multiple species as a means of lowering costs and ensuring a full stocked stand. The slow height growth of redcedar relative to its associated species means that planting density, species proportions, and spatial distribution will have a large influence on differentiation and stand development,especially in Douglas-fir and redcedar mixes with faster initial height growth of Douglas-fir. The two are often mixed where SNC is of moderate or low intensity. Even where pure redcedar has been planted in root disease infected stands, Douglas-fir quickly regenerates naturally due to seedfall from surrounding stands. Although redcedar is shade tolerant, questions remain regarding what Douglas-fir densities will preclude overtopped redcedars from producing merchantable volumes at likely rotation ages. The objective of this analysis were to quantify growth and mortality of redcedar under the influence of Douglas-fir.

METHODS

Sites

The study sites were located in the eastern foothills of the Oregon Coast Range, at approximately 44.7° N latitude, and with elevations ranging from 300-500m. All stands at the two sites had been planted to pure redcedar between 1986 and 1990 due to high levels of *Phellinus sulphurascens* root rot. Naturally regenerated Douglas-fir established shortly thereafter, with Douglas-fir and redcedar density varying by plot (table 1). Two of the plots were pure redcedar due to aggressive removal of Douglas-fir by the landowner. Douglas-fir site index is approximate 47m (Bruce 1981) and redcedar site index was ~33m (Kurucz 1978).

Ten 0.2 ha plots were established in 1994 or 1996 depending on site. On each plot, all trees were tagged and measured for DBH (nearest 0.1 cm), and a subsample of 40 trees of each species was measured for total height and height to lowest live branch (nearest 0.01 m). This subsample included the 10 largest by dbh, the 4

smallest by dbh, and 26 additional trees distributed evenly across the diameter range of the plot.

Table 1—Per hectare density by plot and species

plot	TPH			BA (m²/ha)		
	WRC	DF	Total	WRC	DF	Total
1	717	232	949	15.37	4.35	19.72
2	815	917	1732	16.47	5.92	22.39
4	539	534	1073	5.35	9.62	14.97
5	623	974	1597	5.59	13.67	19.26
6	524	890	1414	4.52	9.71	14.23
p1	519	677	1196	9.42	34.6	44.02
p2	499	756	1255	6.06	31.16	37.22
p3	766	376	1142	24.43	17.56	41.99
w1	801		801	17.93		17.93
w2	939		939	25.43		25.43

Analysis

Basal area and height growth of individual western redcedar trees was assessed over a four year growth period using non-linear regression. Many independent variables were used to quantify tree size, competitive position within the stand, and stand density, including dbh, height, stand basal area, Douglas-fir basal area, relative height (subject tree height relative to the largest 100 tph), basal area in larger trees, and various interactions. Mortality was assessed using logistic regression techniques and the same set of independent variables.

To estimate the implied effects of Douglas-fir on redcedar in different establishment mixes, five hypothetical stands of pure Douglas-fir were produced with SYSTUM-1, a young stand simulator (Ritchie and Powers 1993). These stands were assumed to have a site index of 45 m (maximum allowed with SYSTUM-1). Five densities were projected to 20 years of age (62, 125, 250, 500, and 750 tree per ha), and it was assumed that these projected trees would develop similarly with or without the presence of redcedar. Output from these hypothetical stands was used in combination with values from the measured plots to estimate from the constructed growth equations the effect of different establishment densities on the growth of western redcedar.

RESULTS AND DISCUSSION
Basal area and height growth
Redcedar basal area growth was described by the following equation:

[1] BAG_{wrc}

$= \alpha_1 * dbh^{\beta2} * e^{(\beta3 *BAtot + \beta4 *bal -(exp (\beta5 +BAdf) *relht \beta6))}$

where BAG_{wrc} was redcedar basal area growth

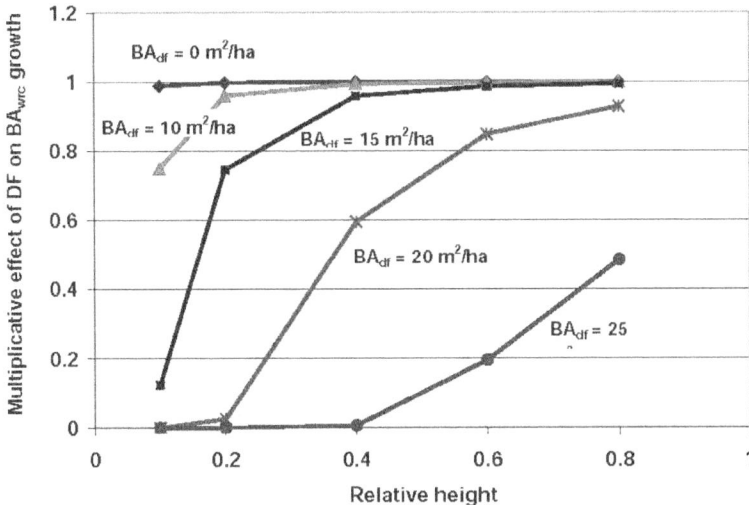

Figure 1—Multiplicative effect of BA_{df} presence on WRC BA growth, by relative height, relative to pure redcedar

(cm^2/4 yrs), Dbh was diameter at breast ht (cm), BA_{tot} was stand basal area (cm^2/ha), BAL was basal area in larger trees (m^2/ha), BA_{df} was Douglas-fir basal area (m^2/ha), and Relht was relative height.

Basal area growth of redcedar mixed with Douglas-fir was negatively correlated with total stand basal area and basal area in larger trees and positively correlated with dbh and relative ht (table 2). However, the positive correlation with relative height diminishes as the amount of Douglas-fir basal area increases (figure 1).

Redcedar height growth was described by the following equation:

[2] $Htgr_{wrc}$
$= \beta1 *ht^{\beta2} * e^{(\beta3 *bal -(e (\beta4 +BAtot) *relht \beta5))}$

where $Htgr_{wrc}$ was height growth (m/4-yr), ht was initial height (m) and BAtot, BAL, and relht are as defined above.

Height growth of redcedar in mixed stands with Douglas-fir is negatively correlated with total basal area in larger trees and positively correlated with initial height and relative height (table 1). However, the positive correlation with relative height diminishes as total stand basal area increases.

Although not specifically tied to above canopy light levels, figure 2 is consistent with findings that redcedar height growth is relatively unaffected by shading until light levels become very low (Carter and Klinka, 1992, Drever and Lertzmann 2001).

Mortality
Redcedar mortality was described by the following equation:

[3] $\log (p/(1-p)) =$
$$\beta_0 + \beta_1 *dbh + \beta_2 *BAL + \beta_3 *BA_{df}$$

where p= probability of mortality over the 4-yr growth period and all other variables are defined as above. The probability of mortality was negatively correlated with dbh, and positively correlated with basal area in

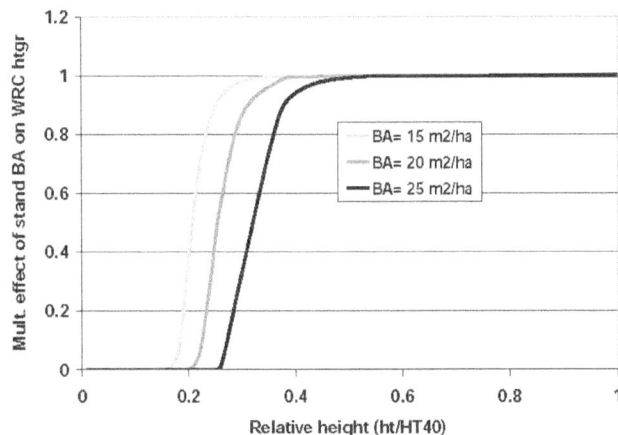

Figure 2—Multiplicative effect of stand BA on WRC height growth by relative height; relative to pure redcedar

111

larger trees and Douglas-fir basal area (table 2). Mortality was greatest for the smallest and most suppressed trees, and particularly where suppressed by Douglas-fir. The four year mortality rate of redcedar trees with dbh=5 cm in a stand containing 20 m^2/ha of Douglas-fir was nearly 50%.

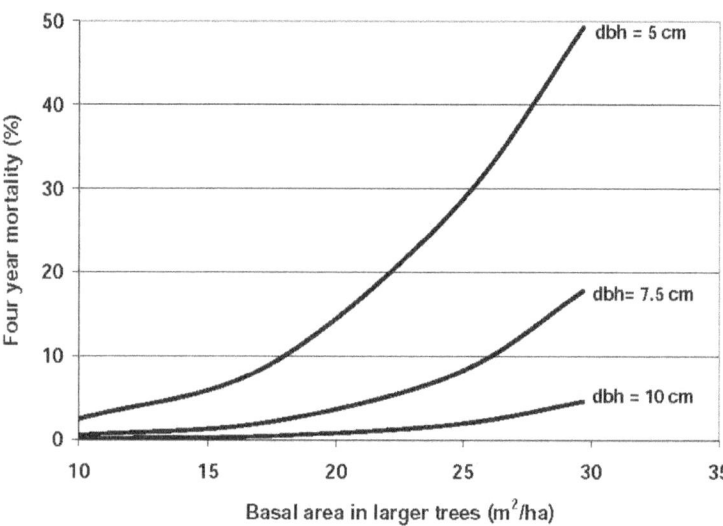

Figure 3—Four yr mortality by tree size and competitive position. Based on a stand with BA$_{df}$= 20 m^2/ha.

In mixed stands of Douglas-fir and redcedar, Douglas-fir is generally assumed to overtop the redcedar the shade tolerant redcedar is assumed to persist. The results from this analysis do not support this generalization, even when stands are only 20-25 yrs old. Although mortality is still relatively low for the larger size classes of trees, as these stands continue to develop, greater mortality rates can be expected for the larger redcedar size classes. Furthermore, although some of these trees may persist, their chances of reaching merchantable size classes at the rotation age of the more dominant Douglas-fir is low, as is likely their ability to release successfully from suppression if left after an overstory harvest.

Growth under different establishment mixes
Using the growth equations [1] and [2], the negative effect of 20 yr old Douglas-fir on the concurrent dbh growth of similarly-aged redcedar was assessed for 5, 15, and 25 cm

redcedar dbh classes, and on height growth for 5, 10, and 13 m ht classes.

Independent variables used in equations [1] and [2] were calculated or estimated for each redcedar size class and specific to each of the Douglas-fir densities (0, 62, 125, 250, 500, and 750 TPH). Average covariate values for the three size classes in a pure redcedar stand were based on the two pure redcedar study plots. Average covariate values for these different size classes in a 750 TPH Douglas-fir stand were based on SYSTUM-1 output, and was similar to measured values on the two study plots with the greatest density of Douglas-fir. Covariate values on the intermediate Douglas-fir density simulations were generally linear interpolations between the values estimated for pure redcedar and high Douglas-fir density plots. However, for the large redcedar size classes (25 cm dbh, 13 m ht), linear interpolation was sometimes inappropriate. For example, because relative height is based on subject tree height relative to the largest 100 TPH, and because low density Douglas-fir can be expected to be larger in diameter than slower growing redcedar, relative height for all

Table 2 -- Parameter estimates for eqns 1-3

Parameter	Eqn [1]	Eqn [2]	Eqn [3]
β$_0$			-4.0452
β$_1$	1.00196	1.5472	-0.6005
β$_2$	1.383	0.2471	0.4605
β$_3$	-0.0492	-0.0314	0.1864
β$_4$	-0.1002	-22.3198	
β$_5$	-10.9885	-10.1395	
β$_6$	-2.8269		

redcedar will always be based on top height of the dominant Douglas-fir. Furthermore, because large redcedar at these stand ages remain free to grow even at the highest densities measured on these study plots, the relative height of a 25 cm redcedar growing with 125 DF per ha will be the same as the same tree growing with 750 DF per ha. In other words, subjectivity was applied in estimating independent variable values for the largest redcedar size classes.

Figure 4 implies that with a relatively low density of Douglas-fir (125 tph), the relative basal area growth loss is independent of size class, amounting to approximately 30% relative to a pure redcedar stand. As Douglas-fir density increases beyond 125 tph, the large size class experiences less relative growth loss. At 750 tph, basal area growth loss of the 25 cm size class is 70% and trees in the 5 cm size class are implied to have stopped growing in diameter.

As with basal area growth, the implied negative effect of 125 Douglas-fir per ha on redcedar height growth is independent of size class (Fig. 5). All of the negative effect on the 25 cm size class is implied to result from the first 100 Douglas-fir per hectare. Increased Douglas-fir density is implied to have no additional negative effect—large redcedar within a young and dense even-aged plantation of Douglas-fir exist because they have had sufficient sunlight and space for crown expansion. At the highest DF densities, height growth of the 15 cm size class is still 80% of that expected in a pure redcedar stand, though 5 cm trees are implied to have stopped growing in height. This is consistent with results shown in figures 2 and 3.

Broader application of these results to other sites or regions may not be appropriate. These sites are very productive with high site indices. Comparison of site curves corresponding to the calculated site indices for each species implies that the height of a dominant redcedar without overstory competition would be about 70% that of its dominant Douglas-fir counterpart on these sites. If on other sites the relative height development rates were more similar, redcedar performance could be expected to improve.

The fact that these stands have developed in harvest units originally considered worthy of *P. sulphurescens* sanitation with a rotation of western redcedar raises questions about the

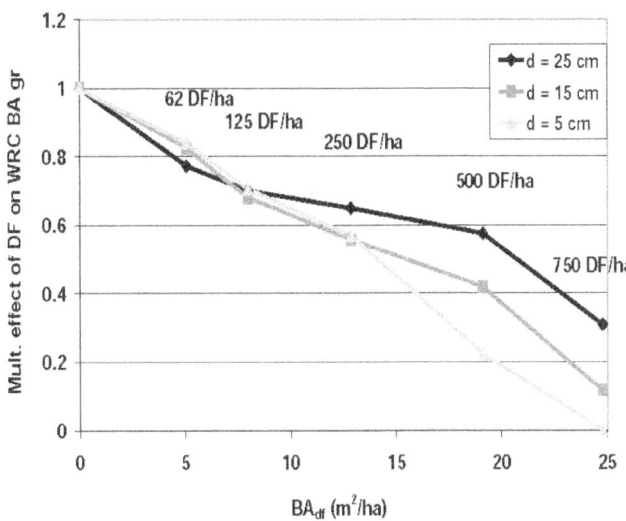

Figure 4—Multiplicative effect of BA_{df} on BA_{wrc} growth, relative to pure redcedar for 5, 15, and 25 cm size classes

broad applicability of these results to healthy sites. Whether or not these plots were installed in areas specifically identified as root rot centers

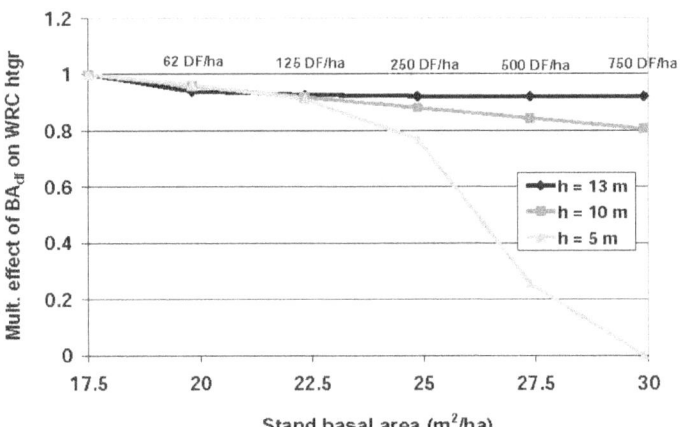

Figure 5—Multiplicative effect of BA_{df} on BA_{wrc} growth, relative to pure redcedar for 5, 10, and 13 cm size classes

is unknown. At this time, the Douglas-fir has shown no obvious signs of infection (thin crowns, slow growth, or mortality), suggesting that the trees are growing normally, and that results of the analysis can be applied outside of *P. sulphurescens* infected stands.

These results are also likely to be affected by the distribution of trees within a stand. On the study sites from which these equations were constructed, the two species were generally interspersed. Clumped distribution would improve the relative performance of redcedar.

LITERATURE CITED

Bruce, D. 1981. Consistent height-growth and growth-rate estimates for remeasured plots. For. Sci. 27:711-725.

Carter, R.E.; Klinka, K. 1992. Variations in shade tolerance of Douglas-fir, western hemlock and western redcedar in coastal British Columbia. For. Ecol. Manage. 55: 87–105.

Drever, C.R.; Lertzman, K.P. 2001. Light-growth responses of coastal Douglas-fir and western redcedar saplings under different regimes of soil moisture and nutrients. Can. J. For. Res. 31: 2124–2133.

Filip, G.; Kanaskie, A.; Kavanagh, K.; Johnson, G.; Johnson, G.; Maguire, D. 2000. Silviculture and Swiss needle cast: Research and recommendations. Research Contribution 30, Forest Research Laboratory, Oregon State University, Corvallis.

Hansen, E.M.; Stone, J.K.; Capitano, B.R.; Rosso, P.; Sutton W.; Winton L.; Kanaskie A.; McWilliams, M.G. 2000. Incidence and impact of Swiss needle cast in forest plantations of Douglas-fir in coastal Oregon. Plant Disease. 84: 773–779.

Kurucz, J.F. 1978. Preliminary polymorphic site index curves for western redcedar *Thuja plicata* Donn in coastal British Columbia. MacMillan Bloedel Ltd., Vancouver, B.C. For. Res. Note 3.

Maguire D.A.; Kanaskie A.; Voelker W.; Johnson R.; Johnson, G. 2002. Growth of young Douglas-fir plantations across a gradient in Swiss needle cast severity. West. Jour. of Ap. For. 17: 86–95.

Ritchie, M.W.; Powers R.F. 1993. User's guide for SYSTUM-1 (Version 2.0): A simulator of growth trends in young stands under management in California and Oregon. General Technical Report. PSW-GTR-147. Albany, CA: Pacific Southwest Research Station, Forest Service, US Department of Agriculture; 45p.

SURVIVAL AND GROWTH OF WESTERN REDCEDAR AND DOUGLAS-FIR PLANTED IN A VARIABLE RETENTION HARVEST UNIT IN THE WESTERN CASCADES, WASHINGTON

Andrew Cockle[1] and Gregory Ettl[2]

ABSTRACT

The effects of light, brush control, and simulated herbivory on the growth and survival of planted western redcedar and Douglas-fir were investigated under variable overstory retention; a factorial combination of two spatial patterns (aggregated vs. dispersed) and two retention densities (25 and 49 trees per ha) was used to vary light. Seedlings were planted and measured for initial height and stem diameter. Prior to budbreak, half of all seedlings were clipped, removing their terminal bud and emulating natural browse observed in adjoining stands. Prior to the onset of summer drought, half of all seedlings were mechanically weeded within a 0.5 meter radius. Seedling mortality and change in height, diameter and volume were assessed after the first and second growing seasons. First-year mortality differed by species, as western redcedar experienced almost double the mortality rate of Douglas-fir. Overstory treatment also affected mortality, with the greatest mortality occurring in the most exposed treatment and the least mortality occurring in the shadiest treatment. Growth rates differed between species, as western redcedar displayed less mean height growth and greater diameter growth after two years, but volumetric growth was similar for the two species. Clipping reduced diameter growth in both species, with western redcedar experiencing a greater reduction in diameter growth than Douglas-fir when clipped. Seedlings were sensitive to total understory cover, displaying an increase in height growth and a decrease in diameter growth as understory cover increased. Results suggest that both species can survive and grow when underplanted in a variable retention harvest site and also exposed to herbivory, and that weeding provides no immediate advantage for seedling growth or survival. Both species experienced the least mortality in the overstory treatment that provided the greatest shade, suggesting some shelterwood benefit may be conferred by retaining more trees in a dispersed spatial pattern. After the earliest stages of stand regeneration following a variable retention harvest, it appears that establishing a two-species cohort is possible.

KEYWORDS: Douglas-fir, seedling herbivory, variable retention harvest, weeding, western redcedar.

INTRODUCTION

In the Pacific Northwest, variable retention harvest treatments are being increasingly utilized to balance ecological management objectives with timber extraction (Franklin et al. 1997). However, the effect of shade provided by retained trees on underplanted seedling growth and mortality remains unclear. Seedling death and impaired growth may be caused by varying species response to low light (Carter and Klinka 1992), competition with understory vegetation (Brandeis et al. 2001) and herbivory (Stroh et al. 2008), leading to delayed establishment. These complications can be exacerbated when planting multiple species with differing life history strategies. Western redcedar (*Thuja plicata* Donn ex D. Don) and Douglas-fir (*Pseudotsuga menziesii* (Mirb.) Franco) are two species that naturally occur in mixed stands throughout the western slope of the Cascades (Franklin and Dyrness 1988), but they differ in shade tolerance. Western redcedar often outperforms Douglas-fir in lower light levels (Carter and Klinka 1992, Drever and Lertzman 2001) but concerns about western redcedar being preferentially browsed by ungulate herbivores

[1] Andrew Cockle is a graduate student at the University of Washington's School of Forest Resources, PO Box 352100, Seattle, WA 98195. andrew.cockle@gmail.com.

[2] Gregory J. Ettl is an Associate Professor and the Director of the Center for Sustainable Forestry at Pack Forest, University of Washington, School of Forest Resources, PO Box 352100, Seattle, WA 98195. ettl@u.washington.edu.

(Maas-Hebner et al. 2005) may lead managers to forgo planting the species in mixed stands. The objectives of this experiment were to determine rates and potential causes of seedling mortality, and to quantify the effects of light, understory competition and browse on the growth of Douglas-fir and western redcedar seedlings in a variable retention harvest system.

METHODS
Study area
The study was conducted at Charles L. Pack Forest (latitude 46° 50' 11" N, longitude 122° 15' 55" W) located within the Puget Sound area of Washington. The study site is a 19 ha stand located on a moderately-dissected south-to-southeast facing slope (mean aspect = 142°, mean slope = 21%). Elevation ranges from 390-575 m, with a mean elevation of 496 m. Site topography is influenced by four perennial or intermittent streams that flow roughly from north to south on the site, with channels creating steep side-slopes. The site has Wilkeson series soil (gravelly silt loam, mixed, mesic Ultic Haploxeralfs, Anderson 1955). Data collected from a weather station at Pack Forest shows an average daily temperature of 9°C and average annual precipitation of 970 mm for the years 1998-2008.

The study site is located within the *Tsuga heterophylla* [Raf.] Sarg. Zone described by Franklin and Dyrness (1988). The upland forest is dominated by Douglas-fir, with black cottonwood (*Populus balsamifera* ssp. *trichocarpa*) and red alder (*Alnus rubra*) present. Understory vegetation is dominated by trailing blackberry (*Rubus ursinus*), salal (*Gaultheria shallon*) western sword fern (*Polystichum munitum*) and low Oregon grape (*Mahonia nervosa*). Weedy invasive species (native and non-native) such as stinging nettle (*Urtica diocia*) bull thistle (*Cirsium vulgare*) and foxglove (*Digitalis purpurea*) are present on the site, as well as rushes (*Juncus* spp.) and sedges (*Carex* spp.) on mesic portions of the site in local concavities (Pojar and MacKinnon 1994).

The stand is dominated by an 80 year-old cohort of Douglas-fir that was treated with biosolids in the 1980's, commercially thinned, and harvested in 2007 for a regeneration cut leaving variable retention, with target residual densities of 25 and 49 trees per hectare, in spatial arrangements of dispersed and aggregated. In December 2007, equal numbers of western redcedar and Douglas-fir seedlings were planted across the site at a density of 740 trees per hectare. Sixteen plots were subjectively established using a stem map to meet designated overstory densities (25 and 49 trees per hectare) within the plot, and all seedlings were placed in Vexar® tubes (8 cm diameter × 80 cm height) to prevent natural browse from local populations of black-tailed deer (*Odocoileus hemionus*) and elk (*Cervus elaphus*).

Experimental Design
The experiment utilized a factorial split-plot combination of four overstory treatments (high vs. low density, aggregated vs. dispersed spatial arrangement), within which four quarter-hectare (2500 m^2) plots were established, creating a total of sixteen plots. Within each plot, 92 western redcedar and 92 Douglas-fir seedlings were tagged to track first-year growth and mortality ($N = 2944$). Additionally, within each plot, 20 western redcedar and 20 Douglas-fir seedlings were randomly selected to collect measurements of light, soil moisture, understory cover, and second-year growth at the seedling level ($N = 640$).

All seedlings were randomly selected for a combination of two different treatment factors: clipping (to simulate natural browse) and weeding (to reduce competition with understory plants); weeding reduced mean understory cover by 35% ($p < 0.0001$). Seedlings were clipped in the spring of 2008 prior to budbreak to mimic natural herbivory by deer and elk observed in adjacent stands, removing 50% and 25% of the mean leader length for western redcedar and Douglas-fir respectively. Understory cover was assessed for a subsample ($N = 640$) of seedlings, with all species located within a 0.5 m radius of selected seedlings being identified and their cover measured to the nearest 5% (after two years, weeding reduced mean understory cover by 6%, $p = 0.014$).

Seedlings were assessed for growth and mortality in January 2009 (at the end of the first growing season) and October 2009 (at the end of the second growing season). Seedling height was measured from the root collar at ground level to the tallest living element of the plant to the nearest 0.5 cm. Seedling diameter was measured 7 cm above the root collar to the nearest 1.0 mm. From height and diameter, volume was calculated using the geometric formula for a cone:

$$volume \ (cm^3) = \frac{\pi \left(\frac{diameter \ (mm)}{20}\right)^2 x \ height \ (cm)}{3}$$

Hemispherical photographs taken above seedlings were used to determine total transmitted light in moles per m^2 per day when processed with Gap Light Analyzer software (Frazer et al. 1999). These photographs capture canopy architecture, and results indicate each overstory treatment has a unique light environment (p-values < 0.001 for all pairwise comparisons with Tukey HSD). The least mean transmitted light is found in the high retention/dispersed treatment (32.53 moles/m^2/day) and the greatest transmitted light found in the low retention/aggregated treatment (38.95 moles/m^2/day).

Statistical Analysis
The effect of overstory treatment, clipping and weeding on mortality was analyzed with a logit-linked generalized linear model (GLM) incorporating species as a term in the model. Logit-linked GLMs assume that the models can be expressed as a linear function of the model parameters and that the errors are independent and from the binomial family of distributions.

The effect of treatments on growth was analyzed using a linear mixed model, with overstory treatment, weeding and clipping being fixed factors and plot being a random factor nested within overstory treatment. In our study, seedlings can be expected to display within-plot

correlation of response variables (height, diameter and volumetric growth) due to geographic heterogeneity naturally present within the study area. Linear mixed models account for the correlation of observations by presuming that the random effects (in this case, plot) are unknown but are randomly generated from some normal distribution with mean zero. Hypothesis tests were conducted using ANOVA with Type II sums of squares; change in height and change in volume were log-transformed for hypothesis testing.

RESULTS
Mortality
There was a significant difference in first-year mortality between species, with western redcedar having a mortality rate of 27.8% and Douglas-fir having a mortality rate of 13.4% (p < 0.0001). Overstory treatment had a significant effect on mortality ($p = 0.0082$), with greatest mortality in the low retention/aggregated treatment (30.9% for western redcedar, 16.2% for Douglas-fir, Fig. 1) and the least mortality in the high retention/dispersed treatment (24.3% for western redcedar, 4.8% for Douglas-fir). First year seedling mortality was unaffected by

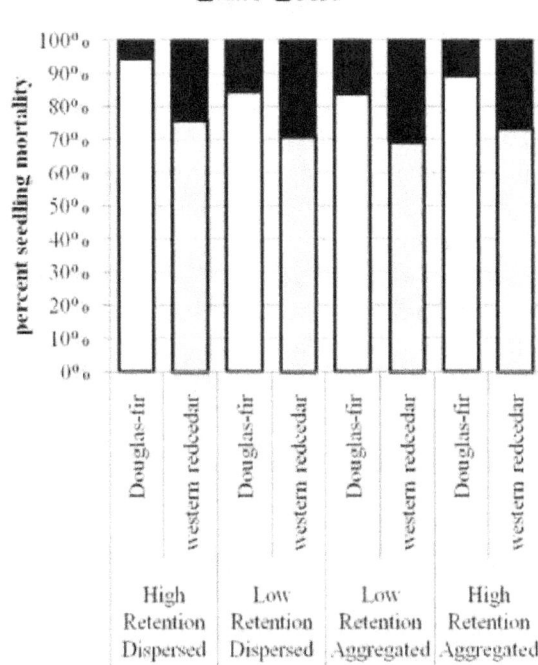

Figure 1. Percent seedling mortality in the first year after planting by overstory treatment. White bars = western redcedar, hatched bars = Douglas-fir.

weeding ($p = 0.93$) and clipping ($p = 0.80$). Second year mortality was very low (0 dead western redcedar, 4 dead Douglas-fir) but there was a significant difference in mortality rate between the two species ($p = 0.0006$). No statistical differences existed in mortality for overstory treatments, clipping, or weeding.

Growth

There was a significant difference in two-year height growth between western redcedar and Douglas-fir ($p < 0.0001$) with western redcedar averaging 21.92 cm to Douglas-fir's 24.73 cm. Overstory treatment ($p = 0.0759$), weeding ($p = 0.0519$) and clipping ($p = 0.1232$) had no-to-marginal significance on seedling height growth, and there were no significant interactions between species, overstory treatment, clipping and weeding. First-year understory cover had a significant effect on two-year height growth ($p = 0.0260$), with a slight positive correlation.

Two-year diameter growth was significantly different between species ($p = 0.0169$) with western redcedar averaging 3.62 mm radial growth over two years and Douglas-fir averaging 3.23 mm. Overstory treatment had a significant effect on diameter growth ($p = 0.0241$) and diametric growth in the high retention/aggregated treatment (average 2.96 mm) was significantly different from growth in both the high retention/dispersed treatment (average 3.63 mm, $p = 0.019$) and the low retention/dispersed treatment (average 3.71 mm, $p = 0.008$). Clipping had a significant effect on two-year diameter growth ($p = 0.0003$), with both species showing reduced diameter growth when clipped. There was a significant interaction between clipping and species ($p = 0.0447$), with clipped western redcedar showing an overall reduction of 0.96 mm in two-year diameter growth as opposed to unclipped western redcedar (Fig. 2). First-year understory cover had a significant effect on two-year diameter growth ($p = 0.0154$), with a slight negative correlation.

Overstory treatment had a significant effect on volumetric growth ($p = 0.0074$) and volumetric growth in the high retention/aggregated treatment (average = 14.48 cm^3) was significantly different from both the high retention/dispersed treatment (average = 19.45 cm^3, $p = 0.0308$) and the low retention/dispersed treatment (average = 19.94 cm^3, $p = 0.0170$, Fig. 3). Clipping treatment also had a significant effect on volumetric growth ($p < 0.0001$) with clipped seedlings of both species averaging 15.29 cm^3 of two-year volumetric growth and unclipped seedlings averaging 20.00 cm^3 of two-year volumetric growth. There was a significant interaction between clipping and species ($p = 0.0213$) with clipped western redcedar showing a marked decrease in volume (23.02 cm^3 unclipped, 16.39 cm^3 clipped). There was no significant different in two-year volumetric growth between species ($p = 0.8098$) or by weeding treatment ($p = 0.8131$).

DISCUSSION

Differences existed between Douglas-fir and western redcedar mortality, height growth and diameter growth, but not volumetric growth. In the first year following planting, western redcedar died at nearly twice the rate as Douglas-fir; however, by the second year, both species had mortality rates below 1%. From an operational perspective, mortality rates of 27.8% for western redcedar and 13.4% for Douglas-fir seem to be high, it is not unprecedented. Brandeis, et al. (2001) reported a first year loss of 40-80% of Douglas-fir and 2-15% of western redcedar when underplanted in evenly thinned stands, with mortality increasing for both species as overstory density increased. The authors attributed this high mortality to desiccation of roots due to cold, windy weather at the time of planting.

The overstory treatments that provided the most shade/least transmitted light had the least mortality. Namely, the high retention/dispersed treatment had the lowest mean transmitted light and the least mortality for both species, while the low retention/aggregated treatment had the greatest transmitted light and the highest mortality rate for both species. There are two possible ways to interpret this: 1) reduced transmitted light leads to a shelterwood effect where overstory trees ameliorate site conditions, allowing for greater seedling survival, or 2) hydraulic redistribution from retained overstory trees assists in seedling survival during summer drought.

When averaged across all treatments, western redcedar experienced less height growth and greater diameter growth than Douglas-fir, but there was no difference in volumetric growth. This could be attributed to the greater intensity clipping treatment given to western redcedar in order to mimic natural herbivory; however, in terms of volume growth, there is little difference between the two species after two years, as western redcedar allocated more carbon to diameter growth and less to height growth. Western redcedar were more sensitive to the clipping treatment, experiencing a significantly greater reduction in diameter and volume growth when clipped than Douglas-fir. So, while clipping does not statistically affect western redcedar mortality, clipped individuals grew less vigorously.

Regardless of species, competition with understory plants had an effect on seedling growth. As first-year understory cover increased, seedlings tended to grow taller, with thinner stems. There was no effect of understory cover on volumetric growth, suggesting seedlings allocate more carbon to height growth as surrounding vegetation increases. There may be a competitive advantage in increased height growth as brush increases, allowing the seedling to overtop the understory vegetation.

Western redcedar and Douglas-fir exhibit equally vigorous post-harvest growth after two years in a variable retention setting, albeit with differing growth patterns. While western redcedar experienced much greater initial mortality, second-year mortality was very low, and seedlings that survive in the post-planting environment should be expected to continue to live until density-dependent mortality begins to take effect. This experiment also demonstrates after two years, Douglas-fir can grow as well or better in shade than in open positions. Future monitoring of seedling mortality and growth in this site should continue to provide insight into relative growth rates of the two species in a varying light environment, as well as the potential for establishing a multi-species, multi-cohort stand.

LITERATURE CITED

Anderson, W.W. 1955. Soil survey, Pierce County, Washington. Washington: US Govt. Print Office.

Brandeis, T.J.; Newton, M.; Cole, E.C. 2001. Underplanted conifer seedling survival and growth in thinned Douglas-fir stands. Can. J. For. Res. 31: 302-312.

Carter, R.E.; Klinka, K. 1992. Variation in shade tolerance of Douglas fir, western hemlock and western red cedar in coastal British Columbia. For. Ecol. Man. 55: 87-105.

Drever, C.R.; Lertzman, K.P. 2001. Light-growth responses of coastal Douglas-fir and western redcedar saplings under different regimes of soil moisture and nutrients. Can. Jour. For. Res. 31: 2124-2133.

Franklin, J.F.; C.T. Dyrness. 1988. Natural Vegetation of Oregon and Washington. Oregon State University Press. Corvallis, OR. 452 p.

Franklin, J.F.; Berg, D.R.; Thornburg, D.A.; Tappeiner, J.C. 1997. Alternative Silvicultural Approaches to Timber Harvesting: Variable-retention Harvest Systems. From: Creating a Forestry for the 21st Century: The Science of Ecosystem Management. Island Press, Washington D.C. 111-139

Frazer, G.W.; Canham, C.D.; Lertzman K.P. 1999. Gap Light Analyzer (GLA): Imaging software to extract canopy structure and gap light transmission indices from true-colour fisheye photographs, users manual and program documentation. Simon Fraser University,

Burnaby, British Columbia, and the Institute of Ecosystem Studies, Millbrook, New York.

Maas-Hebner, K.G.; Emmingham, W.H.; Larson, D.J.; Chan, S.S. 2005. Establishment and growth of native hardwood and conifer seedlings underplanted in thinned Douglas-fir stands. For. Ecol. Man. 208: 331-345.

Pojar, J.; MacKinnon, A. 1994. Plants of the Pacific Northwest Coast. Lone Pine Publishing, Auburn, WA.

Stroh, N.; Baltzinger, C.; Martin, J. 2008. Deer prevent western redcedar (*Thuya Plicata*) regeneration in old-growth forests of Haida Gwaii: Is there a potential for recovery? For. Ecol. Man. 255: 3973-3979

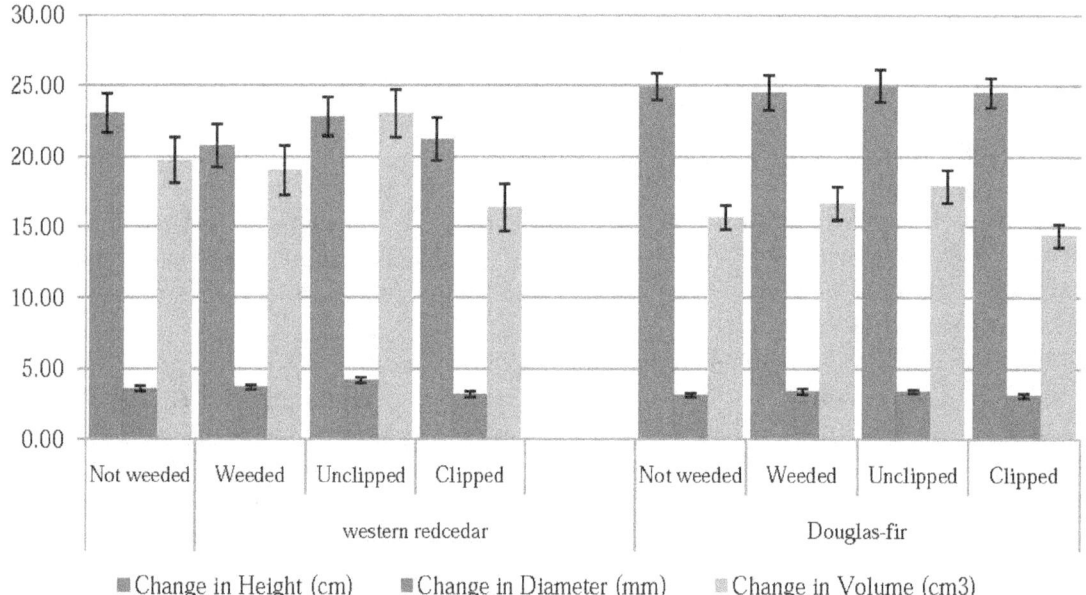

Figure 2. Mean two-year change in height, diameter and volume (± 1 S.E.) for western redcedar and Douglas-fir by weeding and clipping treatment. Because there were no significant interactions for weeding and clipping, all values represent aggregate data for indicated treatment only.

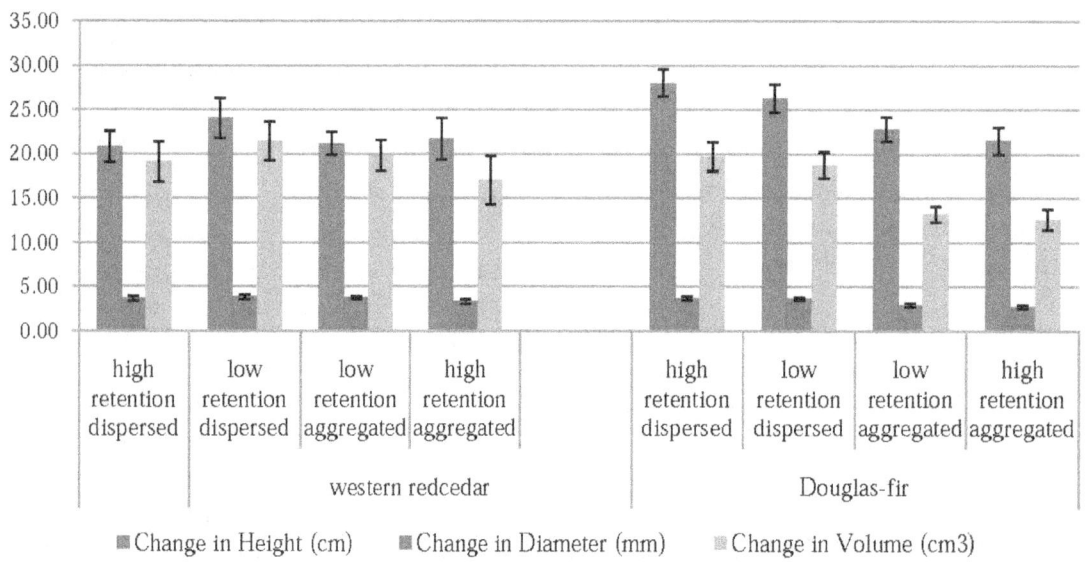

Figure 3. Mean two-year change in height, diameter and volume (± 1 S.E.) for western redcedar and Douglas-fir by overstory treatment.

TEN-YEAR PERFORMANCE OF YELLOW CEDAR AND INTERIOR SPRUCE IN SOUTHERN INTERIOR BRITISH COLUMBIA, CANADA

Clare Kooistra[1], Jonathan D. Bakker[2], and Patience Rakochy[3]

ABSTRACT

Though common on the coast, yellow cedar (*Chamaecyparis nootkatensis* (D. Don) Spach.) (Yc) occurs naturally in two isolated pockets in the Slocan Valley of the BC Southern Interior. A trial was established in the Monashee Mountains to compare the survival and performance of Yc cuttings from one of these sources with that of interior spruce (*Picea glauca* [Moench] Voss, *Picea engelmannii* Parry, and their naturally occurring hybrids) (Sx) seedlings. Trees were planted in the spring of 1999 on a 1580 m elevation site on Currie Ridge and tracked through their tenth growing season. Survival was initially lower for Yc, but after 10 years averaged 86% and did not differ between species. Although Sx seedlings were shorter at planting, they grew more rapidly. After ten years, Sx are larger than Yc in height, ground-level diameter, and stem volume. Yc exhibit more signs of browse and of stem damage, while Sx exhibit more signs of chlorotic foliage and insect damage to foliage. Whether one species is better than the other depends on the objectives for which a stand is being managed. Sx is a common species across the landscape, while Yc provides important diversity. Trends at this site are comparable to those at high elevation plantations on the BC Coast. Yc may provide another reforestation option to the moist ESSF zone of Southern Interior BC.

KEYWORDS: Silviculture, survival, growth, reforestation, yellow cedar, interior spruce

INTRODUCTION

Yellow Cedar (Yc) occurs in two isolated pockets in the Slocan Valley of the BC Southern Interior. The objective of this trial was to explore the possibility of increasing the role of Yc in silviculture and reforestation within the ICH and ESSF biogeoclimatic zones of southern interior BC. Yc cuttings were obtained from wild seed and cuttings obtained at one of these sites, Dago Creek. Yc performance was compared with that of Interior Spruce (Sx). This report focuses on performance during the first ten growing seasons after outplanting.

METHODS

The source material used in this study was Yc cuttings from cutting lot V0327 (cutting hedge established from wild seed and cuttings) and Sx seed from seedlot 06015 (1st generation seed orchard seed).

The trial was established at Currie Ridge (50°15'14" N 118°26'43" W) in the Monashee Mountains. The site is at 1585 m elevation, and is in the ESSF WC2 series 01 biogeoclimatic zone.

Seedlings and cuttings were planted in Spring 1999 in an alternating pattern within 4 four blocks. Each block contained 10 rows, and each row contained 50 trees (25 per species). In total, 2000 trees were planted, 1000 Sx and 1000 Yc. In our analysis, we assumed that blocking occurred on the basis of blocks and rows (40 block/row combinations).

[1] Clare Kooistra is a forest nursery and regeneration specialist with Conifera Consulting, 1-6916 Manning Place, Vernon, BC Canada, V1B 2Y5. Email: cmkooistra@shaw.ca.

[2] Jon Bakker is an Assistant Professor in the School of Forest Resources, University of Washington, Box 354115, Seattle, WA 98195-4115.

[3] Patience Rakochy is a Nursery Services Forester with Nursery Services Interior (North), Ministry of Forests and Range, 2000 South Ospika Blvd, Prince George, BC Canada V2N 4W5

Survival was measured in Fall 1999 and Fall 2000, and tree survival and condition were measured in Fall 2003 (end of the fifth field season) and Spring 2009 (start of the eleventh field season). Stem and foliage faults (broken stems, chlorotic foliage, etc.) were recorded in Fall 2003 and Spring 2009. These categorical variables were analyzed using Cochran-Mantel-Haenszel tests to test for a relationship between the factor (species) and variable of interest after accounting for differences in another factor (block/row). Analyzed variables included survival, condition (live trees only), and various types of foliage damage and growth form differences, including the presence of multiple leaders (forks initiated during the year of measurement) and multiple stems (forks initiated two or more years earlier).

Growth data (stem height and ground-level diameter) were monitored at planting and in Fall 1999, Fall 2000, Fall 2003, and Spring 2009. Four growth characteristics (height, ground-level diameter (GLD), height:diameter ratio (HDR), stem volume) were analyzed. HDR was calculated as height/GLD, and stem volume using the formula for a cone. Height and stem volume increments were calculated as the value in one measurement minus the measurement in the previous measurement. Due to the large differences in diameter over time, diameter growth was calculated as the basal area increment between two measurements. Increments and final (Spring 2009) values were analyzed using ANOVA. All surviving trees were included in these analyses, with $\alpha = 0.05$.

RESULTS
Survival was higher for Sx than Yc after one (99.3 vs 93.6%), two (96.0 vs 90.8%), and five growing seasons (92.1 vs 87.8%). However, survival after ten growing seasons did not differ between species (86.1 vs 86.3%) (Table 1).

Sx trees were in slightly better condition than Yc trees after five and ten growing seasons. However, these differences were diminishing; >90% of surviving trees of both species were in

'Good' or 'Average' condition after ten growing seasons (Table 1).

Table 1—Percent mortality and percentage of live trees in each condition class in Spring 2009. Species data are averaged across blocks/rows.

Species	Live Trees				Mortality
	Good (4)	Average (3)	Poor (2)	Likely to Die (1)	
Sx	44	50	5	<1	13.9
Yc	43	47	9	<1	13.7
Overall	44	49	7	<1	13.8

Several types of foliage and stem damage differed between species in Spring 2009 (Table 2). Sx exhibited more chlorotic foliage, vegetation press, dead or broken tops, and insect (aphid) damage to foliage. Yc exhibited more signs of browse and of stem damage by unknown agents. This stem damage often appeared to be due to branches being stripped off by snow and ice during the winter and/or to deer using the stems as rutting posts.

The proportion of trees with multiple leaders averaged < 1%, and the proportion with multiple stems averaged 3% (Table 3).

Yc cuttings were taller than Sx seedlings at planting, but did not grow as rapidly and were shorter by the end of the first growing season after planting. Sx continued to be taller throughout the trial, and this difference has increased over time (Fig. 1A). Height increments differed between species in all years except 2000.

Sx seedlings had larger GLD at planting, and this difference increased during the first 10 growing seasons (Fig. 1B). Basal area growth

Table 2—Proportion of live trees with chlorotic foliage (FC), vegetation / snow / debris press (VP), broken or dead top leaders (TD), insect-damaged foliage (FI), browse or broken branches (BR), and stem damage by unknown agents (SX) in Spring 2009. Species data are averaged across blocks/rows.

Species	FC	VP	TD	FI	BR	SX
Sx	4	10	6	21	<1	3
Yc	<1	6	3	1	17	7
Overall	2	8	4	11	2	5

increments were larger for Sx than Yc in all measurement intervals. In terms of basal area, Sx seedlings were 11% larger than Yc cuttings at planting, 42% larger after 5 years, and 146% larger after 10 years.

Table 3—Proportion of live trees with various numbers of leaders (shoots originating during previous growing season) or stems (shoots originating two or more growing seasons earlier, including basal forks) in Spring 2009. Species data are averaged across blocks/rows.

	Number of Leaders			Number of Stems		
Species	1	2-3	≥ 4	1	2-3	≥ 4
Sx	99	<1	<1	98	2	<1
Yc	100	--	--	96	3	<1
Overall	99	<1	<1	97	3	<1

Sx seedlings had smaller HDRs (ie, were shorter for a given GLD) at planting, but higher HDRs after one and two growing seasons (Fig. 1C). HDR did not differ between species after five growing seasons, but Sx again had smaller HDRs after 10 growing seasons.

Stem volume did not differ between species at planting, but Sx seedlings grew faster than Yc already in the first year and were larger throughout the first ten growing seasons after planting (Fig. 1D). Compared to Yc, Sx trees averaged 25% larger stem volumes after one growing season, 63% after five growing seasons, and 212% larger after 10 growing seasons.

DISCUSSION

After ten growing seasons in the field, the growth differences between Sx and Yc are increasing. Species are exhibiting different types of foliage and stem damage, and growth of Yc lags that of Sx considerably. However, ten-year survival does not differ between the species. Whether one species is better than the other depends on the objectives for which a stand is being managed. For example, Yc provides important diversity while Sx is a common species across the landscape. Since Yc is holding its own in terms of survival, it appears that it will be able to form crop trees at rotation

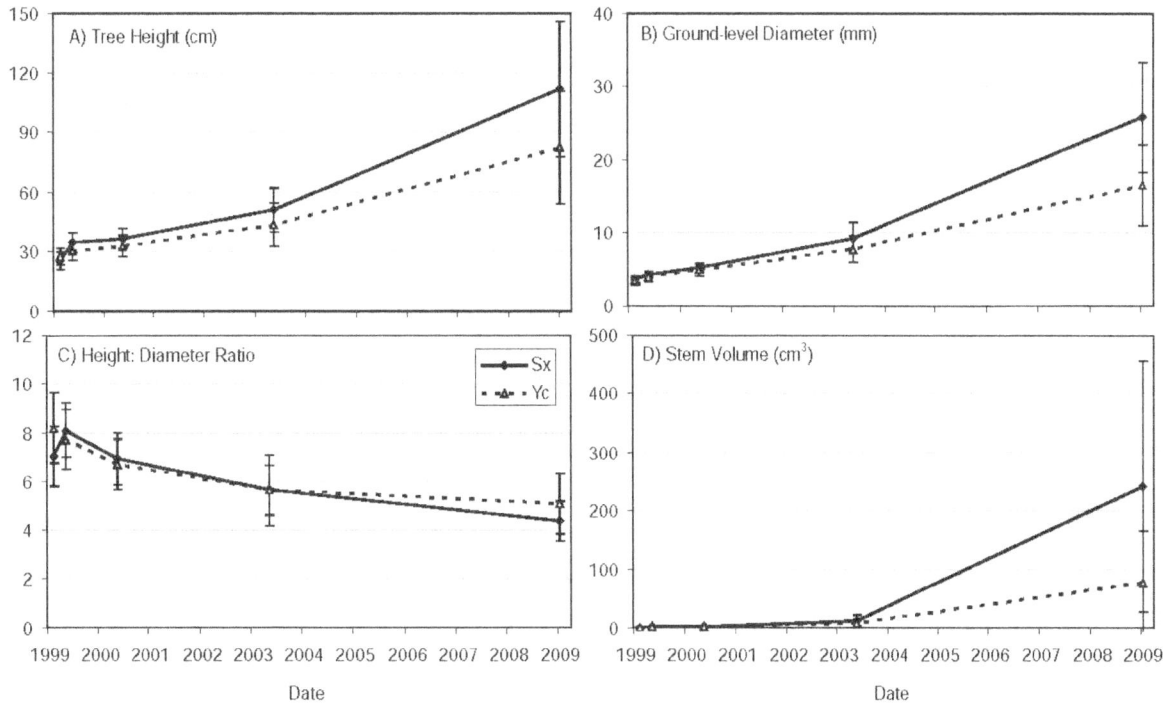

Figure 1—Tree height, ground-level diameter, height: diameter ratio, and stem volume (mean ± SD) for Sx and Yc at planting and after one, two, five, and ten growing seasons.

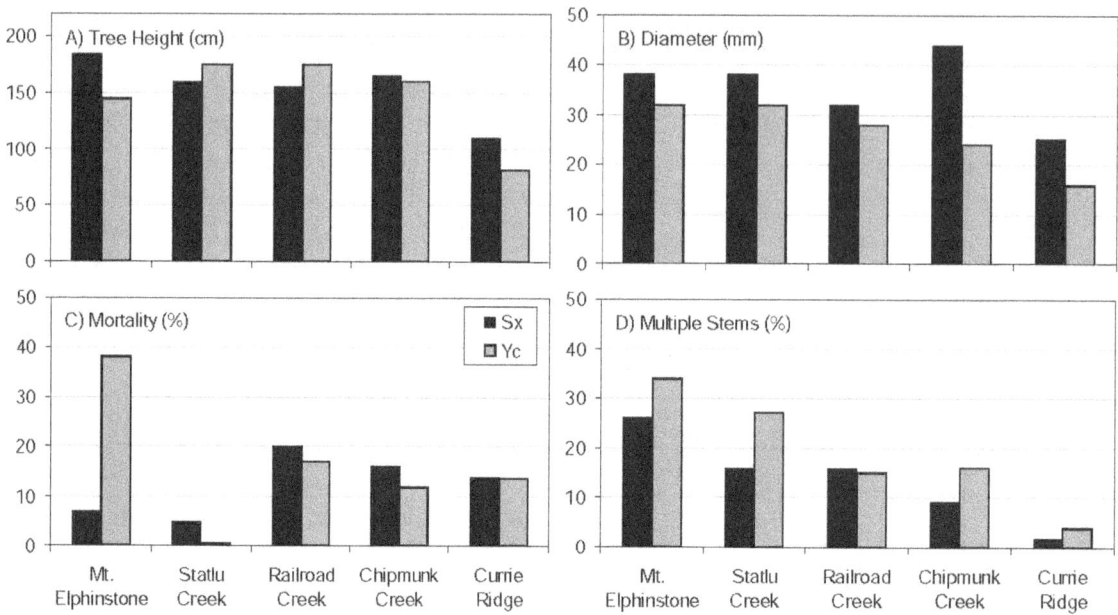

Figure 2—Comparison of ten-year data from four coastal sites with our site at Currie Ridge: tree height, diameter, mortality, and percentage of trees with multiple stems. Sites are arranged in order of increasing elevation (increasing inland influence). Coastal site data were extracted from Scagel et al. (1989). Note that diameter was measured at 30 cm for the coastal sites but at ground level for Currie Ridge.

age, although of a smaller log size than Sx.

To determine if the performance differences that we observed are typical, we searched for other long term reforestation studies that involve Yc. We were unable to find published information from other trials in interior BC, though Yc is currently being tested in the ICH biogeoclimatic zone around Revelstoke (J. Russell and R. Mohr – personal communication).

A few coastal trials have included Yc. Scagel et al. (1989) compared the ten-year performance of a number of high elevation species, including Yc and Engelmann spruce (Se; part of the Sx complex). The comparison is not ideal, as their four sites are located on the southern coast within the normal range of Yc, and are at lower elevations (1030-1200 m) than our site. In addition, their study involved spring and autumn planting dates along with a wide range of stocktypes (e.g., 2+0 Br, 2+0 PSB415, 1+0 PSB211). Finally, some methodological details differed between studies; for example, we measured diameter at ground level while they

measured it at 30 cm height. Nonetheless, it is instructive to put our results in the context of these sites.

Currie Ridge is less productive than the coastal sites (Fig. 2). Mortality is about equal between it and the furthest inland coastal sites (Railway and Chipmunk Creeks). Mean tree heights were taller for Sx than Yc at two coastal sites. Sx consistently had larger diameters than Yc. Coastal sites reported many more problems with multiple stems, particularly for Yc, though this diminished as elevation increased. Over all, it seems that Yc is performing as expected relative to Sx.

Scagel et al. (1989) concluded that Yc was questionable for regenerating high elevation sites because it was much more prone to faults, particularly stem sweep and forks. However, these differences between Yc and other species were less pronounced at the higher elevation (more inland) sites. In comparison, Currie Ridge is at a much higher elevation and has a shorter growing season but also experiences less snow press, so these types of differences between species were minimal (Tables 2 and 3).

Another study compared the performance of Yc with other species (though not Sx) at multiple coastal sites for up to 20 years after outplanting (Arnott and Pendl 1994; Burgess et al. (2003) Yc outperformed other species at some sites, but was susceptible to breakage from heavy snows. Performance once again exceeded that at Currie Ridge.

A third study compared the performance of Yc and other species grown in different silvicultural systems, and concluded that Yc performed better in green tree and patch cut treatments than in clearcuts (Mitchell and Koppenaal 2006).

The performance difference between Yc and Sx could also be due in part to the use of seedlings versus cuttings. Hennon et al. (2009) reported larger height and diameter in seedlings of Yc as compared to cuttings.

Yc populations generally exhibit significant levels of inbreeding, and the interior population of Yc is genetically distinct from those on the coast (Ritland et al. 2001). This may also account for some lower performance in the Yc in our study, though a detailed genetic analysis of this population was obviously beyond the scope of this trial. Recently, the two interior populations of Yc have been crossed and new seed and cutting material are now available from these crosses. Use of this material is recommended.

CONCLUSIONS

The results of this 10-year study show that yellow-cedar is an interesting and acceptable species choice in the ESSF zone in southern interior BC. Older coastal stands of Yc in southern Alaska and northern BC have experienced severe decline (Hennon and Shaw 1997). Therefore, use of Yc as an alternative species in reforestation in the BC southern interior and especially further north, should be tempered with some caution. At this time we do not know if it is appropriate to reforest areas outside the southern interior moist mountain environments with Yc.

This study should be followed for another 10 years to track performance now that the stand is at free-growing and is reaching heights above the depth of the winter snow pack. In addition, the other Yc plantations in the BC southern interior should be examined for performance. While these may not have been planted in trial design, observations on them would be useful to determine the wider application of the results presented in this study.

ACKNOWLEDGMENTS
This trial was designed and installed by Sue Matovich of the Vernon Forest District, Ministry of Forests and Range; we are indebted to her for her efforts on this study in the early years. Wendy Clarke assisted with the repeated measurements of this trial. We thank Stephen Joyce for his direction and support to accomplish the latest measurement. Funding support for this study by the Ministry of Forests and Range, BC Timber Sales, Nursery Services Section is gratefully acknowledged.

LITERATURE CITED
Arnott, J.T.; Pendl, F.T. 1994. Field performance of several tree species and stock types planted in montane forests of coastal British Columbia. Information Report BC-X-347. Victoria, BC: Natural Resources Canada, Canadian Forest Service, Pacific Forestry Centre. 45 p.

Burgess, D; Mitchell, A. K.; Goodmanson, G. 2003. Twenty-year assessment of four species planted in the mountain hemlock zone of coastal British Columbia. For. Chron. 79:280-284.

Hennon, P. E.; Shaw III, C. G. 1997. The enigma of yellow-cedar decline: what is killing these long-lived, defensive trees? J. For. 95:4-10.

Hennon, P.E.; McClellan, M.H.; Spores, S.R.; Orlikowska, E.H. 2009. Survival and growth of planted yellow-cedar seedlings and rooted cuttings (stecklings) near Ketchikan, Alaska. West. J. Appl. For. 24:144-150.

Mitchell, A.K.; Koppenaal, R. 2006. Outplanting performance of western redcedar, yellow-cedar and Douglas-fir in montane alternative silvicultural systems (MASS).

Technology Transfer Note 34. Victoria, BC: Natural Resources Canada, Canadian Forest Service, Pacific Forestry Centre. 4 p.

Ritland, C.; Pape, T.; Ritland, K. 2001. Genetic structure of yellow cedar (*Chamaecyparis nootkatensis*). Can. J. Bot. 79:822-828.

Scagel, R.; Green, B.; von Hahn, H.; Evans, R. 1989. Exploratory high elevation regeneration trials in the Vancouver Forest Region: 10-year species performance of planted stock. FRDA Report 098. Victoria, BC: BC Ministry of Forests. 40 p.

20 YEARS GROWING CEDAR: A SILVICULTURE FORESTER'S EXPERIENCE

Rudi van Zwaaij[1], RPF

ABSTRACT

My presentation will focus on 20 years of experience as a forester establishing and growing western redcedar on the upper Sunshine Coast in BC. The potential for increased yields of growing Yellow cedar will also be touched on briefly. Western redcedar is an exciting species that will be in short supply in the future and will fetch a substantially higher increase in log value over more common species

The presentation will include discussion on suitable ecosystems, considerations in the establishment of western redcedar, elk impacts and successful strategies in mitigating these impacts, and growth and yield data. The presenter will discuss that the potential for successfully growing western redcedar is affected by the lack of collaboration between government agencies and the lack of investment from government in forest management beyond the free growing declaration.

[1] Silviculture Forester, WFP, Stillwater Forest Operation, 201-7373 Duncan Street, Powell River, BC, V8A 1W6, rvanzwaaij@westernforest.com

SIZE HIERARCHY DEVELOPMENT IN JUVENILE WESTERN REDCEDAR (*THUJA PLICATA*) STANDS COMPARED TO WESTERN HEMLOCK (*TSUGA HETEROPHYLLA*)

Roderick W. Negrave[1]

ABSTRACT

Size hierarchies describe size variability within populations and offer insight into inter-plant relations and factors influencing stand development. Factors influencing size hierarchy, including density and nutrient regime, are poorly understood but are important for understanding how diversity develops in stands. This study examined the effects of fertilization, planting density, and site on the development of size hierarchies in juvenile western redcedar (cedar) and western hemlock (hemlock) stands on northern Vancouver Island.

A factorial experiment was established in 1988 to examine the effects of: NPK fertilization versus non-fertilized; three establishment densities of 500 stems per ha (sph), 1500 sph and 2500 sph; the two species; and two sites: Nutrient-poor cedar-hemlock (CH) and nutrient-medium hemlock-amabilis fir (*Abies amabilis*) (HA) sites. The experiment was measured for heights and diameters seven times between 1988 and 2002. Predictive equations for biomass were developed to determine tree- and stand-level biomass estimates. Gini's "G" coefficient was used to quantify size hierarchies (structural diversity) within stands. Development of size hierarch in treatments was analyzed over the 15-year period of stand development for size and biomass variables to determine the effect of site, fertilization and density. Analysis was completed using PROC GLM in SAS ($p<0.05$).

Fertilization reduced size hierarchies i.e. made stands more uniform, by increasing the size smaller individuals, not by increasing their mortality, which is surprising. Density generally did not influence size hierarchy development, although there was a weak trend for more uniformity with increasing density. Size hierarchy varied with site and species: The species with the greater growth response had least diverse size structure on each site. Our results indicate that: Redcedar will tend to produce more structurally diverse stands than hemlock on sites with medium, but not poor, nutrient supply; fertilization reduces stand diversity; and increased soil resource availability does not promote structure-increasing competition.

[1] Coast Forest Region, Ministry of Forests and Range, 2100 Labieux Rd., Nanaimo, BC, V9T 6E9

INFLUENCE OF N AND P SUPPLY ON ROOTING OF YELLOW CEDAR (*CHAMAECYPARIS NOOTKATENSIS*) CUTTINGS FOR PLANTING STOCK PRODUCTION

R. van den Driessche[1] and J. Russell[2]

ABSTRACT

Yellow cedar is a valuable timber species, and reforestation is almost totally with rooted cuttings. Selected elite clones are used to provide cuttings to commercial nurseries where they are then grown into planting stock. Difficulties with rooting and growth of the cuttings encountered by the nurseries prompted work to see if changes in nutrient supply to the elite clones would influence the production of planting stock.

Effect of amount and timing of N and P fertilizer applications to greenhouse grown hedged stock plants was examined in relation to size and survival of cuttings produced in two experiments.

In the first experiment cutting production was from potted hedge plants of two kinds: (1) 2-year old hedges from 9-year-old serially propagated and selected material, and (2) 4-year old seedlings from wild stands. The peat vermiculite growth medium was uniformly fertilized when prepared, but during the experimental growing season applications of N (as Polyon 44-0-0, with a release time of 10 weeks) and P (as H_3PO_4) were made on 4 September (early) or on 1 November (late), or on both dates. Nutrients applied to each stock plant were 2 g N and 0.5 g P. Shoot and root dry mass of cuttings was greater in late applications, but with some differences between serial and wild stock plant sources.

In the second experiment 12 serially propagated clones were subjected to 12 N and P fertilizer level combinations applied at three times during the growing season. Cutting number, survival, shoot dry mass and stem diameter were differently affected by different N and P combinations and application time, with later application times and higher N/P ratios often producing greater responses.

This work showed that nutritional regimes of donor plants can be developed to increase faster rooting and growth of cuttings to produce larger planting stock.

[1] Dept. of Forest Biology, University of Victoria, P.O. Box 3020 STN CSC Victoria B.C. V8W 3N5, rvdd@telus.net
[2] Cowichan Lake Research Station, Ministry of Forests and Range, Research and Knowledge Management Branch, Mesachie Lake, B.C. V0R 2N0, JohnRussell@gov.bc.ca

SECTION D

ABSTRACTS AND PAPERS BASED ON POSTERS

WESTERN REDCEDAR DEER BROWSE RESISITANCE WORKSHOP

FIELD TOURS

THE BALLAD OF TWO CEDARS

PARTICIPANTS

METRIC-ENGLISH EQUIVALENTS

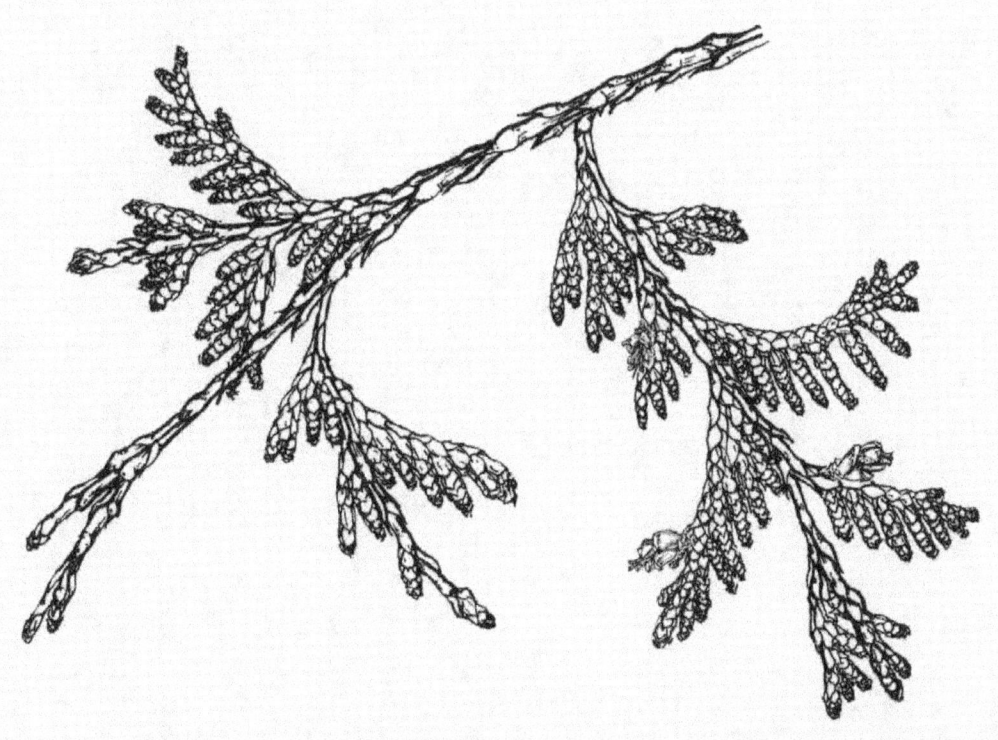

SILVICULTURAL TREATMENT EFFECTS ON ABOVEGROUND BIOMASS GROWTH AND PARTITIONING OF WESTERN REDCEDAR (*THUJA PLICATA* DONN *EX* D. DON) STANDS COMPARED TO WESTERN HEMLOCK (*TSUGA HETEROPHYLLA* (RAF.) SARG.)

Roderick W. Negrave[1]

ABSTRACT

An understanding of the production and allocation of biomass within forest stands is of interest in managing forests for carbon sequestration, managing for biomass-based energy production and increases our comprehension of ecological processes. This study examined the effects of silvicultural treatments and site influences on biomass accumulation and aboveground partitioning in juvenile western redcedar (cedar) and western hemlock (hemlock) stands on northern Vancouver Island. A factorial experiment was established in 1988 to examine the effects of: NPK fertilization versus non-fertilized treatments; three establishment densities of 500 stems per ha (sph), 1500 sph and 2500 sph; and the two species. This design was replicated (4x) on two sites: Nutrient-poor old-growth cedar-hemlock (CH) and nutrient-medium, second growth hemlock-amabilis fir (*Abies amabilis* (Dougl. *ex* Loud.) Dougl. *ex* Forbes) (HA) sites. The experiment was re-measured after 15 growing seasons in 2002. Biomass estimation equations were developed through destructive sampling of 84 cedar and 41 hemlock saplings and applied to plot data to produce estimates of total stand biomass and biomass components for foliage, branches, wood and bark. Analysis was completed using PROC MIXED in SAS ($p<0.05$). Fertilization increased total and component biomasses compared to non-fertilized treatments and increased the proportion of wood in stands. The proportion of foliage in stands increased with establishment density. Proportionally, there was less wood in cedar stands on CH sites. On HA sites, cedar stands had proportionally more foliage than hemlock. Results suggest that: Both total biomass and wood production can be increased through fertilization; cedar responds less strongly than hemlock to fertilization; cedar is the preferred species in managing for both biomass and wood production on the poorer CH site; and return on fertilizer investment, in terms of biomass and wood volume (as opposed to value), is likely maximized by fertilizing hemlock on HA sites.

KEYWORDS: Western redcedar, western hemlock, fertilization, density, biomass, aboveground partitioning

INTRODUCTION

Management of forests for biomass and carbon sequestration has recently become of interest in British Columbia. These approaches to management differ from traditional views in that all of the biomass grown by a stand is of interest as a product, not just stem-wood. An understanding of how biomass is partitioned to stand structural components, foliage versus wood for example, can also further our understanding of how silvicultural treatment influence stand growth by how they affect allocation to these structural components (Gower *et al.* 1993, Retzlaff *et al.* 2001). In 1988, a silvicultural trial was established to study how fertilization and establishment density may be used to reforest former old-growth forest sites that were occupied by salal (*Gaultheria shallon* Pursh) on which it was difficult to establish viable conifer plantations

[1]Roderick W. Negrave is Research Team Leader and research silviculturist, British Columbia Ministry of Forests and Range, 2100 Labieux Road, Nanaimo, BC, V9T 6E9

on. These treatments were also applied to nearby circum-zonal sites that supported acceptable conifer growth in comparison.

We used this established experiment to study how silvicultural treatments during stand establishment might influence total stand biomass growth on different types of sites and the aboveground allocation to stem-wood, bark, foliage and branches.

METHODS
Study Sites
The study site was located on northern Vancouver Island (50° 60'N, 127° 35' W) in the Submontane Very Wet Maritime variant of the Coastal Western Hemlock Biogeoclimatic, or CWHvm1 zone (Green and Klinka 1994). The area receives approximately 1900 mm of precipitation annually, most of which falls as rain. Growing season soil moisture deficits typically do not occur (Lewis 1982).

The experiment was conducted on two common CWHvm1 forest types. Hemlock Amabilis Fir (HA) sites are occupied by stands composed of western hemlock and amabilis fir. Cedar Hemlock (CH) sites are occupied by stands dominated by western red redcedar with lesser amounts of western hemlock and amabilis fir. CH sites support old-growth forests and canopies in these stands are irregular with frequent gaps and the understory is consequently well developed and dominated by salal. The HA sites in this study were second-growth forests that mostly originated from a major windstorm in 1906 (Prescott and Weetman 1994). These forests are more uniform in structure and are composed of younger trees. Canopies in HA forests are uniform and dense with little light penetration to the forest floor.

Nitrogen and P availability is lower on CH sites than on HA sites and the reasons for this phenomenon remain obscure. The wetter nature of CH humus and soil above concreted layers and resulting reduction of biological activity may be responsible for the lower N and P availability that characterizes these sites

(Prescott and Weetman 1994, Prescott *et al* 1996).

Experimental design and treatments
Ninety-six square treatment plots, each containing 64 sample trees were established in 1988. Treatments were arranged in a fully-crossed factorial combination with two levels of fertility (fertilized and unfertilized) and three levels of density (500, 1500 and 2500 stems per ha). The 2 x 3 combination of fertilizer/no-fertilizer by densities was applied to each of redcedar and hemlock and duplicated on both CH and HA sites. The CH and HA sites used in this study were scattered throughout a 3-km^2 area in close proximity to each other. Each fertilization-density-species combination was randomly assigned within four blocks on each site, with a single treatment level replicate per block. Thus, a total of 48 plots examined 12 treatments with 4 replications per treatment level on each site.

Fertilized plots received a 60 g dressing of Nutricote^{TM} controlled-release fertilizer at time of planting. The fertilizer was raked into 15-cm radius areas around each seedling and provided 10 g of N, 2.5 g of P and 5 g of K to each seedling. Total application rates per ha varied with density. All fertilized plots were re-fertilized before the beginning of the growing season in 1993 with a broadcast application of 225 kg of N and 100 kg of P per ha as urea (46-0-0) and triple superphosphate (0-45-0).

Measurements
Height and diameter of each living sample tree within core measurement areas were measured after the completion of growth in late 2002. Diameter was measured 1.3 m above the root collar. Regression equations were developed to predict individual tree total mass and mass of foliage, branch, bark and wood components. Saplings were destructively sampled after growth had ceased in the fall of 2001 and 2002. Dry mass conversion factors were determined for stem wood, stem bark, branch foliage and woody branch components for each sample tree.

A total of 84 cedar saplings were destructively sampled compared to 41 for hemlock, due to the greater variability among mass components of cedar.

Mass Prediction Equations

Biomass estimation equations were developed from the destructive sampling data. These equations were ordinary least-square regressions of the allometric log-log transformed type e.g. Brix (1983). These regressions used height and diameter to estimate mass of stem wood, stem bark, branches, and foliage. Prediction equations were corrected for back-transformational bias. Separate equations were developed for each component for each species, along with equations to estimate total tree mass. All of these predictive equations were significant (p <0.001) with r^2 values ranging from 0.813 to 0.981. The predictive equations were then applied to plot data to produce estimates of total stand biomass and biomass components. Proportional allocation of biomass to components within stands was then derived from these estimates.

Treatment effects on biomass growth and proportional allocation of biomass to components within stands were analyzed using a general linear model approach. Three factors including species, density and fertilization were tested using a mixed-effects model with block-effects assumed to be fixed. Variables analyzed included total stand mass, masses of stem-wood (wood), stem-bark (bark), branches and foliage, and the percentage of total stand mass contained in wood, bark, branches and foliage. Analysis was completed using PROC MIXED in SAS (p<0.05).

RESULTS

Fertilization increased total stand mass and each of the masses of wood, bark, branches and foliage for both species on each site (p values ranging from <.0001 to 0.0225; Table 1). On CH sites, unfertilized cedar masses were greater that those of hemlock, however, hemlock responded more strongly to fertilization than did cedar and no differences existed between the species for masses when fertilized. Fertilization increased total stand and component masses by two to three times for most species-site combinations but up to a 15-times increase was noted for fertilized compared to unfertilized hemlock on CH sites (Table 1). Masses of hemlock exceeded those of cedar on HA sites (p <.0001; Table 1).

On HA sites, total stand mass and the masses of bark and branches were least in the 500 sph treatments (p <.0001; Table 1). Total stand mass did not significantly increase with density on unfertilized CH sites (p = 0.0225; Table 1). The total, foliage, and wood masses of hemlock stands were less at 2500 sph than at 1500 sph on unfertilized CH sites, but these were not significant (Table 1). Although significant three-way treatment effects were present for masses of wood and foliage on CH sites, no clear pattern of effects was evident. Masses of bark and branches tended to be significantly least at 500 sph than at the higher densities on CH sites (p values of 0.0186 and <.0001, respectively; Table 1), although this effect was stronger for cedar and on unfertilized sites.

Fertilization increased the proportion of stand mass in wood for both species on both sites (p values from <.0001 to 0.0307; Table 2). On CH sites, hemlock had proportionally more stand mass in wood than cedar (p = 0.0008, Table 2). Fertilization decreased the proportion of stand mass in foliage for both species on both sites (p values from <.0001 to 0.0438; Table 2). On HA sites, unfertilized cedar had proportionally more mass in foliage than hemlock (p = 0.0438; Table 2). Fertilization decreased the proportion of hemlock stand mass in branches on both sites (p 0.0024 to 0.0293; Table 2). Fertilization decreased the proportion of bark in both cedar and hemlock stands on CH sites and in cedar stands on HA sites (p values from 0.0002 to 0.0003; Table 2). Cedar had proportionally more stand mass in bark than hemlock on CH sites (p = 0.0002; Table 2).

Increasing density reduced the proportion of stand mass in wood for both species on both sites (p values from <.0001 to 0.0307; Table 2). On CH sites, the proportion of stand mass in bark increased with density in cedar and the proportion of mass in branches increased with density in hemlock (*p* values of 0.0006 and 0.0293, respectively; Table 2). On HA sites, proportional stand mass in bark was greater in the 2500 sph treatment compared to 500 sph (*p* = 0.0383; Table 2).

Table 1: Means of total stand mass and mass components with standard errors in brackets.

Species	Fert.	Planting Density (Stems/ha)	Wood (t/ha)	Bark (t/ha)	Branches (t/ha)	Foliage (t/ha)	Total Stand (t/ha)
CH Sites:							
Cw	F0	500	2.12(0.68)	0.35(0.09)	1.33(0.38)	1.10(0.25)	4.92(1.41)
Cw	F0	1500	3.41(1.47)	0.66(0.22)	2.37(0.87)	2.25(0.63)	8.71(3.25)
Cw	F0	2500	3.66(0.73)	0.78(0.13)	2.68(0.49)	2.74(0.43)	9.83(1.81)
Cw	F1	500	5.04(1.03)	0.69(0.11)	2.85(0.51)	2.03(0.28)	10.66(1.92)
Cw	F1	1500	11.86(3.61)	1.77(0.43)	7.05(1.88)	5.35(1.15)	26.22(7.08)
Cw	F1	2500	10.56(4.77)	1.75(0.68)	6.68(2.78)	5.56(1.98)	24.74(10.35)
Hw	F0	500	0.78(0.24)	0.12(0.03)	0.43(0.12)	0.41(0.10)	1.75(0.49)
Hw	F0	1500	1.39(0.52)	0.23(0.08)	0.84(0.28)	0.86(0.26)	3.35(1.15)
Hw	F0	2500	0.72(0.18)	0.13(0.03)	0.49(0.11)	0.54(0.12)	1.89(0.44)
Hw	F1	500	6.96(2.37)	0.84(0.26)	2.99(0.92)	2.53(0.72)	13.18(4.17)
Hw	F1	1500	9.44(3.57)	1.25(0.44)	4.52(1.58)	4.06(1.35)	19.31(6.92)
Hw	F1	2500	14.52(7.86)	1.94(0.93)	7.00(3.30)	6.31(2.73)	29.83(14.68)
HA Sites:							
Cw	F0	500	2.79(1.40)	0.42(0.18)	1.66(0.76)	1.28(0.50)	6.18(2.84)
Cw	F0	1500	4.89(1.99)	0.86(0.28)	3.21(1.16)	2.82(0.83)	11.85(4.32)
Cw	F0	2500	6.17(6.18)	1.07(0.89)	3.99(3.61)	3.46(2.62)	14.74(13.44)
Cw	F1	500	5.31(2.03)	0.70(0.22)	2.94(1.00)	2.03(0.56)	10.99(3.76)
Cw	F1	1500	18.31(6.97)	2.42(0.73)	10.12(3.41)	6.99(1.89)	37.87(12.87)
Cw	F1	2500	22.74(6.64)	3.18(0.74)	13.02(3.36)	9.42(1.94)	48.59(12.65)
Hw	F0	500	6.32(3.97)	0.76(0.44)	2.71(1.54)	2.30(1.22)	11.95(7.00)
Hw	F0	1500	15.05(11.04)	1.86(1.24)	6.65(4.39)	5.73(3.53)	29.09(19.82)
Hw	F0	2500	21.06(19.38)	2.61(2.23)	9.34(7.92)	8.06(6.48)	40.80(35.50)
Hw	F1	500	11.90(1.69)	1.34(0.18)	4.74(0.63)	3.84(0.49)	21.38(2.87)
Hw	F1	1500	45.69(7.95)	5.08(0.82)	17.94(2.88)	14.41(2.21)	81.24(13.36)
Hw	F1	2500	56.64(14.78)	6.48(1.52)	23.00(5.30)	18.84(4.02)	103.13(24.70)

Cw = Cedar, Hw = Hemlock, Fert. = Fertilization; F0 = Unfertilized, F1-= Fertilized

DISCUSSION

Fertilization was effective at increasing total stand mass and increasing the proportion of wood in stands. Increasing density was more ambivalent in this regard: the highest density did not always yield the greatest biomass, as with hemlock on CH sites. Increasing density also resulted in proportionally less wood in stands but more in branch and bark components.

Table 2: Mean mass component percentage of total stand mass with standard errors in brackets.

Species	Fert.	Planting Density (sph)	Wood (%)	Bark (%)	Branches (%)	Foliage (%)
CH Sites:						
Cw	F0	500	42.57(2.07)	7.11(0.30)	27.00(0.10)	22.66(1.83)
Cw	F0	1500	38.52(2.08)	7.72(0.34)	27.20(0.11)	26.43(2.14)
Cw	F0	2500	37.16(0.62)	7.95(0.12)	27.28(0.04)	27.96(0.78)
Cw	F1	500	47.08(1.22)	6.51(0.14)	26.79(0.05)	19.14(0.78)
Cw	F1	1500	44.93(1.57)	6.78(0.20)	26.88(0.07)	20.62(1.14)
Cw	F1	2500	41.91(2.48)	7.21(0.39)	27.03(0.13)	23.23(2.49)
Hw	F0	500	44.34(1.24)	6.65(0.05)	24.39(0.28)	23.77(0.81)
Hw	F0	1500	41.33(1.26)	6.77(0.05)	25.09(0.31)	25.78(0.92)
Hw	F0	2500	38.15(0.62)	6.91(0.03)	25.93(0.17)	28.42(0.54)
Hw	F1	500	52.38(1.78)	6.37(0.06)	22.75(0.33)	19.36(0.82)
Hw	F1	1500	48.49(1.52)	6.49(0.06)	23.48(0.32)	21.25(0.85)
Hw	F1	2500	47.92(2.10)	6.51(0.07)	23.60(0.42)	21.56(1.12)
HA Sites:						
Cw	F0	500	44.16(2.98)	6.91(0.41)	26.93(0.14)	21.49(2.48)
Cw	F0	1500	40.83(1.55)	7.36(0.24)	27.08(0.08)	24.17(1.48)
Cw	F0	2500	39.45(3.60)	7.62(0.58)	27.17(0.19)	25.95(3.76)
Cw	F1	500	47.77(2.42)	6.45(0.28)	26.76(0.11)	18.85(1.54)
Cw	F1	1500	47.58(3.03)	6.47(0.36)	26.77(0.13)	18.95(2.00)
Cw	F1	2500	46.39(2.17)	6.61(0.27)	26.82(0.10)	19.68(1.54)
Hw	F0	500	51.58(2.85)	6.39(0.09)	22.91(0.53)	19.78(1.33)
Hw	F0	1500	50.02(3.45)	6.45(0.12)	23.20(0.67)	20.55(1.73)
Hw	F0	2500	48.54(4.94)	6.50(0.18)	23.52(1.02)	21.44(2.76)
Hw	F1	500	55.61(0.908)	6.27(0.03)	22.19(0.15)	17.99(0.36)
Hw	F1	1500	56.17(0.70)	6.25(0.02)	22.09(0.12)	17.77(0.27)
Hw	F1	2500	54.69(1.28)	6.29(0.04)	22.34(0.22)	18.36(0.52)

Cw = Cedar, Hw = Hemlock, Fert. = Fertilization; F0 = Unfertilized, F1-= Fertilized

These results suggest that combined high-density planning with fertilization will not always yield the greatest biomass and therefore both site and species factors need to be considered in management for biomass. Findings also suggest that the greatest return on fertilizer investment, in terms of biomass and wood mass production, is achieved by fertilizing hemlock on HA sites.

Stand level results likely occurred via treatment effects on tree size and the mix of tree sized produced. Larger trees tend to consist of proportionally more wood and less foliage, bark and branches than smaller trees (Barclay *et al.* 1986, Newton and Jolliffe 1993). In our experiment, fertilization increased tree size, tended to favour the growth of smaller trees, and produced more uniformly-sized stands, while increasing density tended to decrease tree size but not affect size-distribution of individual trees within the stand (Negrave 2004, Negrave *et al.* 2007).

LITERATURE CITED

Barclay, H.J., Pang, P.C. and D.F.W. Pollard. 1986. Aboveground mass distribution within trees and stands in thinned and fertilized Douglas-fir. Can. J. For. Res. 16: 438 – 442.

Brix, H. 1983. Effects of thinning and nitrogen fertilization on growth of Douglas-fir: relative contribution of foliage quantity and efficiency. Can. J. For. Res. 13: 167 – 175.

Green, R.N. and K. Klinka. 1994. A Field Guide to Site Identification and Interpretation for the Vancouver Forest Region. British Columbia Ministry of Forests, Research Branch, Victoria.

Gower, S.T., Hayes, B.E. and K.S. Fassnacht. 1993. Influence of fertilization on the allometric relations for two pines in contrasting environments. Can. J. for. Res. 23: 1704 – 1711.

Lewis, T. 1992. Ecosystems of the Port McNeill block (Block 4) of Tree farm License 25. Western Forest Products Ltd., Vancouver, BC. 75 p.

Negrave, R.W. 2004. Nutrient and Establishment Density Effects on Structural Development and Growth Processes in Juvenile Western Redcedar and Western Hemlock Stands on Northern Vancouver Island. PhD Thesis, University of British Columbia, Dept. of Forest Sciences, Vancouver, BC. 289 p.

Negrave, R.W., Prescott C.E., and J.E. Barker. 2007. Growth and foliar nutrition of juvenile western hemlock and western redcedar plantations on low- and medium-productivity sites on northern Vancouver Island: response to fertilization and planting density. Can. J. For. Res. 37: 2587 – 2599.

Newton, P.F. and P.A. Jolliffe. 1993. Aboveground dry matter partitioning, size variation and competitive processes within second growth black spruce stands. Can. J. For. Res. 20: 1720 – 1731.

Prescott, C.E. and G.F. Weetman (eds.).1994. Salal Cedar Hemlock Integrated Research Program: A Synthesis. Faculty of Forestry, University of British Columbia, Vancouver, BC. 85 p.

Prescott, C.E., Weetman, G.F. and J.E. Barker. 1996. Causes and amelioration of nutrient deficiencies in cutovers of redcedar-hemlock forests in coastal British Columbia. For. Chron. 72: 293 – 302.

Retzlaff, W.A., Handest, J.A., O'Malley, D.M., McKeand, S.E. and M.A. Topa. 2001. Whole-tree mass and carbon allocation of juvenile trees of loblolly pine (*Pinus taeda*): influence of genetics and fertilization. Can. J. For. Res. 31: 960 – 970.

RESPONSE OF WESTERN REDCEDAR TO RELEASE AND FERTILIZATION IN A MIXED-SPECIES STAND

Leslie Chandler Brodie and Constance A. Harrington[2]

ABSTRACT

Western redcedar (*Thuja plicata* Donn ex. D. Don) is of high commercial value, is considered highly shade tolerant and occurs more commonly in mixed-species, uneven-aged stands than in pure stands. Successful maintenance of redcedar as a component of mixed-species stands to enhance diversity or to overcome the difficulties of establishing redcedar regeneration is dependent on its response to release and other silvicultural treatments. To assess the response of western redcedar to release and fertilization in a mixed-species stand, 74 western redcedar trees were selected to represent a wide distribution of diameter and crown classes in a stand in which the overstory had been recently removed in Capitol State Forest near Olympia, WA. Three types of competition indices were calculated for each study tree in order to quantify the extent of the release treatment as well as to characterize the current growing conditions. Pre-treatment values for the competition indices were calculated retrospectively using the number and size of stumps present. Half of the study trees were fertilized with urea at the rate of 200 kg of N/ha. Percent DBH growth increased significantly in response to fertilization every year for 3 years following fertilization with the greatest effect the first growing season after application. Percent height growth was more affected by the presence of overtopping trees following the release treatment than by fertilization. Of the competition indices modeled, the percent overlap of influence areas (based on tree size) was the most consistently effective at predicting percent diameter and height growth at all years when measurements were taken up to year 15. Western redcedar responded positively to removal of overtopping trees; thus, this type of release should be considered a viable management option. Response to fertilization was positive but short lived.

KEYWORDS: redcedar, release, fertilization, management, height growth, diameter growth

INTRODUCTION

Western redcedar (*Thuja plicata* Donn ex. D. Don) is a highly shade-tolerant tree species found in western North America and occurs more commonly in mixed-species, uneven-aged stands than in pure stands (Minore 1990, Klinka and Brisco 2009). Because of its shade tolerance, it can survive in the understory or midstory of forests, and thus, can be an important contributor to the structural diversity associated with old-growth stands (Old-growth Definition Task Force, 1986). It has been recommended that forest managers interested in wood production grow redcedar in relatively high density, pure-species stands because wood quality and growth will be reduced when redcedar is overtopped by faster growing trees (Oliver et al. 1988). Managers interested in wildlife habitat, biodiversity, accelerating the development of late successional characteristics, or maintaining visual quality, however, may be interested in managing redcedar as a component of more complex stands. Redcedar is difficult to regenerate in many locations due to browsing by deer and elk. For these reasons, it may be especially desirable to retain existing redcedar trees when harvesting the overstory, even if many of these trees may not be valuable for future timber harvest.

Substantial information is available on the tree and site factors which influence response of

[1,2] Leslie Brodie is a forester and Constance Harrington is a research forester with the Genetic and Silvicultural Foundations for Management team, PNW Research Station, 3625 93rd Ave SW, Olympia WA 98512. [1]email address: lbrodie@fs.fed.us

redcedar to release in the northern Rocky Mountains (Graham 1982) but very little has been reported for redcedar in the coastal portion of its range and some foresters have suggested that overtopped redcedar would not respond well to release as shade-formed leaves will not be able to function well in a higher light environment or root systems developed in a forest stand will not be adequate when the species is exposed to a more stressful environment. Redcedar has been shown to be responsive to fertilization (Devine and Harrington 2009, Walker et al. 1955, Weetman et al. 1988, Prescott 1996) and could possibly respond more quickly to release if fertilized with nitrogen. In this experiment, we followed the fate of redcedar trees for 15 years in a stand near Olympia, WA after overstory removal and fertilization. Because the stand conditions were irregular, we evaluated competition indices for their efficacy in reducing variation in tree growth response and used release and overtopping codes to further partition responses in a meaningful way.

MATERIALS AND METHODS

The study area is located in the northern portion of the Washington State Department of Natural Resources Capitol Forest near Olympia, WA, USA. It was in Unit 1 of the 'Poria' sale area (Fig. 1) which covered 11.3 ha; the unit is relatively flat and at an elevation of 180 m. The dominant soil type is Grove very gravelly sandy loam. In March 1995, the overstory was removed except for approximately 25 Douglas-fir trees per hectare and all western redcedar—primarily understory and midstory—was retained. We selected 74 western redcedar trees for the study which were free from obvious logging damage and represented a wide range in stem diameter and crown position. Diameter at 1.3 m (DBH) of selected study trees ranged from 0.8 to 24.8 cm and heights ranged from 1.6 to 18.3 m. Half of the selected trees were chosen on the basis of crown class, diameter and distance to other selected trees to be fertilized with nitrogen such that fertilized trees were approximately the size and crown position as the non-treated trees and were well distributed

throughout the stand. All study trees were measured for DBH, height, height to live crown, and crown width soon after logging in 1995 (end of the 1994 growing season is year 0), prior to fertilization in the early spring of 1995 (year 1), and at years 2, 3, 4, 5 and 15.

We evaluated three competition indices (CI's) for their efficacy in reducing variation in tree growth response and to help quantify conditions pre- and post-release. The CI's were calculated for each study tree both for past status (retrospectively, using stumps) and in their current status. The level of release was defined as the difference between the two values. Any tree or stump with a diameter at 0.3 m greater than 15 cm and within 10.3 m distance from the study tree was considered a competitor. Trees and stumps with a basal diameter 5.0 cm to 14.9 cm and located within a distance of 2.56 m were also considered competitors. In addition, study trees and surrounding trees and stumps were assessed post-harvest and used to estimate the tree's crown position both before and after the harvest. As a result, study trees were coded as either 'over-topped' or 'released'.

The three competition indices (CI's) used to quantify the extent of the release treatment and current growing conditions were 'sum line length', 'area', and 'percentage overlap'. Their calculation and descriptions are presented in Table 1 (see Brodie and DeBell 2004 for additional detail). For 'sum line length', the length of each line is proportional to the ratio between the DBH of the 2 trees. The competition index 'area', is similar to 'sum line length, but 'area' accommodates the differences in distribution of line lengths by going one step further to calculate the area enclosed by joining the endpoints of adjacent lines. For calculation of 'percentage overlap', each tree is considered to have a circular influence area estimated as ¼ of total height. The CI is the percentage of the study tree's area of influence that is overlapped by those of competitors.

In the early spring of 1996, urea at the rate of 200 kg of N/ha was manually applied to individual trees in a circular area centered on the stem and with a radius equal to one-half of the tree height.

Table 1 -- Competition indices used in the study		
Competition Index Name	Definition/Description	Representation
Sum Line Length	———	
Area	Area delineated by the endpoints of the lines defined by the CI 'Sum Line Length'	
Percent Overlap	———	

Where CI_i =competition index of subject tree i, DBH_i =diameter at 1.3 m of subject tree i, DBH_j =diameter at 1.3 m of competitor j, $DIST_{ij}$ = distance between trees i and j, and O_j =portion of the influence area of competitor j (radius=0.25 x height j) that overlaps influence of subject tree, and I_i = influence area of subject tree i.

Annual and periodic percent DBH and height growth were analyzed by a series of general linear models (GLM) using fertilization treatment, crown position, the CI's and initial size class as covariates (SAS Institute Inc. 2005).

RESULTS AND DISCUSSION
Residual Stand Damage
Selected study trees exhibited little or no damage from the removal of the Douglas-fir overstory either directly or as a result of the change in environment. Wind damage to the study trees during the course of the study was minimal. During the 15-year period, 4 trees were blown down or damaged by other blown down trees and two trees suffered broken tops. Excluding these trees from the study affected initial mean diameter and heights only minimally, so did not affect the overall study design. As a side note, in the months just prior to the last measurement, 3 of the study trees (and several others within the stand) were severely pruned by unauthorized bough harvesters. Generally, well over half of the crown was removed. The harvest of the overstory and subsequent crown development of the redcedar trees created a condition where the cedar boughs were not only more obvious, but more plentiful and may have subjected the stand to more damage of this type.

Response to Fertilization
Because of the wide range in initial diameter of study trees, growth response was expressed as percent DBH growth. Percent DBH growth increased significantly in response to fertilization every year for 3 years following fertilization with the greatest effect the first growing season after application (Fig. 2). Treated trees responded to fertilization with a 44% increase in percent DBH growth the first year, a 97% increase the second year and a 60% increase the third year. Trees did not respond differentially by initial size class. Height growth (figure 3) was much more influenced by the presence of overtopping trees following the release treatment than by fertilization (height growth response to fertilization not statistically significant). Over the first 5 years of the study, trees with an over-topping crown grew a mean of 0.57 m while those without the presence of an over-topping crown grew 1.24 m—a 118% increase. Long-term (15-year) response to fertilization was not statistically significant for either diameter or height growth, nor was the interaction between CI and fertilization significant.

These findings concur with the findings of previous studies where western redcedar has been shown to be consistently responsive to nitrogen additions in relatively even-aged stands during the years immediately following treatment (as opposed to the more erratic response of western hemlock) (Harrington and Wierman 1985, Weetman et al., 1987, Weetman et al. 1989, Weetman et al., 1993, Devine and Harrington 2009). Significant differences were found in diameter and height growth (although in those studies the presence of over-topping trees was not a factor) and it was suggested that early response to thinning alone would be quite small in comparison to thinning and fertilization combined, as this study suggests as well. Also similar to other studies, the increase in periodic growth rate produced by the addition of nitrogen was not sustained over a longer period of time (Weetman et al. 1989, Devine and Harrington 2009), dissipating sometime between 4-10 years after treatment (Blevins et al., 2006).

Competition Index Evaluation
For each measurement interval, an analysis of variance was performed for percent DBH and height growth using crown position, fertilization treatments, and 1 of the 3 CI's as covariates. Of the 3 CI's, 'Percentage Overlap' most consistently produced the highest R^2 values and was used to quantify levels of competition in further analysis.

We believe that the other 2 CI's did not perform as well in an unevenly spaced, mixed-species stand for several reasons. The CI 'sum line length' did not account for the spatial distribution of tree size in the area immediately adjacent to the study tree; in its calculation, it could not give value to a group of smaller trees to one side providing a gap for the study tree. Although the calculation of the CI 'area' did take the spatial distribution of competitor trees into account, it could not quantify the amount that competitors' effects overlapped. By contrast, the value of 'percent overlap' has no upper limit. If a smaller competitor is slightly more distant from the study tree than a larger competitor, the influence of both is quantified. Although 'sum line length' and 'area' may work well in evenly-spaced stands where trees are similar in size, the CI 'percent overlap', with its higher sensitivity, performed better as a modeling tool within this more variable stand.

Response to Competition and Release
Percent DBH growth and percent height growth were both significantly increased by the release treatment (Figs. 4 and 5). Two factors contributed to the growth response to treatment. First, and most significant ($p<0.05$), was the reduction of competition within the immediate area (as quantified by 'percent overlap'). Once percent overlap reached approximately 125,

further increases in competition level had little or no effect on either DBH or height growth.

The second factor contributing to response was crown position (over-topped or released). Although not as significant as 'percent overlap', crown position was significant at $p<0.10$. The response of released trees to their crown position was dependent on the level of competition present after treatment (Figs. 4 and 5, inset graphs). If competition in the immediate area remained high (percent overlap greater than 125), the trees did not respond to the removal of crowns directly above. If competition in the immediate area was low, there was greater differentiation in growth between those trees that remained over-topped in contrast to those that had been released.

A related study in southwest Washington (Deisenhofer, 2010) found similar results although in that study, height growth response to release was slower and less pronounced than that of diameter growth. Redcedar's response to release in the northern Rocky Mountains (Graham, 1982) was highly dependent on several site factors including aspect, initial tree size, and soil and foliar characteristics. Although this study did not evaluate all site factors, initial tree size was not a statistically significant predictor of response to release.

CONCLUSIONS
Anecdotal information suggests that western redcedar may suffer from 'thinning shock' as has been documented for Douglas-fir on poor sites resulting in short-term height growth reduction (Harrington and Reukema, 1983). Such was not the case in this study. The trees responded well to release from over-topping crowns and a reduction in the number of competitors in the immediate area, thus these treatments represent viable management options. Although diameter growth responded well to fertilization, the response was not sustained in the long-term, however, fertilization my still be a valuable silvicultural tool depending on the short-term management objectives.

Figure 1 -- The study site in 2000 (year 6 of the study). The overstory had been removed except for approximately 25 Douglas-fir trees per ha.

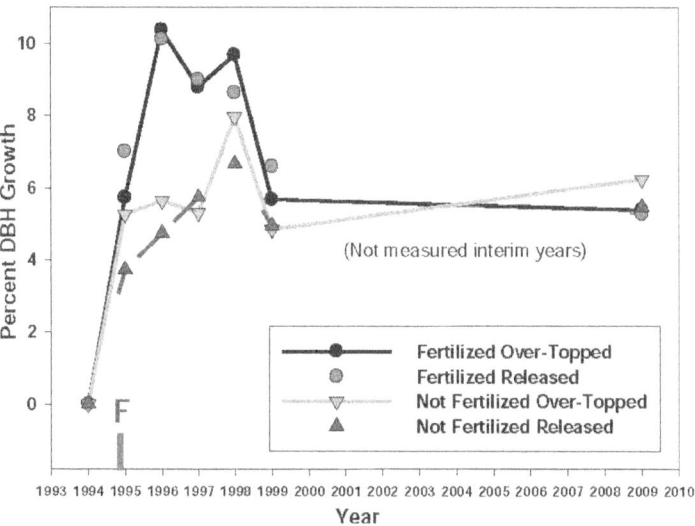

Figure 2 -- Mean annual percent DBH growth by treatment and crown position.

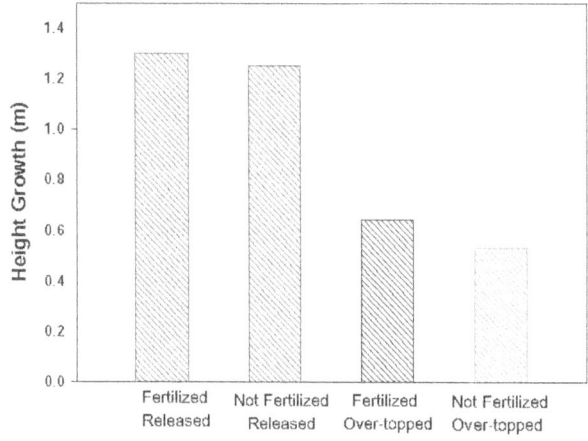

Figure 3 -- Mean height growth from 1994-1999 by treatment and crown position

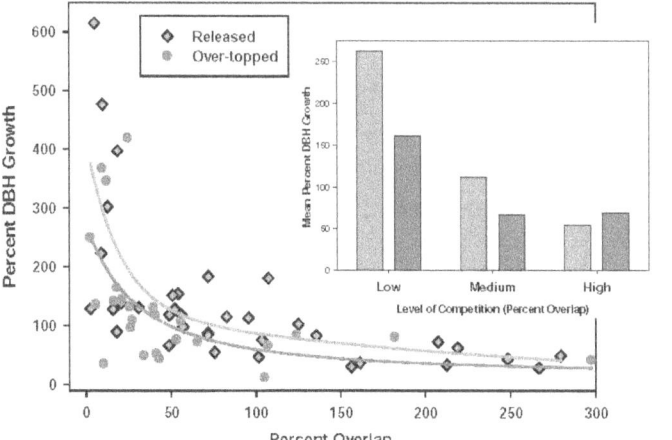

Figure 4 -- Percent DBH growth per tree by the CI, "overlap" and crown position. Note that the release was ineffective at high CI levels. Note: Percent Overlap may exceed 100% where multiple influence areas overlap.

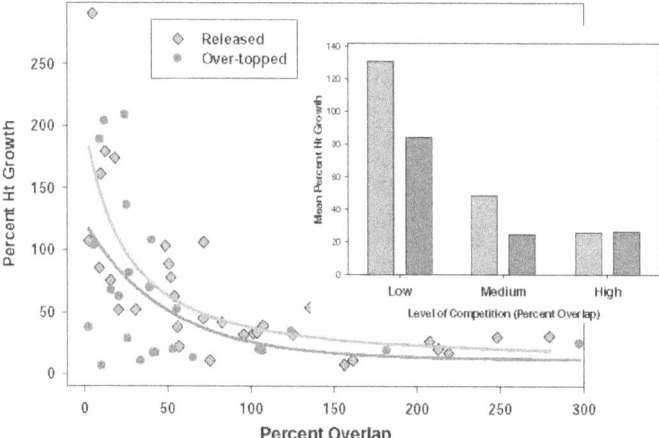

Figure 5 -- Percent Height growth per tree by the CI, "overlap" and crown position.. Note: Percent Overlap may exceed 100% where multiple influence areas overlap.

ACKNOWLEDGMENTS
We thank the Washington State Department of Natural Resources for their cooperation and assistance with this study, particularly in the selection of the study site; Angus Brodie for his help in study establishment; and the former members of the Silviculture and Forest Models Team who assisted with data collection, particularly Mike Gloss, Chris Sato, and Jeanette Robbins. We also thank Dean DeBell and Florian Deisenhofer for their manuscript reviews.

LITERATURE CITED
Blevins, L.L., Prescott, C.E., and Van Niejenhuis, A. 2006. The roles of nitrogen and phosphorus in increasing productivity of western hemlock and western redcedar plantations on northern Vancouver Island. For. Ecol. Manage. **234**: 116–122.

Brodie, L.C.; DeBell, D.S. 2004. Evaluation of field performance of poplar clones using selected competition indices. New For. 27:201-214.

Devine, W.D.; Harrington, C.A. 2009. Western redcedar response to precommercial thinning and fertilization through 25 years post treatment. Can. J. For. Res. 39: 619–628.

Deisenhofer, F. 2010. Western redcedar (*Thuja plicata*) advanced regeneration response to variable retention harvesting in Southwest Washington. *In*: Gen. Tech. Rep. PNW-GTR-828. Portland, OR: U.S. Department of Agriculture, Forest Service. Pacific Northwest Research Station. p.157.

Graham, R.T., 1982. Influence of tree and site factors on western redcedar's response to release: A modeling analysis. USDA Forest Service, Intermountain Forest and Range Experiment Station, Research Paper INT-296, Ogden ,UT.

Harrington, C.A.; Reukema, D.L. 1983. Initial shock and long-term stand development following thinning in a Douglas-fir plantation. Forest Sci. 29:33-46.

Minore, D. 1990. *Thuja plicata* (Donn ex D. Don) Western redcedar. In Burns and Honkala (tech. coords.), Silvics of North America: 1. Conifers. Agricultural Handbook 654. USDA, For. Serv., Washington, D.C. vol. 1, 675 p.

Old-growth Definition Task Group. 1986. *Interim definitions for old-growth Douglas-fir and mixed-conifer forests in the Pacific Northwest and California.* USDA Forest Service, Pacific Northwest Research Station, Res. Note PNW-447. Portland, OR.

Oliver, C.D.; Nystrom, M.N.; DeBell, D.S.1987. Coastal stand silvicultural potential for western redcedar. In N.J. Smith (ed.)Western redcedar - Does it have a future?. Conf. proc., Univ. of B.C., Vancouver, B.C., Canada. pp 39-46.

SAS Institute Inc. 2005. The SAS System for Windows. Version 9.1. SAS Institute Inc., Cary, N.C.

Weetman, G.F., Fournier, R.; Barker, J.; Schnorbus-Panozzo, E. 1989. Foliar analysis of fertilized chlorotic western hemlock and western red cedar reproduction on salal-dominated cedar-hemlock cutovers on Vancouver Island. Can. J. For. Res. 19:1512-1520.

Weetman, G.F.; McDonald, M.A.; Prescott, C.E.; Kimmins, J.P. 1993. Responses of western hemlock, pacific silver fir, and western redcedar plantations on northern Vancouver Island to applications of sewage sludge and inorganic fertilizer. Can. J. For. Res. 23: 1815-1820.

Weetman, G.F.; Radwan, M.A.; Kumi, J. Schnorbus, E. 1987. Nutrition and fertilization of western redcedar. In N.J. Smith (ed.)Western redcedar - Does it have a future?. Conf. proc., Univ. of B.C., Vancouver, B.C., Canada. pp 47-59.

SENSITIVITY OF WESTERN REDCEDAR GROWTH TO CLIMATE AND WESTERN HEMLOCK LOOPER IN BRITISH COLUMBIA'S INLAND TEMPERATE RAINFOREST

Chris Konchalski[1]

ABSTRACT

Conflicting future predictions for British Columbia's inland temperate rainforest under climate change scenarios make it an area of special concern for research, management, and conservation. The inland temperate rainforest results from a globally unique combination of humidity and continental climate, and is host to tree species that are normally considered coastal and rare lichens and bryophytes. Dendrochronology has the ability to describe and quantify the sensitivity of western redcedar (*Thuja plicata*), a dominant canopy tree, to climate and western hemlock looper by analyzing the annual growth increments. The influence of slope position, aspect, elevation, and biogeoclimatic subzone on the sensitivity of western redcedar to climate and western hemlock looper will be analyzed. One elevational transect consisting of three sites will be placed in the two available biogeoclimatic subzones in the study area, as well as one putatively sensitive climate site and one level, well drained site. Nine chronologies will be obtained during the field season. Understanding the sensitivity of western redcedar to climate and western hemlock looper in different areas will help predict future forest responses and processes in the inland temperate rainforest.

[1] MSc NRES (Forestry) Student, University of Northern British Columbia, 3333 University way, Prince George, British Columbia. V2N 4Z9

ETHANOL SYNTHESIS BY ANOXIC ROOT SEGMENTS FROM FIVE CEDAR SPECIES RELATES TO MESIC HABITAT ATTRIBUTES BUT NOT THEIR VULNERABILITY TO *PHYTOPHTHORA LATERALIS* ROOT DISEASE

Rick G. Kelsey[1], Gladwin Joseph[2], and Michael G. McWilliams[3]

ABSTRACT

Ethanol synthesis by anoxic root segments from yellow (*Chamaecyparis nootkatensis*), western red (*Thuja plicata*), Port-Orford (*C. lawsoniana*), Atlantic white (*C. thyoides*), and incense (*Calocedrus decurrens*) cedars were compared to determine whether ethanol released during anoxic stress from flooding could influence their vulnerability to the root pathogen, *Phytophthora lateralis.* Roots were incubated in water at 5, 15, 25, and 35 °C for 14 days. The water was periodically analyzed for ethanol. After a short 12 hour period of anoxia, Atlantic white- and yellow-cedar produced equal but significantly higher ethanol in about twice the amounts than the other three species that showed no differences. After an extended 14 days of anoxia, Atlantic white-cedar ethanol yields remained significantly higher, at about 2 to 3 times the other species, while incense-cedar produced the lowest quantities. Yellow, western red, and Port-Orford-cedar had intermediate ethanol yields, but only yellow-cedar was significantly higher than incense-cedar by about 1.6 times. In general, root incubation temperature affected all species' ethanol synthesis similarly. Anoxic root ethanol production did not correlate with the cedars vulnerability to *P. lateralis.*

Anaerobic tolerance for all five cedars in this study has been estimated in the USDA PLANTS database, with Atlantic white-cedar rated high, yellow-cedar low, and the other three species as none. Ethanol synthesis is essential for roots to survive anoxia, but the quantities produced over time are not always a reliable indicator of a species tolerance to anoxic stress, as there are many contributing factors. However, the quantities of ethanol synthesized by detached roots over 14 days seems to align with the species associations with wet, mesic habitats and their likelihood of experiencing anaerobic stress from flooding. This suggests their ranking for anaerobic tolerance would be Atlantic white-cedar high, yellow, western red, and Port-Orford-cedar low to possibly moderate, and incense-cedar as none.

[1] USDA Forest Service, Pacific Northwest Research Station, 3200 Jefferson Way, Corvallis, OR, 97331, USA

[2] ATREE, 659, 5th A Main Rd, Hebbal, Bangalore 560024, India

[3] Oregon Department of Forestry, Salem, OR, 97310 USA, rkelsey@fs.fed.us.

CHARACTERIZATION AND BIOCIDAL ACTIVITY OF SOME YELLOW-CEDAR HEARTWOOD COMPOUNDS

Joe Karchesy[1], Rick Kelsey[2], Daniel Manter[3], Marc Dolan[4], Nick Panella[4], Javier Peralta-Cruz[5], Mohammad Khasawneh[1], Yeping Xiong[1]

ABSTRACT

The essential oil from yellow-cedar heartwood and its constituent compounds were investigated for their ability to control arthropods of public health concern and forest microbial pathogens. Comparisons were made for the activities of the essential oil, isolated compounds, and derivatives against mosquitoes (*Aedes aegypti*), ticks (*Ixodes scapularis*), fleas (*Xenopsylla cheopis*), and the microbe responsible for Sudden Oak Death (*Phytophthora ramorum*).

Laboratory bioassays showed that nootkatin and carvacrol are strong inhibitors of *P. ramorum* zoospore and sporangia germination and hyphal growth. Zoospore germination was reduced to 0% with 10 ppm of nootkatin, or 100 ppm carvacrol. Nootkatin instantaneously destroys the membrane surrounding zoospores and sporangia, but not the hyphae.

Biocidal assays against arthropods showed that nootkatone, valencene-13-ol, and carvacrol were the most effective, while nootkatin was not effective. Nootkatone was the most effective against ticks (LC_{50} = 0.0029%) and valencene-13-ol the most effective against mosquitoes (LC_{50} = 0.0024%). Carvacrol showed activity against ticks, fleas, and mosquitoes with LC_{50} values after 24 hours at concentrations of 0.0068, 0.0059, and 0.0051% (wt:vol), respectively. Residual activities were good for nootkatone and valencene-13-ol for up to four weeks. Repellency of yellow-cedar compounds against ticks compared to DEET showed that nootkatone and valencene-13-ol had repellent concentration (RC_{50}) values of 0.0458 and 0.0712% (wt:vol), respectively, compared to DEET (RC_{50} = 0.0728%).

[1] College of Forestry, Oregon State University, Corvallis, OR, 97331

[2] USDA, Pacific Northwest Research Station, Corvallis, OR 97330

[3] USDA, Agriculture Research Service, Fort Collins, CO 80526

[4] Centers for Disease Control and Prevention, Division of Vector-Borne Infectious Diseases, Ft. Collins, CO 80521

[5] Escuela Nacional de Ciencias Biologicas, Department of Organic Chemistry, Instituto Politecnico Nacional, 11340 D.F, Mexico

VITALITY AND DEFENSE MECHANISMS IN BARK-STRIPPED CEDAR TREES

Paul E. Hennon[1] and Nancy Turner[2]

ABSTRACT

Native people of the Pacific Northwest Coast collect the bark from live Western redcedar (*Thuja plicata*) and yellow-cedar (*Chamaecyparis nootkatensis*) that results in large bole injuries. How do these culturally modified cedar trees appear so healthy, and live so long, after injury? This poster reviews studies on heartwood chemistry, deterioration in dead trees, and bole injuries caused by brown bears to propose a scenario that explains how static and active mechanisms in cedar trees compartmentalize wood decay and allows bark-stripped trees to survive for centuries.

Cedars have defenses that are both passive (existing heartwood) and active responses (production of suberized layers, heartwood compounds in live sapwood, and callus growth. Many culturally modified trees are found on productive soils because this is where people find large trees free of lower branches. The long term viability of culturally modified trees may be explained by several defense mechanisms of trees growing on favorable sites…and the practice of never removing bark on too much of the tree's circumference.

[1] Pacific Northwest Research Station, Juneau, Alaska, USA, phennon@fs.fed.us
[2] University of Victoria, Victoria, British Columbia, Canada

THE NATURAL RANGE OF YELLOW-CEDAR:
A PHOTOGRAPHIC TOUR OF DIVERSE LOCATIONS

Marshall D. Murray[1]

The natural range of yellow-cedar (*Callitropsis nootkatensis*) is along the Pacific Coast from northern California to Prince William Sound, Alaska. Within this range yellow-cedar occurs from sea level to 2300 m elevation. Yellow-cedar is not ubiquitous throughout its total range and is absent from many areas where the habitat is suitable for this species. Yellow-cedar occasionally grows in pure stands but is usually found singly or in scattered groups mixed with other conifers. The purpose of this study was to locate and photograph yellow-cedar growing on diverse habitats throughout a subset of its natural range from northern California to southern British Columbia. Potential locations of yellow-cedar were found from range maps, hiking guides, personal observation and other reports. Yellow-cedar was found and photographed by using roads, hiking trails and by "bush whacking." Photographs were taken at a total of 264 locations. This report shows a representative sample of 38 locations. Photographs illustrate the variation in stem and stand structure at locations from Memekay River, British Columbia to Elk Hole, California (the southern-most known occurrence of this species). The yellow-cedar trees photographed vary in size from krummholz to a tree 418 cm in diameter. The photographs show trees growing on bogs, shallow acidic soils, well-drained soils, rocky ridges, talus and along lake margins. Elevations ranged from near sea level to 1850 m. Four locations are east of the crest of the Cascade Mountains, Washington, with one location 35 km east of the crest. Yellow-cedar growing within this wide geographic and elevational range has value for ecological as well as genetic and seed source studies. Locations of these stands (Table 1) are being documented to share with other researchers.

KEYWORDS: Yellow-cedar, range, habitat, ecology, soils, British Columbia, Washington, Oregon, California.

REFERENCES
Burns, R.M.; Honkala, B.H. 1990. Silvics of North America. Vol. 1, conifers. Agri. Handbook 654. USDA Forest Service, Washington, DC. 675 p.

Griffin, J.R.; Critchfield, W.B. The distribution of forest trees in California. Res.Paper PSW-82/1972. Berkeley, CA: USDA Forest Service, Pac. SW For. & Range Exp. Stn. 114 p.

ACKNOWLEDGEMENTS
Many thanks to Joe Kraft for his assistance with the map and photographs and to Connie Harrington for her unwavering support.

[1] Marshall D. Murray is a volunteer forester, Pacific Northwest Research Station, Olympia WA.. Murray can be contacted at: 3689 Cooks Hill Road, Centralia, WA 98531-9011. Email: skookum@localaccess.com

Table 1 -- Photo locations for yellow-cedar stands sampled in British Columbia, Washington, Oregon and northern California. Numbers under Site name correspond to numbers on the photos in Fig. 1 and the map in Fig. 2.

Site name	Lat. (N)	Long. (W)	Elev (m)
1 - Bog forest, Pacific Rim National Park, BC	49.0200	125.6200	30
2 - Memekay River, BC	50.0852	125.8627	1100
3 - Cypress Provincial Park, BC	49.3900	123.1900	880
4 - Mount Bolduc, BC	48.7130	124.3000	1120
5 - Forbidden Plateau, BC	49.7000	125.3000	1080
6 - Near Mt. Stickney, Mt. Baker-Snoqualmie NF	47.8980	121.6050	1200
7 - Goat Creek, Goat Rocks Wilderness, Gifford Pinchot NF	46.4820	121.4850	1460
8 - Miners Ridge, Wenatchee NF[1]	46.9680	121.3470	1580
9 - Near Silver Star Mountain, Gifford Pinchot NF	45.7470	122.2000	1110
10 - Ipsut Creek, Mt. Rainier NP	46.9633	121.8374	1010
11 - Duck Lake, Mt. Baker-Snoqualmie NF	46.6630	122.3300	970
12 - Rat Trap Pass, Mt. Baker-Snoqualmie NF	48.2030	121.3750	1050
13 - Canyon Lake Community Forest, Whatcom County, WA	48.8220	122.0290	1320
14 - Burnt Mountain, Wenatchee NF[1]	46.7130	121.1790	1850
15 - White Pass, Highway 12, WA	46.6470	121.3850	1370
16 - Ridge above Kettle Lake, Wenatchee NF[1]	46.8800	121.3330	1850
17 - Goat Creek, Mt. St. Helens National Volcanic Monument	46.4000	122.1350	1140
18 - Windy Point, WA[1]	46.7035	120.9000	600
19 - Owyhigh Lakes, Mt. Rainier NP	46.8673	121.5822	1580
20 - Granite Creek, North Cascades Highway, WA	48.5640	120.7760	1170
21 - Echo Basin, Willamette NF	44.4130	122.0960	1380
22 - Middle Pyramid, Willamette NF	44.4960	122.0760	1710
23 - Thorn Mountain, Umpqua NF	43.3540	122.4150	1430
24 - Twin Lakes, Umpqua NF	43.2300	122.5920	1540
25 - Pansy Lake, Bull of the Woods Wilderness, Mt. Hood NF	44.8900	122.1110	1210
26 - Moss Mountain, Willamette NF	43.5780	122.2600	1690
27 - Opal Lake, Opal Creek Wilderness, Mt. Hood NF	44.7920	122.2200	1030
28 - Pup Prairie, Rogue-Umpqua Divide Wild., Umpqua NF	43.0330	122.4700	1650
29 - Elk Hole, Klamath NF	41.6083	123.7083	1530
30 - Frog Pond, Red Buttes Wilderness, Rogue River NF	41.9800	122.2600	1520
31 - Mink Lake, Olympic NP	47.9474	123.8633	910
32 - Near Wagonwheel Lake, Olympic NP	47.5293	123.3000	1160
33 - Matheny Ponds, Olympic NF	47.5640	123.8580	850
34 - Buckhorn Mountain, Buckhorn Wilderness, Olympic NF	47.8260	123.0980	1550
35 - Three Peaks, Olympic NF	47.4940	123.5600	960
36 - Big Creek Meadows, Olympic NP	47.6016	123.7133	880
37 - Mt. Angeles, Olympic NP	47.9945	123.4583	1800
38 - Royal Creek, Olympic NP	47.8540	123.2160	1430

[1] -- East of the Cascade Crest.

Figure 1 -- Photographs of yellow-cedar sites. Numbers correspond to those on Table 1 and Fig. 2.

Figure 2 -- Locations of yellow-cedar locations photographed for this study. Numbers correspond to those under "Site name" in Table 1 and on Fig. 1.

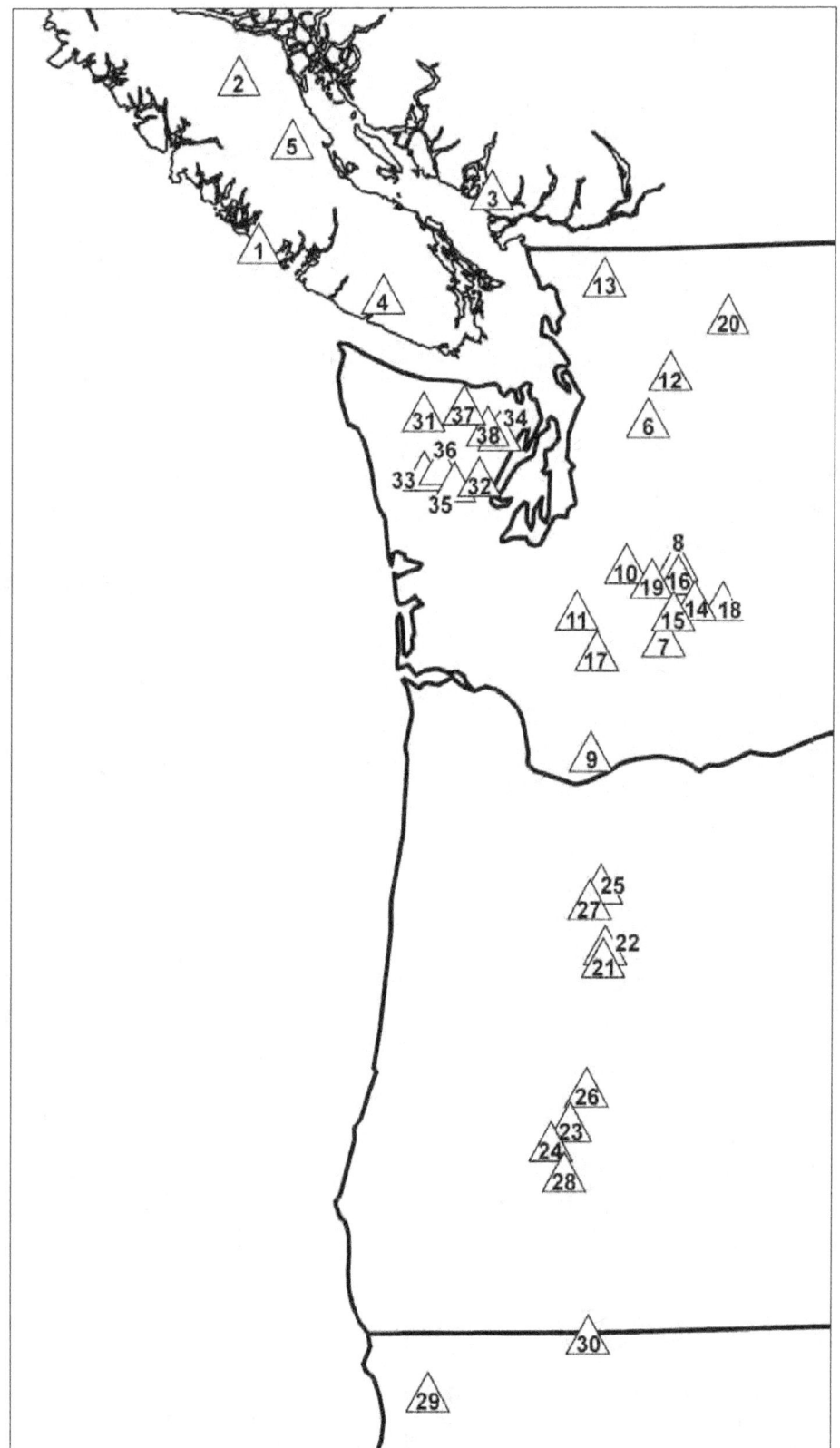

ANCIENT YELLOW-CEDAR GROVES IN THE OLYMPIC MOUNTAINS, WASHINGTON

Marshall D. Murray[1]

Yellow-cedar (*Callitropsis nootkatensis*) grows throughout the Olympic Mountains, Washington at elevations of 500-2200 m. Recent surveys have found ancient yellow-cedar in this area range in size from a 365-cm diameter giant to shrubby krummholz at timberline. Eight groves of ancient yellow-cedar have been found on the windward side of the Olympic Mountains at elevations of 800 to 1000 m where precipitation is high and fire frequency is low (Fig. 1). These groves have not burned for more than 1000 years and contain the oldest trees in Washington. Large yellow-cedar in the groves range in diameter at breast height from 150 to 365 cm. The actual age of the largest trees cannot be determined because of rotten centers and their large size. The 365-cm diameter tree, the largest yellow-cedar in the United States, has been estimated to be more than 2000 years old. Growth of these yellow-cedars is slow. Snow accumulation in the groves is often greater than 3 m per year and growth is affected by the short snow-free growing season. Large decadent trees continue to live and grow for a long time and paper-thin growth rings are common. A tree 180 cm in diameter had 922 annual growth rings on the outer 30 cm of its radius. Photographs from these ancient groves show the physical characteristics of the trees including large burls, rotten, hollow living trees, standing dead hollow trees, and dead trees that fall to the ground and leave a 3 to 5 m high hollow stump. The groves are accessible by road or trail, but most of the groves are not well known. Some visitors may not realize the significance of the large, old yellow-cedar or perhaps mistake them for western redcedar (*Thuja plicata*). The groves have a mystic aura of great antiquity and have important scientific and recreational value. This paper includes geographic coordinates for the eight major groves known to the author.

KEYWORDS: Yellow-cedar, old-growth, ancient groves, Olympic Mountains, Washington.

REFERENCES

Henderson, J.A.; Peter, D.H.; Lesher, R.D.; Shaw, D.C. 1989. Forested plant associations of the Olympic National Forest. R6 Ecol Tech. Paper 001-88. USDA Forest Service, Pac. NW Region. 502 p.

Van Pelt, R. 2001. Forest giants of the Pacific Coast. Univ. Wash. Press, Seattle, WA 191 p.

ACKNOWLEDGEMENTS

Many thanks to Joe Kraft for his assistance with the map and photographs and to Connie Harrington for her unwavering support.

[1] Marshall D. Murray is a volunteer forester, Pacific Northwest Research Station, Olympia, WA. He can be contacted at: 3689 Cooks Hill Road, Centralia, WA 98531-9011 email: skookum@localaccess.com

Table 1 -- Locations of ancient yellow-cedar stands visited on the Olympic Peninsula, Washington.

Site name	Lat. (N)	Long. (W)	Elev. (m)
Pine Mountain, Olympic NP	47.946	123.971	1000
3 - Lakes, Olympic NP	47.604	123.729	970
Big Creek Meadows, Olympic NP	47.602	123.692	800
3 - Peaks, Olympic NF	47.492	123.548	960
West Fork Humptulips River, Olympic NF	47.479	123.629	820
Quinault Ridge, Olympic NF	47.475	123.750	910
Matheny Ridge, Olympic NF	47.579	123.833	880
Matheny Ponds, Olympic NF	47.564	123.858	850

3 - Lakes

Figure 1 -- Photographs of trees & locations of ancient yellow-cedar groves in the Olympic Mountains, WA.

Pine Mountain

Big Creek Meadows

Matheny Ridge

3 - Peaks

Matheny Ponds

Quinault Ridge

W. Fork Humptulips R.

GENE RESOURCE MANAGEMENT FOR WESTERN REDCEDAR AND YELLOW-CEDAR

John Russell[1] and Jodie Krakowski[1]

ABSTRACT

Conservation and management of tree populations in BC is based on the assumption of local adaptation, which is tested using long-term genecological research such as provenance and progeny trials. Since the climate at a given site is expected to change faster than the rate of population migration via seed and pollen, we need more proactive management and conservation to ensure adequate conservation of the genetic capacity to adapt to environmental stresses, provide ecosystem services, and withstand pests and diseases.

BREEDING AND DEPLOYMENT FOR WESTERN REDCEDAR DEER RESISTANCE

John Russell[1] and Jodie Krakowski[1]

ABSTRACT

Ungulate browse damage to redcedar seedlings costs approximately \$20-25 million in BC per year, at \$5-6/tree to reach free-to-grow status. Browse damage levels were found to be directly related to foliar monoterpene concentrations which have high heritability. These naturally occurring chemicals increase as seedlings age. Western redcedar is unique since it can have a generation time as short as 2 years, and also is easy to successfully root cuttings, which allows for clonal testing and deployment, as well as deployment of material from older plants that cuttings can be taken from. Western redcedar shows no trade-off between high monoterpenes and height growth. Field trials in BC rely on natural deer populations to access a planted trial, and may be affected by adjacent stand composition and the design of the experiment in terms of the deer feeding behaviour. An important component of these ongoing studies is to determine how best to deploy resistant material. Planting 100% resistant redcedar stock would effectively force deer to forage on that, since no alternative food source is available, possibly applying selection pressure to the deer to overcome their aversion to high terpene concentrations. Studies are currently underway to determine appropriate levels and spatial distribution for deploying resistant redcedar while meeting stocking standards and other key objectives.

[1] Cowichan Lake Research Station, BC Ministry of Forests, P.O. Box 335 Mesachie Lake, BC, Canada, V0R 2N0

WESTERN REDCEDAR *(THUJA PLICATA)* ADVANCED REGENERATION RESPONSE TO VARIABLE RETENTION HARVESTING IN SOUTHWEST WASHINGTON

Florian Deisenhofer[1]

ABSTRACT

Western redcedar *(Thuja plicata)* is a disease resistant, valuable conifer species in the Pacific Northwest desirable for reforestation. In Southwest Washington many landowners are not planting western redcedar due to heavy ungulate browse. Using advanced regeneration of western redcedar may be a viable method of integrating this species into plantations at little cost, while adding economic value, diversity, habitat structure, disease resistance and resilience.

The response of twenty eight western redcedar mid- and understory trees, ranging in diameter from 12 to 38 cm and relatively free of logging damage on a site infected by *Phellinus weirii*, was studied after a variable retention harvest (20 trees per hectare, mostly scattered) in 2003. Trees selected for the study averaged 22 cm at DBH, 15 m in height with an average height-to-diameter ratio of 66 and an average live crown ratio of 73%.

Within three years of harvest three of the 28 trees selected for the study died. All three trees had above average height-to-diameter ratios; two of the three trees had the greatest height-to-diameter ratios observed, 94 and 107 respectively. Over the six observed growing seasons post-release, average diameter growth has been accelerating from 1cm per year in 2004 to 2 cm per year in 2009. Average diameter increased from 22 cm at breast height to 31 cm over the six year period with trees in excess of 75% live crown responding the most. Height growth in contrast has been slow with no measurable response in the first 3 post-release growing seasons and an average height growth response of 26 cm per year over the last 3 years. Average height-to-diameter ratios have decreased at an annual rate of 2.7.

Advanced regeneration of western redcedar with little or no logging damage responded well to release following variable retention harvesting. Diameter growth response was greater than height growth response thus reducing height-to-diameter ratios. Trees with initial height-to-diameter ratios of less than 80, live crown ratios greater than 75% and free of logging damage are most likely to respond well.

[1] Washington Dept. of Natural Resources, 601 Bond RD, Castle Rock, WA 98611, Florian.Deisenhofer@dnr.wa.gov

SIX-YEAR WESTERN REDCEDAR *(THUJA PLICATA)* HEIGHT GROWTH PERFORMANCE IN SOUTHWEST WASHINGTON

Florian Deisenhofer[1] and Chris Rasor[1]

ABSTRACT

Disease resistance, shade tolerance, and high economic and wildlife value make western redcedar *(Thuja plicata)* a desirable component of commercial forests in Southwest Washington. Due to heavy ungulate browse, achieving survival and tree heights above browse level (1.4 m) are major reforestation challenges. We studied the effects of two repellents, Plantskydd® and Deer Away Big Game Repellent® (BGR), applied to seedlings at the nursery on tree survival and subsequent six year height growth.

In 2003 five sites in southwest Washington were planted with adjacent 10-tree rows of Plantskydd, BGR and a control replicated five times at each site for a total of 150 trees per site. Both repellents kept browse levels low during the first growing season. Treated trees were on average 2-3 cm taller (5-7 cm more growth) than the control. Half of the repellent-treated trees were retreated with BGR in early December after the first growing season. After six growing seasons, there are no significant differences in survival with 80 to 83% of the trees still alive. Trees treated two times with repellents are significantly larger (73 cm) than trees treated once or the control (both 67 cm). Only 2.5% of all surviving trees have reached or exceeded 1.4 m in height and 14% are between 1 and 1.4 m. 22% of all surviving trees are shorter after six growing seasons than when they were planted.

Three of the sites were chemically site prepared before planting. Regardless of treatment, trees planted on sites with chemical site preparation had higher survival (85% versus 77%), were significantly taller (71 cm versus 64 cm) and had a higher percentage of trees exceeding 1.4 m (3.7% versus 0.9%) than non-treated sites.

Planting western redcedar without physical protection in southwest Washington will cause substantial reforestation delays. Management of competing vegetation and the repeated application of repellents significantly improve western redcedar growth. A combination of site preparation, physical protection or repeated application of repellants will most likely be required for success.

---

[1] Washington Dept. of Natural Resources, 601 Bond RD, Castle Rock, WA 98611,
Florian.Deisenhofer@dnr.wa.gov

WESTERN REDCEDAR DEER BROWSE RESISTANCE WORKSHOP
COWICHAN LAKE RESEARCH STATION
WEDNESDAY, JUNE 2ND, 2010

A post meeting satellite workshop on western redcedar deer browse resistance was offered at Cowichan Lake Research Station. The workshop involved presentations and field trips describing the current breeding program and deployment studies that have been ongoing for the last few years. The workshop was attended by over 50 people from Oregon, Washington and British Columbia including nursery growers, seed orchard managers, foresters and research scientists. At the end of the meeting the purpose, structure and function of a cooperative effort to deploy deer resistance material in operational trials across the landscape was discussed. The following two presentations describe the western redcedar deer browse resistant breeding program and a summary of deployment trials accomplished to-date.

WESTERN REDCEDAR BROWSE RESISTANCE BREEDING AND DEPLOYMENT MATERIAL

John H. Russell and Daniel C. Ferguson[1]

ABSTRACT

This presentation reviews progress of the British Columbia Ministry of Forests and Range deer browse resistant breeding program. Tremendous progress has been made in a short period of time selecting for foliar monoterpenes. We are currently in the third generation of breeding and testing. In addition, selected phenotypes have been bulked up through controlled crossing and vegetative propagation for future operational deployment trials.

INTRODUCTION

A breeding program for deer browse resistance was initiated mid-2000 after preliminary studies showed a linkage between foliar phytochemistry and deer preference, high genetic variation and heritabilities in these secondary chemicals that influence deer browsing, and the potential for an efficient and economically viable delivery program. The program has made tremendous progress in breeding and developing deployment material due to high selection efficiency and heritabilities, fast generation turnover, early seedling evaluation, ability to propagate vegetatively, and solid financial and institutional support. This report summarizes the progress to date for the western redcedar deer resistance breeding program.

FIRST GENERATION SELECTIONS

Initial observations at a southern Vancouver Island provenance trial at Holt Creek showed a causal relationship between deer browse preference and needle phytochemistry; high monoterpene trees were less likely to be browsed. We measured needle monoterpenes, browse severity and height on 2200 7-year-old trees at the Holt Creek provenance trial (60 open-pollinated families from 14 BC range-wide populations) and multiple copies from 1000 range-wide parent trees at Cowichan Lake research Station. Individual western redcedar monoterpenes had high additive genetic

variations (21.2% to 30.7%) and narrow sense heritabilities (0.33 to 0.57). The genetic correlation between needle monoterpenes and height growth was 0.1.

Selections were made from both sites for two populations: 1) preferred (30 selections: total monoterpenes less than 20,000 ppm) and 2) not preferred (120 selections: total monoterpenes greater than 30,000 ppm). Scions were taken for grafting from all selected trees. In addition, cuttings from the 7-year-old Holt Creek trees were rooted and subsequent rooted cuttings used for deployment trials at Olympia, WA and in the field on southern Vancouver Island.

SECOND GENERATION BREEDING

Selected parents were crossed in partial diallels including selfs (there is minimal inbreeding depression in western redcedar – even from self-fertilization), both on grafted selections in greenhouses at CLRS, as well as in the field, to help speed up the breeding process. Seed from the over 300 families was sown in 3 series across five years. Foliage samples were taken for monoterpene analysis at the end of the first growing season. Selections were subsequently made for both preferred (<10,000 ppm total monoterpenes) and not-preferred (>65,000 ppm total monoterpenes) populations. Figure 1 illustrates the frequency of individuals for total monoterpene classes from the first and second generation populations, as well as the not-preferred selections from each generation. Note

[1]Cowichan Lake Research Station, Ministry of Forests and Range, Box 335, Mesachie Lake, BC V0R 2N0. John.Russell@gov.bc.ca

the high number of trees with foliar concentrations greater than the maximum class from the first generation. Vegetative material from the second generation selections was grafted for future breeding.

THIRD GENERATION BREEDING
Limited third generation breeding has been undertaken. However, further breeding may not be necessary depending on results from deployment trials. It may be more important to integrate other correlated fitness traits including heartwood durability, growth, and cedar leaf blight resistance into the breeding population (Fig. 2).

MATERIAL FOR DEPLOYMENT TRIALS AND OPERATIONAL PLANTINGS
There are currently two populations available for operational deployment testing and eventual reforestation: preferred and not-preferred, both selected from the second generation populations. Vegetative material from second generation one-year-old select seedlings was grafted for seed production and rooted for clonal production.

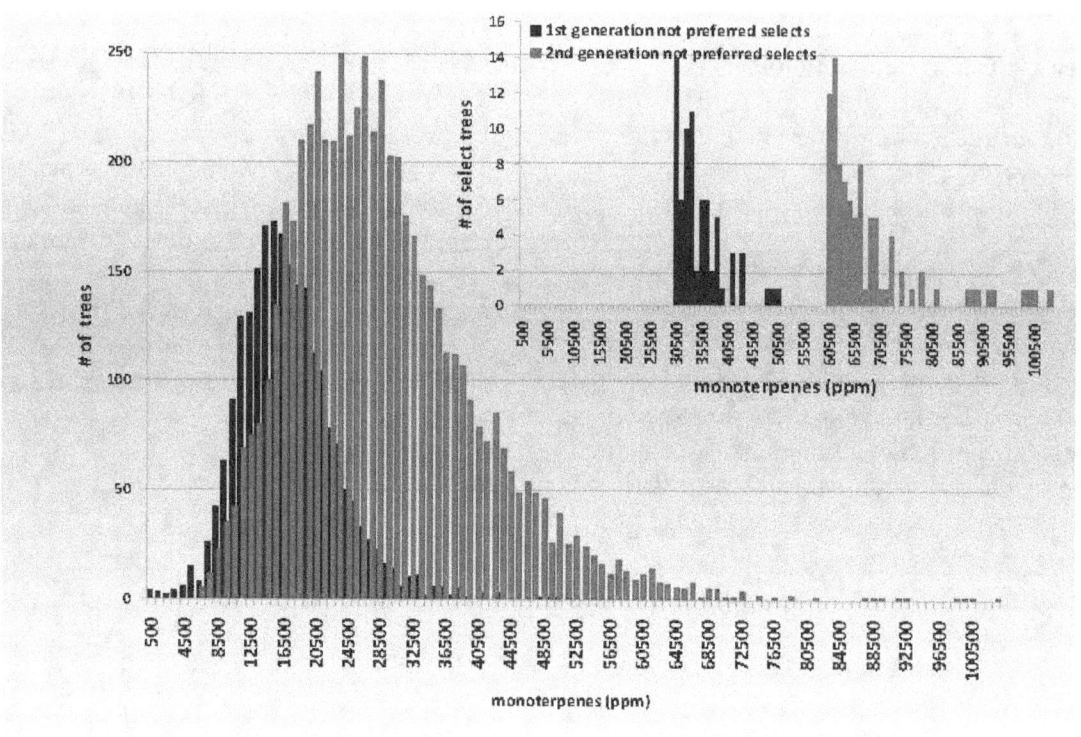

Figure 1 -- Foliage monoterpene classes and frequency of first (blue) and second (red) generation individuals from the main population and the select not preferred population.

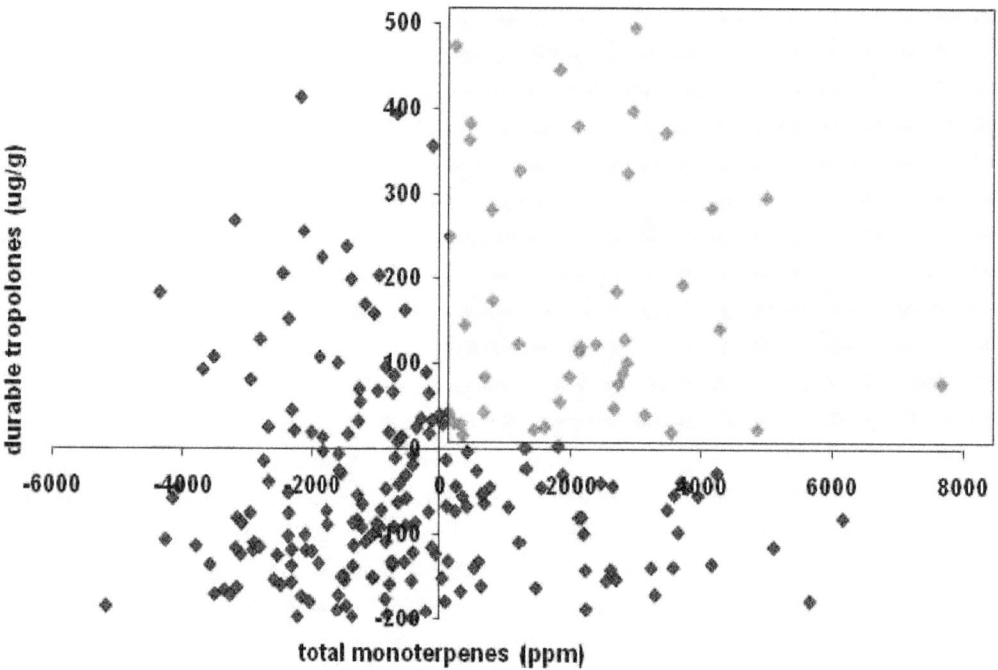

Figure 2 -- Relationship between individual tree heartwood extractive effects (BLUPs) and total foliar monoterpene effects (BLUPs) from CLRS western redcedar parent trees. Shaded box indicates potential future selections for developing durable breeds.

SUMMARY OF WESTERN REDCEDAR BROWSE RESISTANCE RESEARCH

John Russell[1] and Bruce Kimball[2]

ABSTRACT

This presentation reviews browse resistant field trials that have been conducted to measure deer responses to experimental manipulations of western redcedar foliar chemistry. Selective breeding was employed to produce planting stock of seedlings and cuttings with varying levels of monoterpenes. These studies examined black-tailed deer preferences among individual seedlings, how deployment of "browse resistant" seedlings influenced deer browsing behavior and the relative impacts of monoterpene content and tree maturation. Implications for future research and operational deployment of deer resistant material are discussed.

INTRODUCTION

Deer browsing has a detrimental effect on productivity in managed plantations. Diversity may decrease when certain seedling characteristics are specifically targeted by foraging deer. Previous studies have suggested that much of the variability observed in deer preferences for individual conifer seedlings can be attributed to the phytochemical content of the plant tissues. Beginning in 2006, the USDA-APHIS-WS National Wildlife Research Center and British Columbia Ministry of Forests and Range jointly conducted a series of studies to measure deer responses to experimental manipulations of western redcedar foliar chemistry. Selective breeding was employed to produce seedlings (and cuttings) with varying levels of monoterpenes. These studies examined deer preferences among individual seedlings (tree selection) and also evaluated how deployment of "browse resistant" (not-preferred) seedlings influenced deer browsing behavior (plot selection) and assessed the relative impacts of monoterpene content and tree maturation (ontogeny).

METHODS

Plant experimental material

Individual trees were selected from a 7-year-old *Thuja plicata* open-pollinated provenance trial with family structure established at Holt Creek, southern Vancouver Island, British Columbia (48° 45' N, 123° 53' W, elev. 212m). Selections were included from three browse potential categories based on foliar needle monoterpene and deer browse intensity observed in the provenance trial: not preferred (no browse and high monoterpene content), preferred (high browse and low monoterpene content), and intermediate (low browse and average monoterpene content). Selected trees were then cloned through propagation by cuttings and selfed/outcrossed using controlled crossing techniques. For trials using rooted cuttings, cuttings were taken from serial propagated clonal donors established from the original cuttings and for seedling trials. For seedlings, seed was sown from either selfed or full-sib families. Both rooted cuttings and seedlings were grown in greenhouses according to standard nursery protocol. The resultant one-year-old rooted cuttings and seedlings of various ages were used for all subsequent experiments.

Trials

There were three studies as follows:
Tree selection. Multiple clones varying in foliar monoterpene concentrations were planted at two locations: USDA-APHIS-WS National Wildlife Research Olympia Field Station using penned

[1]Cowichan Lake Research Station, Ministry of Forests and Range, Box 335, Mesachie Lake, BC V0R 2N0. John.Russell@gov.bc.ca

deer and a field plot at Fairservice, south Vancouver Island.

Plot Selection. Various percentages of not preferred seedlings and cuttings (33%, 66% and 100%) were planted in large plots with preferred material at the Olympia Field Station.

Ontogeny. Preferred and not preferred rooted cuttings and seedlings were outplanted together at the Fairservice field trial. At the Olympia Field Station, 1-, 2- and 3-year-old preferred and not preferred seedlings were outplanted in 16 tree plots.

RESULTS

Tree selection

Browse damage varied significantly among three redcedar browse categories (preferred, intermediate, and not-preferred) that varied by monoterpene content. Similar damage observations were made in field and pen trials. Among the spatial parameters assessed, trees were more likely to be browsed in discreet areas where many surviving trees were available. Further, individuals near many not-preferred trees were very likely to be browsed themselves.

Plot selection

Data from the initial experiments demonstrated that when deer are browsing in a patch, phytochemical content and spatial variables directly influence which individual trees are browsed. However, these data provide no information regarding factors that influence which patches are selected for browsing. When deer were required to select from distinct plots varying in distribution of not-preferred trees (33%, 66%, or 100%), browse damage decreased with increasing percentage of not-preferred seedlings: 33% > 66% > 100%. Within plots, deer did not eat higher proportions of preferred seedlings than expected by chance encounter – indicating that deer do not simply eat all the preferred trees in each plot, and then move on to the next (Fig. 1).

Ontogeny

Seedlings from both preferred and not preferred groups were significantly browsed more than

rooted cuttings from either monoterpene group at the Fairservice field trial (Figure 2). The greatest browse resistance was observed in two- and three-year-old seedlings with high monoterpene content in the penned deer trials at Olympia Field Station. Although not explicitly evaluated in the plot selection trial, a dramatic decrease in deer browsing was observed when cuttings were employed (versus seedlings). These results suggest that chemical or physical characteristics of redcedar trees in addition to monoterpenes may dramatically influence deer foraging behavior. Results of field and pen studies indicate that both plant tissue development (ontogeny) and monoterpene concentration contribute toward reduced browsing by black-tailed deer.

IMPLICATIONS

Phytochemical content of individual seedlings directly influences palatability and the likelihood of being browsed. However, once a patch has been selected, the presence of highly defended individuals may not confer significant browse protection to other seedlings in the patch. Deployment options should focus on aspects which influence patch selection. Among-plot foraging behaviour observed in plot selection experiments suggests that increasing the distribution of high monoterpene-containing trees is desirable to promote patch avoidance. Thus, a management strategy should incorporate greater than 66%, but less than 100%, high monoterpene trees at a given location. Our results further indicate that a promising strategy for reducing browse damage to redcedar seedlings in reforestation operations should include both breeding for higher monoterpene defenses and exploiting tree maturation in the nursery. Ultimately, successful deployment of browse resistant redcedar requires further study. Among the questions left unanswered are: 1) importance of different age distributions, 2) critical spacing and plot sizes, and 3) importance of species diversity.

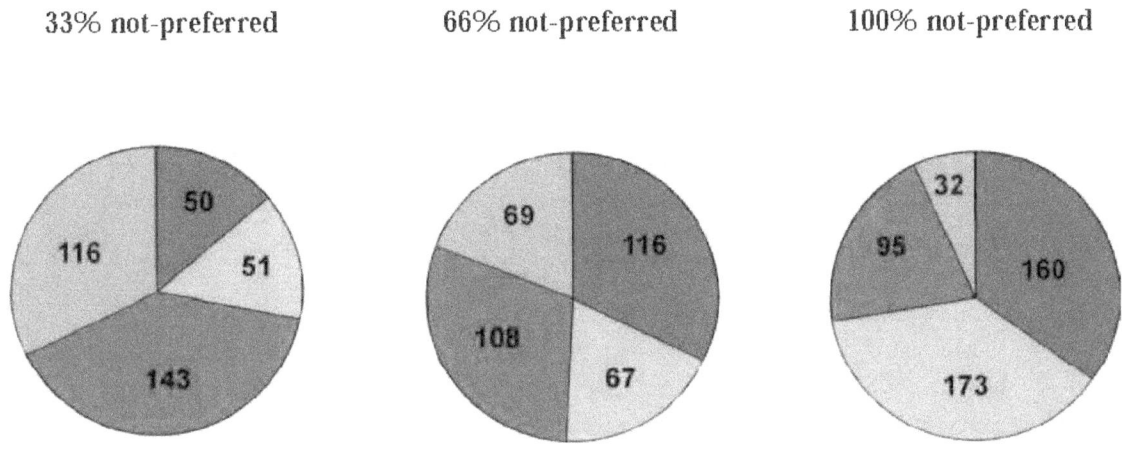

Figure 1 -- Number of trees receiving no damage (blue), minor damage (light blue), significant damage (green), or complete loss (light green) in 3 plot mixtures of preferred and not preferred seedlings.

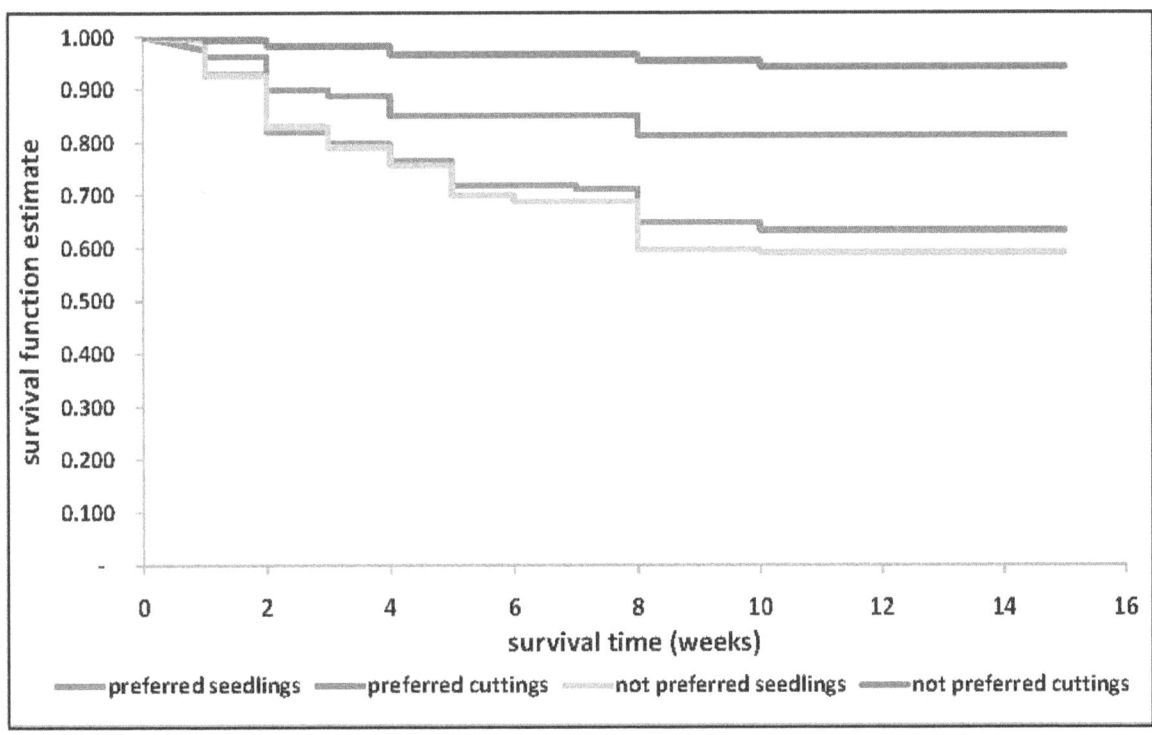

Figure 2 -- Survivability curves of 1-year-old seedlings and rooted cuttings with both stocktypes categorized as having high or low monoterpene content.

FIELD TRIP 1 – MAY 25: CAPITAL REGIONAL DISTRICT WATERSHED

Don Herriott[1]

The public is not permitted access to the watershed, except on guided scheduled tours. Access restrictions and careful stewardship has preserved unique pockets of pristine old-growth right in the backyard of Victoria. Forest harvesting ceased in the watershed in the 1990s. The focus has shifted to water quality, ecosystem restoration, forest health, and fire hazard abatement.

Stop 1: Old-growth forest in the dry maritime coastal forest

Old-growth western redcedar (Cw) stands like this are extremely rare so near to an urban centre and represent some very unique intact old growth remnants of Coastal Douglas-fir and very dry Coastal Western Hemlock forests. This forest contains Douglas-fir (Fdc) and Cw with some western hemlock (Hw). Average age is estimated under 250, but there are many older veterans. Heights average 60-64 m, with a site index (bh age 50) of 32 m.

Stop 2: Western redcedar used to mitigate *Phellinus weirii*

The original Fdc stand was harvested with mini tower and rubber tired skidder in 1993 using a variety of selection systems including strip shelterwood (60-200 residual stems per ha), group selection (in root rot pockets), and single stem selection. It was fall planted in 1994 and 1995, with Cw and western white pine (Pw) in the root rot pockets. Planting stock was: Fdc 1+1, Cw 1+2, Cw 1+1 bareroot, Pw 2+0 styroblock, and Pw 3 year old stock in 6" pots. Since planting, the area experienced windthrow in 1995, 1996 and 1999 and periodically since then.

---

[1] Senior Supervisor, Watershed Operations, CRD Integrated Water Services, Watershed Protection

FIELD TRIP 2 - MAY 27: JORDAN RIVER WESTERN FOREST PRODUCTS LANDS

Annette Van Niejenhuis[1]

Western Forest Products Ltd. (WFP) holds harvesting rights to 3.1 million hectares of Crown land on the BC coast under a variety of renewable forest tenures granted by the provincial government. These tenures allow the sustainable harvest of approximately 7.5 million cubic metres of high quality first- and second-growth logs each year. WFP also holds 30,000 hectares of private lands. The main species harvested are western hemlock and Pacific silver fir (Hem-Fir), western redcedar, Douglas-fir and Sitka spruce.

Principal activities conducted by WFP include timber harvesting, reforestation, sawmilling logs into lumber and wood chips, and value-added remanufacturing. WFP's operations, employees and corporate facilities are located in coastal BC, while its products are sold in more than 20 countries worldwide. The company has a lumber capacity in excess of 1.5 billion board feet produced from 8 sawmills and 4 remanufacturing plants.

Our Timberland Operations staff manage the company's forestry program from initial inventories, assessments and plans, through road building and harvesting, to reforestation and second-growth stand management. Company and contract crews carry out these activities at more than 30 locations.

All timberland activities are governed by an Environmental Management System registered to ISO 14001 standards. The majority of WFP's harvested volume is also certified to CSA standards as coming from sustainably managed forests. Both ISO registration and CSA certification are verified annually through a program of internal and independent third-party audits.

WFP plants approximately 8 million trees each year, with a third of these grown at WFP's nursery near Victoria and the balance contracted out to other private nurseries. Of these, 2.5 million are western redcedar, and 0.7 million are yellow-cedar.

Jordan River Operations occur on Tree Farm License (TFL) 25, Block 1, and associated private lands on the southwest coast of Vancouver Island. It has a total area of 32,200 ha of which 30,477 ha are productive forest and a Timber Harvest Land Base (THLB) area of 25,562 ha comprised of 16,754 ha of Crown land and 8,808 ha of privately owned land. These Operations extend from sea level to the height of land on Loss and San Juan Ridges. This area has been managed as a separate, sustained yield unit within the TFL since its inception in 1958. The original TFL 25 was granted to a WFP predecessor company, Alaska Pine and Cellulose, on May 21, 1958.

Recently, the Capital Regional District (CRD) has entered into agreement to purchase three parcels of the private lands (2,350 ha) previously managed by Jordan River Operations. These include the lands adjacent to the Sooke Potholes Regional Park, the lands adjacent to the CRD water supply, and the shorefront properties from Jordan River to Sandcut Beach. Additional parcels of these private lands remain on the real estate market.

---

[1] FIA Coordinator, Western Forest Products Inc., 118-1334 Island Highway, Campbell River, BC V9W 8C9, Canada

Stop 1: Yellow-cedar and western redcedar provenance trials

Populations from the entire range of both species were planted on multiple sites throughout each species' range in British Columbia. Regional population differentiation can be observed for both species. Adaptability, productivity and health information from these studies has been used to develop breeding zones and operational seed transfers for current and future climates.

There are four provenance trials in Jordan River: two in this low elevation, productive site (150 m; Cwhxm1/01) and two at a high elevation, low productivity site (1000m; MHmm1/01). This yellow-cedar (Yc) provenance trial is 20 years old, and the western redcedar (Cw) trial is 18 years old.

The local populations of both Cw and Yc have low mortality and good height growth here, compared to other test sites around B.C. However, local populations are not always the best. California populations showed severe maladaptation for both species at all sites. Interior Cw populations did best at the high elevation site. Yc populations were better adapted (better survival, less mortality) at the high elevation site, but this low elevation site had better height growth on average than the nearby high elevation site.

Cedar leaf blight (CLB) incidence is high on Cw across the coastal low elevation region, allowing us to test for resistance. Although populations from the local region (south coast low elevation) were more resistant than average, the most resistant population was from the wet northern Coast-Interior transition. Local populations had the best survival and height at the low elevation site.

Stop 2a: Mature second growth forest of Douglas-fir, western redcedar, western hemlock, Sitka spruce in the transition between drier and wetter maritime habitats

This area is typical of the transition between the Coastal Western Hemlock very dry maritime western (CWHxm2) and the Coastal Western Hemlock very wet maritime submontane (CWHvm1) biogeoclimatic units. The site is characterized as CWHxm2/05(01), slightly richer than typical, with some zonal areas. This mature stand is approximately 70 years old with a site index of 32 (age 50). Thinning has occurred in these stands in the past.

Stop 2b: Mixed species plantings in the transition between drier and wetter maritime habitats

The Hw/Fdc/Sitka spruce (Ss)/Cw (65/25/5/5) forest was logged in 2002 and 2003, slashburned, and planted in 2004 with a mix of Fdc and Cw seedlots with improved growth, wildstand seedlots of grand fir (Bg) and Pacific silver fir (Ba), blister rust-resistant western white pine (Pw), and weevil-resistant Ss. Minor fill planting was done in 2005. Target stocking is 900 stems per ha. This nutrient-rich ecosystem has a site index of 32. Western hemlock (Hw) has regenerated naturally. There is a 1st-generation Cw progeny trial on the site that will yield information for improving the species' productivity, and a 1st generation Ss trial testing seedlings for white pine weevil resistance.

Stop 3: Western redcedar plantation on a nutrient-poor ecosystem

This ecosystem is classified as CWhvm1/01/06s, a nutrient- poor to -very poor "salal phase" which occurs in subdued terrain. The site index is 20. The original stand was harvested in 1990 and replanted in 1992 with 90% Cw and 10% Hw. It was declared free-growing in 2000 with no silvicultural inputs. Hw ingress is abundant.

Stop 4: Plantation including yellow-cedar and western hemlock on a poorly drained site

This nutrient-poor and poorly drained ecosystem, classified as CWhvm1 (T. Lewis series 04) has a site index of 16. It is dominated by species that indicate acidic soils such as salal, *Vaccinium membranaceum*, *V. ovalifolium*, and *V. parvifolium*. The original stand was harvested in 1995, replanted in 2 sections in 1996 with 70% Yc rooted cuttings and 30% Hw; and 100% Yc. It was declared free-growing in 2006 with no silvicultural inputs. There is substantial ingress of Pacific silver fir (Ba).

Stop 5: Old-growth yellow-cedar and western redcedar forest

This moderately productive old-growth forest is typical of montane coastal sites, with substantial snowpack, classified as CWHvm2/01(06). Major species include Yc, Cw, Ba, Hw, and mountain hemlock (Hm). Note the abundant natural regeneration of all species present in the overstorey stand.

THE BALLAD OF TWO CEDARS

Come listen to a story 'bout a cedar that is red
The native folk say that it kept their family fed
Even though they didn't use the cedar tree for food
They used the bark for baskets, and made houses from the wood
Long houses, sturdy walls, totem poles

Well the next thing you know those burly loggers came
The locals said, "Weyerhaeuser is to blame!"
They said "California is the place you ought'a be"
But they cut a lot of cedar and they left woody debris
Coarse woody, rotten logs, habitat

Well red cedar has a cousin and its wood is kind' a yellow
Most folks say he's a mighty handsome fellow
They say *Callitropsis* is the name we ought'a use
Don't say *Chamaecyparis* or folks will be confused
Alaska cedar, Nootka cypress, Cupressaceae

Now folks did some retention and they left some scattered trees
Franklin and Bunnell said it's good for birds and bees
Along came the wind and it blew some cedars down
But they'll still have a life just lying on the ground
[If the salvagers don't get 'em!] **Shake** cutters, chainsaws

So now you've heard the story of the yellow and the red
Yellow is declining and a lot of trees are dead
They're worth a lot of money making houses in Japan
And we want them in the future so we're doin' what we can
Research, management, conservation

Yes, we love both of these cedars
So we're doin' all we can.

<Da dada da da, da da>

Bill Beese, 26 May 2010
Written for the "Tale of Two Cedars" International Workshop, Univ. of Victoria, BC
Tune: The Ballad of Jed Clampett (Beverly Hillbillies theme), Lester Flatt & Earl Scruggs

INTERNATIONAL CEDAR SYMPOSIUM PARTICIPANTS

Kim Allan, RPF District of Mission Director of Forest Management Box 20, 33835 Dewdney Trunk Road Mission, BC V2V 4L9 604.820.3764 Work (Direct) 604.302.4082 (Mobile) 604.826.8633 (Fax) kallan@mission.ca	Bryce Bancroft RPBio. Symmetree Consulting Group Ltd. 6301 Rodolph Road Victoria, B.C. Canada V8Z 5V9 250.652.6509 http://symmetree.ca BryceB@telus.net
Bill Beese Professor, Forestry Department Faculty of Science and Technology Vancouver Island University 900 Fifth Street, Nanaimo, BC V9R 5S5 Bill.Beese@VIU.ca	John Caouette Forest Statistician The Nature Conservancy 416 Harris Street, Suite 301 Juneau, AK 99801 907.523.1983 (Phone) 907.586.8622 (Fax) jcaouette@tnc.org
Andy Cockle University of Washington Home address: 401 14th St. Bellingham, WA 98225 360.393.4347 (Home Phone) andrew.cockle@gmail.com	David D'Amore Research Soil Scientist Pacific Northwest Research Station 11305 Glacier Highway Juneau, Alaska 99801 Phone: 907-586-7955 Fax: 907-586-7848 ddamore@fs.fed.us
Florian Deisenhofer Region Silviculturist Pacific Cascade Region Washington Department of Natural Resources (DNR) 360.666.6005 / 666.9400 (Work center) 360.773.5724 (Cell) 360.577.2025 (Main office) Florian.Deisenhofer@dnr.wa.gov	Louise de Montigny, Ph.D., RPF Research Leader, Silvicultural Systems and Forest Dynamics Research and Knowledge Management Branch B.C.Ministry of Forests and Range PO Box 9519 Stn. Prov. Govt., Victoria, BC V8W 9C2 250.387.3295 (Phone) 250.387.0046 (Fax) Louise.demontigny@gov.bc.ca
Diane Douglas Tree Improvement Branch British Columbia Ministry of Forests and Range 2nd Floor - 727 Fisgard Street Victoria BC V8W 9C1 250.356.6721 Diane.L.Douglas@gov.bc.ca	Ivan Eastin **Professor/Director, CINTRAFOR** *Center for International Trade in Forest Products* *University of Washington* *Seattle, WA* 206.543.1918 eastin@u.washington.edu

Robert L. (Bob) Edmonds, Denman Professor in Sustainable Resource Sciences, and Interim Director, The Water Center School of Forest Resources Box 352100 University of Washington Seattle, WA 98195 Office - 264 Bloedel Hall 206.685.0953 (Phone) 206.685.3091 (Fax) bobe@u.washington.edu	Gregory J. Ettl, Associate Professor, Ridgeway Chair, and Director Center for Sustainable Forestry at Pack Forest School of Forest Resources University of Washington Box 352100 Seattle, WA 98195-2100 206-616-4120
Shalima Devi Ganesan Meenakshy PhD student Faculty of Forestry, UBC Dept. Of Forest Sciences 3041-2424 Main Mall University of British Columbia Vancouver, BC V6T1Z4 shalimag@interchange.ubc.ca	Chris Gaston *FPInnovations* *2665 East Mall* *Vancouver, BC V6T 1W5* chris.gaston@fpinnovations.ca
Rolf Gersonde Silviculturist Watershed Services Division Seattle Public Utilities 19901 Cedar Falls Way SE North Bend, WA 98045 206.233.1513 (Phone) rolf.fersonde@seattle.gov	Laura Gray PhD Student Forest Conservation Department of Renewable Resources 815 GSB (SIS Lab) 780.492.2540 lkgray@ualberta.ca
Steven C. Grossnickle, Ph.D. **CellFor Inc.** Senior Manager, DownStream - Development & Quality 250.544.3073 (Phone) 250.889.3187 (Cell) SGrossnickle@cellfor.com	Joshua Halman University of Vermont 705 Spear St. South Burlington, VT 05403 802.656.0567 jhalman@uvm.edu
Kevin J. Hardy, RPF Growth and Yield Forester Ministry of Forests and Range Coast Forest Region 2100 Labieux Rd. Nanaimo, B.C. V9T 6E9 250.751.7093 (Phone) 250.751.7190 (Fax) Kevin.Hardy@gov.bc.ca	Constance A. Harrington Research Forester Pacific Northwest Research Station Forestry Sciences Laboratory 3625 93rd Avenue SW Olympia, WA 98512-9193 360.753.7670 (Phone) 360.753.7737 (Fax) charrington@fs.fed.us http://www.fs.fed.us/pnw/olympia/silv/

Dr. Barbara J. Hawkins Centre for Forest Biology University of Victoria PO Box 3020, STN CSC Victoria, BC, CANADA V8W 3N5 250.721.7117 (Phone) bhawkins@uvic.ca	Paul Hennon Resilience and Ecosystem Disturbance Team PNW Research Station 11305 Glacier Highway Juneau, AK 99801 907.586.8769 (Phone) 907.586.7848 Fax phennon@fs.fed.us
Clare M. Kooistra, RPF Forest Nursery and Regeneration Specialist Conifera Consulting 1-6916 Manning Place Vernon, BC V1B 2Y5 250.549.2322 cmkooistra@shaw.ca	Jodie Krakowski Research Scientist British Columbia Ministry of Forests and Range Cowichan Lake Research Station Box 335 Mesachie Lake, BC V0R 2N0 250.749.6811 ext. 43 (Phone) Jodie.Krakowski@gov.bc.ca
Terri Lacourse Department of Geography University of Victoria Victoria, British Columbia V8W 3R4 tlacours@uvic.ca	Joe LeBlanc, RPF Senior Forester, Coastal Woodlands International Forest Products Ltd. 1250A Ironwood Street Campbell River, B.C. V9W 6H5 250.286.5148 (Phone) 604.422.3259 (Fax) joe.leblanc@interfor.com
Robin Lesher Ecologist, Western Washington Ecology Program Mt. Baker-Snoqualmie National Forest rlesher@fs.fed.us	Thomas J. Link District Silviculturist Newport/Sullivan Lake R.D's, Colville N.F. U.S. Forest Service Sullivan Lake Ranger Station 12641 Sullivan Lake Rd Metaline Falls, WA 99153 509.446.7527 (Phone) tjlink@fs.fed.us
Damon Little *Cullman Program for Molecular Systematics* *The New York Botanical Garden* *Bronx, NY USA 10458-5126* dlittle@nybg.org	Thomas Brian Maertens PhD student Tree Ring Lab, Department of Geography University of British Columbia 1984 West Mall Vancouver, BC V6T 1Z2 maertens@forestmail.com
Doug Mainwaring Oregon State University Dept of Forest Engineering, Resources, and Management 204 Peavy Hall Corvallis, Ore. 97331 541.737.8107 doug.mainwaring@oregonstate.edu	Brian Marcus Western Forest Products Port Alberni, BC BMarcus@westernforest.com

Carol McKenzie Regional Silviculturist, Alaska Region USDA Forest Service P.O. Box 21628 Juneau AK 99802-1628 907.586.7915 (Phone) cmckenzie@fs.fed.us	Rick Monchak RPF Operations Forester TimberWest Forest Corp. Box 2500 Campbell River BC V9W 5C5 250.286.7364 MonchakR@TimberWest.com
Paul I Morris PhD Group Leader - Durability and Protection FPInnovations - Wood Products Division 2665 East Mall Vancouver, BC 604.222.5651 (Phone) 604.222.5690 (Fax) paul.morris@FPInnovations.ca www.fpinnovations.ca www.durable-wood.com	Roderick Negrave PhD, PAg, RPF Research Team Leader Coast Forest Region Ministry of Forests and Range 250.751.7160 (Phone) Roderick.Negrave@gov.bc.ca
Victor Nery Forest Engineer - Masters Candidate 2625E Forest Sciences Centre 2424 Main Mall UBC, Vancouver BC V6T 1Z4 604.866.5952 victornery@gmail.com	Elisabeth Pittl Department of Forest Sciences 3621-2424 Main Mall University of British Columbia Vancouver, BC V6T 1Z4 lisa.pittl@gmail.com
Dr Cindy Prescott Professor and Associate Dean, Graduate Studies and Research Faculty of Forestry University of British Columbia 2005-2424 Main Mall Vancouver, BC, V6T 1Z4 604.822.4701 Cindy.Prescott@ubc.ca	John Russell Research Scientist, Coastal Forest Genetics British Columbia Ministry of Forests and Range Cowichan Lake Research Station Box 335 Mesachie Lake, BC V0R 2N0 250.749.6811 Ext.26 John.Russell@gov.bc.ca
Toktam Sajedi PhD candidate Department of Forest Sciences 3621-2424 Main Mall University of British Columbia Vancouver, BC, V6T 1Z4 tsajedi@gmail.com	Brian Saunders Area Forester Island Timberlands Ph: 250 468 6838 bsaunders@Islandtimberlands.com
Paul G. Schaberg, Ph.D. Research Plant Physiologist NRS-10-Burlington Northern Research Station Forest Service, U.S. Department of Agriculture 705 Spear Street South Burlington, VT 05403 USA 802.951.6771 Ext.-1020 (Phone) 802.951.6368 (Fax) pschaberg@fs.fed.us	Mel Scott 250.598.7228 melscott@shaw.ca

Ted Stevens, RPF, AScT Forestry Coordinator, Gwa'sala-'Nakwaxda'xw Nation and General Manager, Gwa'Nak Resources Ltd. PO Box Port Hardy BC V0N 2P0 250.949.8393 (Phone) 250.949.8301 (Fax) 250.949.0344 (Cell) forestry@gwanak.info	Rod Stirling FPInnovations 2665 East Mall Vancouver, BC V6T 1W5 604.222.5712 (Phone) 604.222.5690 (Fax) rod.stirling@fpinnovations.ca
Rona Sturrock Research Scientist NRCAN-CFS Pacific Forestry Centre 506 West Burnside Road Victoria BC V8Z 1M5 250.363.0789 (Phone) 250.363.0775 (Fax) Rona.Sturrock@nrcan.gc.ca	Kwang-IL (Leo) Tak ISEE (International School For Environmental Education, Korea) 7305 Rossiter Ave. Lantzville, B.C. V0R 2H0 250.390.3711 (Phone) leotak@i-see.or.kr leotak@kookmin.ac.kr
Mark Tressel, RFT Tamihi Logging Co. Ltd. 42255 Arnold Road Chilliwack, B.C. V2R 4H8 604.823.4830 ext.109 (Phone) 604.823.7150 (Fax) mark.tamihilog@shaw.ca	Robert van den Driessche 2361 Queenswood Drive Victoria, B.C. V8N 1X4 (Ret.) Research Branch, BC Min Forests New Dendrology Inc. robtvdd@telus.net
Annette van Niejenhuis RPF FIA Coordinator Western Forest Products Inc. 118-1334 Island Highway Campbell River, BC V9W 8C9 250.286.4109 (Phone) AVanniejenhuis@westernforest.com	Rudi van Zwaaij, RPF Area Forester WFP Stillwater Forest Operation 604.485.3110 (Phone) RVanZwaaij@westernforest.com
Dave Weaver RPF Silviculture Survey Specialist BC Ministry of Forest and Range Forest Practices Branch Box 9513 Stn Prov Govt Victoria, BC VW 9C2 250.387.4768 (Phone) David.Weaver@gov.bc.ca	Craig Wickland, RPF Silviculture Forester Coast Forest Region, Nanaimo. 250.751.7094 (Phone) Craig.Wickland@gov.bc.ca
Ralph Winter Stand Mgmt Officer Harvesting and Silvicultural Practices Forest Practices Branch Ministry of Forests and Range 9th Floor - 727 Fisgard Street Victoria, BC V8W 9C2 250.387.8906 (Phone) Ralph.Winter@gov.bc.ca	Claire Wooton, MSc. Student Department of Geography University of British Columbia 1984 West Mall Vancouver, BC V6T 1Z2 604.822.6212 (Phone) cwooton@geog.ubc.ca http://www.geog.ubc.ca/~brian/cwooton

METRIC - ENGLISH EQUIVALENTS

When you know:	Multiply by:	To find:
Degrees Celsius (°C)	(°C * 9/5) + 32	Degrees Fahrenheit (°F)
Centimeters (cm)	0.3937	Inches (in)
Meters (m)	3.2808	Feet (ft)
Square meters per hectare (m^2/ha)	4.36	Square feet per acre (ft^2 /ac)
Cubic meters per hectare (m^3/ha)	14.30	Cubic feet per acre (ft^3 /ac)
Kilograms per hectare (kg/ha)	0.89	Pounds per acre (lb/ac)
Kilometers (km)	0.6214	Miles (mi)
Hectares (ha)	2.470	Acres